LABOR MARKET ADJUSTMENTS IN THE PACIFIC BASIN

LABOR MARKET ADJUSTMENTS IN THE PACIFIC BASIN

edited by
**Peter T. Chinloy and
Ernst W. Stromsdorfer**

Kluwer-Nijhoff Publishing
a member of the Kluwer Academic Publishers Groups
Boston   Dordrecht   Lancaster

Distributors

for the United States and Canada: Kluwer Academic Publishers,
101 Philip Drive, Norwell, MA 02061, USA

for the UK and Ireland: Kluwer Academic Publishers, MTP Press
Limited, Falcon House, Queen Square, Lancaster LA1 IRN, UK

for all other countries: Kluwer Academic Publishers Group, Distribution
Centre, P.O. Box 322, 3300 AH Dordrecht, The Netherlands

Library of Congress Cataloging-in-Publication Data

Labor market adjustments in the Pacific basin.

    Bibliography: p.
    Includes index.
    1. Labor supply—Pacific Coast (North America)
2. Labor supply—Japan.   3. Foreign trade and employment—
Pacific Coast (North America)   4. Foreign trade and
employment—Japan.   I. Chinloy, Peter T., 1950–
II. Stromsdorfer, Ernst W., 1934–
HD5722.L33 1986   33.12′099   86-15350
ISBN 0-89838-180-0

Contents

Contributing Authors and Participants

Joseph G. Altonji
Department of Economics
Columbia University
New York, NY 10027

Masahiko Aoki
Department of Economics
Stanford University
Stanford, CA 94305

G.C. Archibald
Department of Economics
University of British Columbia
Vancouver, BC V6T 1W5
CANADA

Peter T. Chinloy
Department of Economics
University of Santa Clara
Santa Clara, CA 95053

Joseph J. Cordes
Department of Economics
The George Washington University
Washington, DC 20052

Jean-Michel Cousineau
School of Industrial Relations
University of Montreal
Montreal, Quebec H3C 3J7
CANADA

Ben Craig
Department of Economics
Washington State University
Pullman, WA 99164

Juan Diez-Canedo Ruiz
Superente de Financiamento Externo
Banco de Mexico
Cond. 6, 90 Piso
Cent. Deleg Cuauht., 06059
MEXICO, DF

Gregory M. Duncan
Department of Economics
Washington State University
Pullman, WA 99164

Robert S. Goldfarb
Department of Economics
The George Washington University
Washington, DC 20052

John C. Ham
Department of Economics
University of Toronto
Toronto, Ontario M5S 1A1
CANADA

Daniel S. Hamermesh
Department of Economics
Michigan State University
East Lansing, MI 48824

Masanori Hashimoto
Department of Economics
Indiana University
Bloomington, IN 47402

Laurence R. Iannacone
Department of Economics
University of Santa Clara
Santa Clara, CA 95053

Nicholas M. Kiefer
Department of Economics
Cornell University
Ithaca, NY 14853

Kazuo Koike
Institute of Economic Research
Kyoto University
Yoshida-Honmachi, Sakyo-ku
Kyoto 606, JAPAN

Duane E. Leigh
Department of Economics
Washington State University
Pullman, WA 99164

Hajime Miyazaki
Department of Economics
Ohio State University
Columbus, OH 43210

Ronald Oaxaca
Department of Economics
University of Arizona
Tuscon, AZ 85721

Isao Ohashi
Department of Economics
Nagoya University
Furo-cho, Chikusa-ku
Nagoya 464, JAPAN

Edgar Ortiz
Universidad Autonoma de Mexico
Civdad Universitaria
Alvaro Obregon, 04510
MEXICO, DF

John Raisian
Unicorn Research Corporation
10801 National Boulevard
Los Angeles, CA 90064

Susan Ranney
Department of Economics
University of Washington
Seattle, WA 98195

Jaime Serra-Puche
El Colegio de Mexico
Camino Al Ajusco 20
Codigo Postal 01000
10740 MEXICO, DF

Ernst W. Stromsdorfer
Department of Economics
Washington State University
Pullman, WA 99164

Acknowledgments

This project arose from initial discussions on how to examine the effects on labor markets of rapid changes in exchange rates and the decline of goods producing sectors in the economies of the United States and Canada. Discussions with colleagues in Canada, the United States, Mexico, and Japan suggested that there was extensive international interest in how labor markets adjust to external shocks. This book is a product of that interest. The intention throughout has been to include explicitly the institutions of the labor market, as they are manifested in different societies. The Chapters are all directed to the topic of international labor market adjustment, and contain theoretical modelling, empirical work, and discussion of significant labor market institutions.

We acknowledge the research support of the U.S. Department of Labor. This support covered the researchers in the United States, Mexico, and Japan. The researchers in Canada have been supported by the Social Sciences and Humanities Research Council of Canada. Support for the preparation of the manuscript has also been provided by a Presidential Grant from the University of Santa Clara and from the College of Business and Economics at Washington State University.

There are several individuals who have provided assistance. This is an incomplete list, as justice cannot be done to all. Dr. William Barnes of the U.S. Department of Labor has provided his personal interest and encouragement. Daniel Hamermesh gave several valuable suggestions on the design of this project. Joy Congdon and Laura Beach have made suggestions on the logistical aspects of the project. The research library at the Massachusetts Institute of Technology has aided with information retrieval on Mexico. The Word Processing Center of the Washington State University, through Helen Stevens and her staff, produced the book in a most skillful and timely way.

ix

LABOR MARKET ADJUSTMENTS IN THE PACIFIC BASIN

1 INTRODUCTION

Peter T. Chinloy and Ernst W. Stromsdorfer

I. Background to Adjustments in Labor Markets

The book examines the process of adjustment in labor markets across countries arising from external shocks and shifts in international competitiveness. The examination of specific countries and their data permits a comparison of alternative institutions for compensating and redeploying labor. Four countries are involved, whose labor markets are both competitive and complementary: Canada, Japan, Mexico, and the United States.

Both public labor market institutions, such as direct government compensation of displaced workers and the effect of unemployment insurance, and private market arrangements, such as emloyer-employee agreements on layoffs, the work contract, and severance pay, are considered. Comparative examination across countries of labor market and related insitutions is thus possible. The book has a common theme, namely the adjustment of labor markets to exogenous shocks, particularly those externally induced. The unifying focus in on workers whose specific skills in an industry or firm render them relatively immobile.

Institutional arrangements in the labor market vary among countries. In Canada and the United States, wages are relatively rigid in the short run, but workers in sectors vulnerable to foreign competition can typically be permanently discharged or temporarily laid off during a downturn. This limited job security may make workers less willing to invest in firm-specific or industry-specific human capital. In other jobs, such as within the public sector, both wages and employment are relatively rigid. By comparison, Japan has more rigid employment levels but more flexible compensation,[1] including bonus payments to productive workers and regular renegotiation of wage contracts or payments, at least for large manufacturing firms.

The book is divided into four sections. Part I deals with theoretical developments that can lead to different labor market institutions across countries. The subsequent three sections all contain empirical work. Part II is concerned with the observed phenomena associated with dislocations in labor markets. These phenomena include the degree of wage and employment flexibility, the degree and management of redundancy, and the nature and extent of migration in the Mexico−United States case. Part III examines the effect of external shocks on domestic aggregate employment. Part IV discusses compensation alternatives to workers displaced by these shocks.

II. Theoretical Framework: Institutions and the Labor Market

The theoretical aspect in this section discusses institutional arrangements in the labor market. In chapter 2, Nicholas Kiefer examines how labor market differences can arise across countries when individuals may have the same underlying utility functions.

It is assumed that the same utility and production functions obtain, that all agents optimize, and that there is no economic profit. Four alternative institutions are considered, three obtaining in capital markets and one in the labor market. For capital markets, these are complete anonymity, or intertemporal separability, the presence of a bond market, and contingent markets for all claims. The capital market institutions remain relevant for labor markets. If complete bond markets exist, for example, workers can hedge the risk of layoff or decline in demand.

For labor, there are contracts on employment. Models with and without fixed employment are presented. It is shown that the effect on wages, consumption, and employment, and the correlation between them, varies depending on the institutions considered. Hence, institutions have an effect on observed data, even where the underlying preferences are the same. In part, this sets the stage for the subsequent differences in labor markets across countries.

III. Observed Dislocations: International Comparisons

This section examines specific dislocations in labor markets, by comparison across countries. This permits the determination of whether one country has relatively flexible wages with respect to another. On this issue, the first two chapters compare, respectively, the United States and Japan, and the United States and Canada. Comparisons can be made on the quantity, or employment side, as well on the wage side between countries.

The remaining two chapter compare the degree of flexibility in redundancy between the United States and Japan, and the degree of migration in response to external shocks between Mexico and the United States. Aggregate wages in the United States and Japan are compared by Masanori Hashimoto and John Raisian in chapter 4.[2] One conventional observation is that aggregate wages in the United States are relatively rigid. Using microdata, Hashimoto and Raisian indicate that there is less rigidity in the United States wage structure than appears based on earlier analysis performed with aggregate data. Layoffs occur among low wage workers, reducing the average skill level of those remaining employed. A wage adjusted for employment composition has more procyclical behavior than an unadjusted wage. Among specific worker characteristics, wages do not differ in procyclical behavior by race or eduction. Those with low or high on-the-job experience have procyclical wages.

One method by which the Japanese labor market is said to adjust is through flexible wages with inflexible quantities, at least for total employment, if not for hours worked. The principal mechanism of wage flexibility is the bonus, amounting to up to one-third of annual compensation in manufacturing. (Compensation in Japan is defined as including base earning and bonus.) The bonus-earnings ratio in Japan is compared across firms and time. The cyclical wage variation, including bonus, is shown to be more pronounced than in the United States. If there is a trend away from longterm employment contracts, the bonus-earnings ratio will decline. There does not appear to be a trend away from long-term arrangements. Finally, it is noteworthy that the bonus is not the only source of wage flexibility in Japan, as the wage base itself fluctuates a great deal depending on economic conditions.

The issue of wage flexibility between Canada and the United States, and response of the Canadian economy to external shocks, is examined by Jean-Michel Cousineau in chapter 5. Although wages in Canada and the United States are more rigid than in Japan, Canada has more flexible wages than the United States[3]. It is hypothesized that flexible wages arise because Canada more closely approximates a small, open economy where an exposed sector is sensitive to international market conditions.

The exposed sector is defined for empirical purposes as containing all industries where exports or imports amount to at least 25% of industry gross domestic product. Remaining industries are grouped into a sheltered sector. In the exposed sector, for Canada over the time period 1967I to 1984I, United States output is shown to be highly correlated with wages. Hence, wages are flexible with respect to the United States business cycle.

On the quantity side, Kazuo Koike deals with the effect of labor market institutions such as permanent employment, promotion on the basis of seniority, mandatory retirement, and delayed labor market entry, on the ability of the Japanese economy to respond to external shocks. There are two aspects of Japanese labor markets that differ from comparable United States institutions. First, layoffs and redundancies in Japan do not occur on predetermined criteria such as inverse seniority. Second, the "ratio of internal production," or proportion of gross output undertaken within a firm, is relatively low. There is less vertical integration in production than in the United States.

Lower skill jobs in manufacturing tend to be subcontracted, given that large firms offer lifetime job security, while small firms do not offer such security. When a large firm engages in layoffs, relatively older, more experienced workers suffer, in contrast with the United States. This is because of the absence of seniority rules on layoff, and the greater proportion of experienced workers in employment among large firms in Japan. The resulting loss of firm-specific human capital can be relatively large.

Layoffs in the United States are concentrated among less experienced workers. These workers have more general skills and are more mobile. Those who invest in firm-specific skills both experience and impose higher costs upon layoff, since their mobility is limited. Japanese workers may have relatively more firm-specific skills than their United States counterparts. Yet, the Japanese labor market as a whole may provide less employment security than a superficial review of Japanese institutions might suggest.

Empirical evidence is presented on the layoff experience of Japanese workers. During the period 1976–79, 20% of Japanese firms engaged in layoffs, a proportion not dependent on firm size. Regarding layoffs, the average redundant worker is older than the average worker remaining with the firm.

Juan Diez-Canedo Ruiz examines the exit and return flow of Mexican migration to the United States. There are two sectors to the migration process in Mexico. Relatively affluent workers migrate temporarily to the Unite States in response to labor market opportunity. At the same time, low income Mexican workers migrate to urban areas of Mexico. Given the large real wage disparity between the United States and Mexico, a natural issue is why a larger flow of migration from Mexico to the United States does not take place. Language apparently is not a barrier. Rather, the opportunity costs of migration to the United States are high enough to cut off the flow of the very poor potential migrants—the minimal cash savings required are a constraint.

The empirical section of the chapter provides an estimate of the number of undocumented migrants from Mexico working in the United States. Financial data are employed that use bank checks originating in the United States and clearing commercial banks in Mexico to determine the total flow and average size of remittances from Mexican migrants in the United States. From these, estimates of migrant population sizes are constructed. The principal conclusion is that the number of undocumented workers in the United States from Mexico is substantially lower than that from alternative estimates. The estimate of undocumented Mexican workers in 1975 is about 800,000, as opposed to alternatives between two and five million. At the same time, the distribution indicates pockets of Mexican migrants in areas previously not thought to have large such populations, notably New York City.

IV. Domestic and International Shocks: Effects on Employment and Wages

Part III presents two chapters examining the effect of domestic and international shocks on employment and wages. Wage and employment adjustments are developed by Isao Ōhashi in an efficiency wage model. Labor productivity, output per worker, depends on hours worked, training costs, and effort. Effort depends on the differential between the wage offered and the return to alternative labor force activity. The latter is an unemployment rate-weighted average of the alternative wage and unemployment insurance benefits. An increase in wage offered increases effort by inducing increased loyalty and reducing incentives to shirk. Reduced form models, each containing a wage and employment adjustment equation, are obtained from a dynamic version of the general model. Wage and employment adjustments depend on the unemployment rate and average wage, through effort.

The wage and employment adjustment equations are estimated for Japanese manufacturing over the 1970–82 time period.[4] The hypothesis that Japanese employment is inflexible while wages are flexible is tested.

Employment and wages respond negatively to unemployment for all sizes of firm. The response of employment to the average wage varies by the size of firm. Larger firms reduce employment when average wages increase, but smaller firms maintain employment levels.

The responsiveness in employment and wages among Canadian industries to internal and external shocks is explored by Joseph Altonji and John Ham. Separate equations estimating employment and wages by industry and region are estimated. The disturbances have components for domestic effects from Canada, external effects from the United States, specific industries and provinces, and random effects. Whether an external shock has the same impact on employment as on wages can be determined. The empirical results suggest that about 60% of the fluctuations in aggregate Canadian employment are accounted for by aggregate shocks in the United States, with another 25% arising from aggregate shocks in Canada, while the remainder arises from specific industry and province shocks.

V. Compensation of Displaced Workers

Part IV discusses whether displaced workers ought to be compensated, and if so, how much. A model of the preferences of workers for security and wages at the job is developed by G.C. Archibald and Peter Chinloy. Security of income can be provided either by jobless payments if unemployment arises or by maintaining employment. Income security reduces the demand for job security and permits labor markets to be more flexible. On the demand side, where workers have conceded wages to gain job security, lacking income security, markets may operate less efficiently.

An empirical examination is carried out of the employment performance of five countries for the 1964–82 time period: Canada, Japan, Germany, the United Kingdom, and the United States. The two North American countries have the most rapid growth in employment and the smallest growth in the user cost of labor. This user cost is the price of hiring the services of one worker for one hour, given eventual completed tenure duration, opportunity cost of capital, and wages. Japan has the lowest user cost of labor at the beginning of the sample period and the highest at the end. While the United Kingdom and Germany have the lowest user costs, they have the largest barriers to firing. These data are not inconsistent with the hypothesis that the underlying demand for security by workers has been channelled into the employment contract in the last three countries. Conversely, general labor market institutions such as unemployment insurance in Canada and Social Security in the United States may engender flexibility in the labor market.

In the United States, a large number of workers have lost their jobs through plant closures. High estimats of this number generally exceed one million per year. Daniel Hamermesh, Joseph Cordes, and Robert Goldfarb examine how to compensate displaced workers. Two separate cases of job loss are identified. The first is as a consequence of a specific governmental action such as airline deregulation. The second arises from shifts in demand from tastes or from technological change. Since the first case cannot easily be anticipated, there is an argument in favor of compensation.

Workers have lost a property right in their firm- or industry-specific skills. Calculations of the loss based on the price of time or reservation wage can be in error, if these delcine rapidly during a search period. This suggests that compensation be paid on a lump sum basis. The lump sum form avoids distorting the marginal price of time during the search for another job.

VI. Concluding Remarks

A common theme in the empirical chapters is the degree of flexibility of labor markets, both in wage and employment. It is shown that flexibility must be carefully defined. While Japan has more flexible total compensation than the United States, the latter has more flexible employment adjustment. For the United Staes, this can permit the movement of workers to other sectors of the economy. For Japan, workers may be more inclined to acquired firm- or industry-specific skills because their mobility opportunities are limited by institutional or legislative constraint.

Another issue is the degree to which the cost of employment dislocation is shared among the displaced worker, the employer, the industry and the labor market as a whole. A major distinction exists in whether and how much to compensate displacement that destroys specific human capital based on whether the displacement can reasonably be anticipated by the worker.

Two main conclusions appear from our international comparison of labor markets. The first is concerned with the theoretical developments in labor markets surrounding implicit contracts. The second is on the stylized facts arising in North America regarding the perception of Japanese labor markets.

Implicit contracts occur where an insurance policy is offered by a firm to protect workers against fluctuations in demand. The theory applies to real as opposed to nominal wages.

To observe implicit contracts, certain empirical observations are required. First, wages are relatively rigid, with employment relatively flexible.

Second, there are long-term attachments between firms and workers. The spot wage is not an indication of the long-term cost of retaining labor services nor is it the market clearing wage. Third, there is exogenous unemployment insurance to divert instability in labor markets to employment as opposed to wages. Fourth, financial markets are either incomplete or imperfect, so workers do not have an incentive to self-insure against layoff except through wage rigidity and, presumably, some layoff rule on the basis of seniority.

The chapters in this book shed some light on the observed environment in Canada, the United States, and Japan. The implicit contract argument appears not to be directed at countries such as Mexico. First, consider the evidence that wages in the United States are relatively rigid. Hashimoto and Raisian, for the United States, indicate that although wages measured by aggregate average are relatively rigid, at least in comparison with Japan, when using microdata and adjusting for age, sex, race, and experience, there is more volatility in wages.

Second, of the countries studied, average job attachment is longest in Japan, where wages are most flexible, and shortest in the United States, where there is less wage flexibility. Third, the country with the most generous unemployment insurance program among those examined is Canada. Among Canada, the United States, and Japan, Japan is the least generous. Yet there appears to be wage flexibility in Canada than the United States, as indicated by Jean-Michel Cousineau. Unemployment insurance generosity and tenure appear to be negatively correlated, rather than positively.

Fourth, Kiefer suggests that workers can use financial markets to hedge against layoffs. If so, workers in more risky employment could ask for higher wages and engage in bond financing to lay off the risk. Implicit contracts may not necessarily characterize the arrangements by which bonding occurs between firms and workers.

The second lesson is on the nature of labor markets in Japan. The stylized facts, as they appear to observers in Canada and the United States, are that there is long-term tenure, and that promotion occurs on seniority. The evidence, from Koike, is less certain. Japanese firms engage in redundancies. Promotion does not necessarily occur on the basis of seniority. Up to certain levels on the shop floor, this may be the case, but it is not universal. For top management, and for most white collar workers, seniority promotion does not appear to be the method used. On layoff, Japanese labor markets do not have organized methods such as seniority for determining who is to be removed. The United States labor market may be more characterized by promotion on seniority, and layoff on inverse seniority, than Japan.

Notes

1. See Sekscenski [1979], Table D, p. A-14. For males, median tenure in years, for those still employed in the reported job, is 4.5 years. However, median job tenure in the United Stated federal public administration is 7.7 years, and it is 11.7 years in the United States Postal Service.
2. See Tau [1982].
3. See Orr, Shimada, and Seike [1985].
4. The first part of this has been documented by Gordon [1982].

References

Gordon, R.J. 1982. "Why U.S. Wage and Employment Behavior Differs from That in Britain and Japan." *Economic Journal* 92, 13–44.
Orr, James A., Haruo Shimada, and Atsushi Seike. 1985. *United States–Japan Comparative Study of Employment Adjustment*. Washington, D.C.: United States Department of Labor, Bureau of International Labor Affairs.
Sekscenski, Edward S. 1979. "Job Tenure Declines as Work Force Changes." Special Labor Force Report 235. Washington, D.C.: United States Department of Labor, Bureau of Labor Statistics.
Tan, Hong W. 1982. "Wage Determination in Japanese Manufacturing: A Review of Recent Literature." *The Economic Record* 58 (March): 46–60.

I THEORETICAL FRAMEWORK: INSTITUTIONS AND THE LABOR MARKET

2 A COMPARISON OF LABOR MARKET EQUILIBRIA UNDER DIFFERENT INSTITUTIONAL ORGANIZATIONS

Nicholas M. Kiefer

I. Introduction

It is a widely accepted "stylized fact" that the United States economy exhibits rigid wages and flexible employment over the business cycle. Hall (1980) and Gordon (1982) document this phenomenon using aggregate time series data. A widely cited example of an economy with a different organization is Japan. There wages are extremely flexible: typically a base wage is renegotiated each year and then supplemented with bonuses depending on profitability, and employment is fairly rigid. Canada and many other countries line up somewhere in between the United States and Japan in the relative flexibility of wages and employment. Stable employment is often taken to be more desirable than stable wages, and the Japanese

This is a revision of a paper for the conference on Adjustments in Labor Markets, Santa Clara, CA, June 6–8, 1985. I would like to thank Randy Wright of the IBW and the members of Cornell's Labor Economics workshop for their help. I have also benefitted from the comments of Chris Pissarides, Torben Andersen, and my discussant at the conference, Duane Leigh. This research was partly supported by the National Science Foundation.

13

economy attracts attention as perhaps providing clues about introducing more wage flexibility, and presumably consequently less employment flexibility, into the United States economy.

However, it is not clear that a remuneration system with fixed employment and flexible wages is better than one with flexible employment and fixed wages, or indeed better than one with wages and employment flexible, in an efficiency sense or in a welfare sense. The interpretations of movements in observables like labor earnings per time unit, profits, employment and output, depend crucially on the contractual arrangements in the labor markets and on the access of workers to securities markets. The contractual arrangements need not be explicit; they could be part of the customary operation of the labor market, or they could be established by government or other institutions. The point is that a worker's utility depends on his or her path of consumption (ignoring for the present the utility of leisure), and the path of consumption need not be closely related to the path of wages. If we wish to make welfare comparisons between workers with the same utility function in different economic organizations, we would need data on consumption paths, not on earned income sequences. When employment is variable, workers care about their utilities; in the time separable case, on the path of utility over time. This will depend on the paths of consumption and of leisure, which in turn depend on the paths of employment and earned income, the observables (in principle). The employment pattern over time is, of course, directly related to the pattern of leisure over time, so there is some hope of making inferences about welfare or efficiency from observations on employment over time. As in the case of fixed hours, however, the relationship between the path of wages and the path of consumption may be too imprecise to allow any inference about welfare or efficiency from patterns of wages.

Comparison of economies with different institutional characteristics is a complicated task. Normally, we would like to explain not only behavioral differences on the part of economic agents due to differing institutions but the source of variation in institutional structures. Data on this interesting problem are scant—how much variation is there in institutional organization within economies? And, theoretical models are rarely rich enough to characterize the formation and change of economic institutions. It is much simpler to study the first question mentioned above. This can be usefully reformed as: What do differences in economic institutions imply for observable variables?

In this chapter we study the equilibrium dynamics of a number of labor market variables in the presence of stylized labor market institutions. The economies we study have three important features in common: (1) utility and production functions are identical; (2) all agent optimize, subject to institutional constraints; and (3) firms operate at zero (longrun or expected) economic profit. The assumption of common utility and production functions is necessary so that differences across economies with different institutions can legitimately be ascribed to differences in the institutions, and not to differences in technology or tastes. Our analysis here is merely theoretical. An attempt to bring data to bear on these questions would doubtless have to consider differences in technology, especially in the short run, due for example to variations in the quality and variety of capital stocks. Similarly, the assumption of common tastes may require appropriate adjustments for demographic characteristics of the populations. For present purposes, however, we abstract from these issues. The production functions we consider are subject to "shocks." The stochastic processes generating these shocks are also assumed to be common across economies. The assumption that agents optimize is a behavioral assumption, unlike the assumption on tastes and technologies. Consumer-workers maximize utility and firms maximize profits. The institutional constraints we consider are described fully below; mostly they restrict access to credit or contract markets. The zero profit condition is imposed as an equilibrium condition. "Entry" is the economic mechanism we have in mind as the background force leading to zero long-run or expected profit, though entry, and the number of firms, are not modelled explicitly.

The institutions we focus on are the presence or absence of credit markets, ranging from the case of "complete anonymity," with no transfer of assets across periods whatever, through an example with bond markets, to the Arrow-Debreu case of complete contingent securities markets. In addition, we consider the presence or absence of employment contracts, implicit or explicit, in which workers and firms enter into a long-term agreement, under terms agreeable to both parties.[1] As we shall see, payment schemes under contract equilibrium can be quite different from those under the non-contract competitive equilibrium. Finally, we study equilibrium dynamics when wages are fixed, and when employment is fixed.

The case of complete anonymity is a useful starting point not because it is realistic but because it is the simplest extension of the simple static model of consumption and labor supply. In this case assets are not transferred across periods, and spot market equilibrium holds in every period. Behavior in each period follows the rules of the static analysis, applied to the conditions (prices, wages, productivity) in that period. Implications for dynamics are obtained in this case (in a great tradition of economics) by applying the static model sequentially. This approach can lead to insight. The major misleading implication concerns the magnitude of income effects, which are attenuated since they cannot be distributed across the future.

The model with a market for bonds perhaps most closely parallels actual economies. Here, workers can buy bonds, payable next period, at a discount determined in equilibrium. There is no uncertainty about the return on these investments, since payouts do not depend on the state of the world. Thus, bonds can be used to spread surprises (pleasant and unpleasant) over time, but not to eliminate risk altogether. Eliminating risk requires the introduction of contingent securities. These are studied in the third model developed below. Once securities markets are introduced, the time pattern of wages has little relevance for welfare.

The contract models we study consist of equilibrium agreements specifying the wage paid and, in the case of variable labor supply, the level of employment as functions of the current period's technology shock. This shock is assumed to be observable to both the firm and the worker. More complicated contracts arise in the case of asymmetric information; these are not treated here.[2]

In section II the model is introduced. To keep the mathematics simple while focusing attention on the role of differing institutions we use a particular, specific example, namely quadratic utility and linear technology. The case of fixed labor supply is considered first, in part of fix ideas and in part because it corresponds to the case of rigid employment, which is sometimes alleged to be an important feature of some economies. The following sections treat the equilibria corresponding to the three credit market assumptions—complete anonymity, bond markets, and contingent securities. The next sections parallel these analyses, except that variable labor supply is introduced. This allows us to study wage and employment variations as functions of the worker's access to the credit market.

The next part of the chapter introduces the employment contract. In two sections we consider in turn the equilibrium employment with fixed labor supply and with variable labor supply. Here, the assumptions about the credit markets are irrelevant, since the worker can incorporate any financial transaction desired into the employment contract. Of course, if the forms of the employment contracts are constrained, it may be optimal for the worker to enter the credit markets, but this case is not developed here.

II. The Economy with Fixed Labor

The first models to be treated fix labor supply, at one unit, say, and deal with the determination of consumption. Assume that the production function is linear, so that the side issues of the determination of the number of firms and of the distribution of profit can be ignored. Suppose that the marginal product of labor, there the return to one unit of labor, is given by the stochastic process $\{x_t\}$, where the x_t are independent and identically distributed random variables. Agents in the economy observe x_t at the beginning of period t and plan their allocations accordingly. The distribution of the x_t is known to all agents in the economy. The firm (or firms) pays wage w per unit of labor in period t and maximizes the expected present value of profits discounted at the rate β,

$$E \sum_{t=0}^{\infty} \beta^t (x_t - w_t).$$

With labor fixed, and therefore leisure fixed, the worker's utility is a function of consumption alone. Assume that the utility function is intertemporally separable and identical over time. Then the worker's problem is to maximize expected discounted utility,

$$E \sum_{t=0}^{\infty} \beta^t U(c_t),$$

where for simplicity the worker discounts at the same rate as the firm. The worker's maximization problem is subject to constraints that depend on the nature of the credit markets available.[3] Clearly, however, the equilibrium solutions to the two maximization problems must satisfy the resource constraint:

$$\sum_{t=0}^{\infty} \beta^t (c_t - x_t) = 0.$$

The assumption of zero long-run profits also implies that

$$\sum_{t=0}^{\infty} \beta^t (x_t - w_t) = 0.$$

When we wish to use a specific solution, we will specify the utility function:

$$u(c_t) = \alpha c_t - \frac{1}{2} c_t^2.$$

A. Spot-Market (Complete Anonymity) Equilibrium

The spot market equilibrium in this model is particularly simple. Here workers cannot transfer assets through time, so the worker's budget contraint is

$$c_t = w_t,$$

and equilibrium in the spot market for labor implies that

$$w_t = x_t.$$

In this equilibrium, consumption and wages are the same i.i.d. stochastic process.

B. The Model with Bonds

A more realistic specfication allows the worker to access to a bond market. A bond purchased in period t at discount rate q_t pays face value in period t. Then dynamic programming can be used to solve the problem:

$$V(s_{t-1}) = \max_{s_t} \{u(c_t) + \beta EV(s_t)\},$$

Subject to:

$$c_t = w_t + s_{t-1} - q_t s_t,$$

where $V(\cdot)$ is the value function and s_{t-1} is the stock of assets brought into period t and s_t is the face value of bonds purchased in period t (paying face value in period $t + 1$). Equilibrium in this set up will require.

$$w_t = x_t, \quad q_t = \beta.$$

The first condition is again a result of the operation of the spot market for labor; the second condition equates the demand for and supply of bonds (the risk-neutral firm will supply to meet any demand at discount β). What are the dynamics of consumption and savings in this model? The first order condition for maximization with respect to s_t is

$$\beta u_t' + \beta EV'(s_t) = 0$$
$$\Rightarrow u_t' = Eu_{t+1}',$$

so the worker will attempt to equate the expected marginal utility of consumption across periods. At this point it is useful to simplify the problem by restricting attention to our quadratic utility function

$$u(c) = ac_t - \frac{1}{2}c^2.$$

With this specification the condition on expected marginal utilities becomes:

$$\alpha - x_t + \beta s_t - s_{t-1} = E(\alpha - x_{t+1} + \beta s_{t+1} - s_t).$$

Since this equation is linear in x and s, we can appeal to certainty equivalence and remove, temporarily, the expectation operator. Upon rearranging we have:

$$(1 - L)x_{t+1} = (\beta - (1 + \beta)L + L^2)s_{t+1},$$

where L is the lag operator $L_{xt} = x_{t-1}$. Factoring the quadratic on the rhs and applying L to both sides (to simplify notation) gives

$$(1 - L)x_t = \beta(1 - L)(1 - \beta^{-1}L)s_t.$$

The next step toward a solution for s_t in terms of the xs is to invert $(1 - \beta^{-1}L)$. This operator is not invertible in the usual way (a power series in L) since $\beta^{-1} > 1$. The "trick" (important in Minnesota macro-economics) is to look for an inverse in a power series in L^{-1}. Note that $(1 - \beta^l) = -\beta^{-1}L$ $(1 - \beta L^{-1})$ (both factors are invertible), so

$$\beta(1 - L)s_t = -\beta L^{-1}(1 - \beta L^{-1})(1 - L)x_t$$
$$= -\beta \sum_{j=0}^{\infty} \beta^j L^{-j} L^{-1}(1 - L)x_t$$
$$= -\beta \Sigma \beta^j L^{-j}(x_{t+1} - x_t)$$
$$= -\beta \Sigma \beta^{-h}(x_{t+1+j} - x_{t+j}).$$

Cancelling β and taking expectations at time t gives the decision rule

$$s_t = s_{t-1} + (x_t - Ex).$$

The stock of wealth follows a random walk.

Turning to implications for consumption we can use the budget constraint to write:

$$c_t = x_t - \beta s_{t-1} - \beta(x_t - E_x) + s_{t-1}$$
$$= Ex + (1 - \beta)(x_t - Ex) + (1 - \beta)s_{t-1}.$$

Consumption in any period is equal to expected earnings plus the return on this period's wage shock plus the return on bonds. Thus the effect of a (positive or negative) shock is spread over the current and all future periods. Note that:

$$E_t c_{t+1} = Ex + (1 - \beta)E_t s_t$$
$$= Ex + (1 - \beta)s_{t-1} + (1 - \beta)(x_t - Ex)$$
$$= c_t,$$

so the consumption process is a martingale.[4]

C. The Model with Complete Contingent Securities Markets

Let us calculate the competitive equilibrium with complete contingent securities markets. Suppose the distribution of x is the discrete distribution

$$P(x_t = x(i)) = P_i \qquad i = 1, \ldots, I$$
$$t = 1, \ldots, \infty.$$

Let $s_t(i)$ be an investment purchased in period t that pays $s_t(i)$ in period $t + 1$ if $x_{t+1} = x(i)$, and pays nothing otherwise. The consumer's period t budget constraint is:

$$c_t = x_t - \sum_{i=1}^{I} q_t(i)s_t(i) + \sum_{i=1}^{I} D_t(i)s_{t-1}(i),$$

where $q_t(i)$ is the price in period t of the investment $s_t(i)$ and $D_t(i) = 1$ if $x_t = x(i)$, zero otherwise. Equilibrium requires $w_t = x_t$ (this was imposed in writing the budget constraint) and $q_t(i) = \beta p_i$, for all i and t. The consumer's problem is then to maximize

$$V(\Sigma D_{t-1}(i)s_{t-1}(i)) = u(c_t) + \beta EV(\Sigma D_t(i)s_t(i)).$$

The first order conditions determining securities purchases and hence consumption are:

$$\beta p_i u_t' - \beta E_t D_{t+1}(i)u_{t+1}' = 0.$$

Now,

$$E_t D_{t+1}(i)u_{t+1}' = p_i u'(x_{t+1} - \beta \Sigma p_i s_{t+1}(i) + s_t(i))$$
$$= p_i u'(c_{t+1}(i)).$$

Therefore the optimal policy equates consumption across states and across periods. Investment in each security is constant over time; the relative amounts are given by the condition

$$x(i) + s(i) = \text{constant},$$

and the levels are determined by initial conditions. Note as an aside that this allocation of investments does not minimize the variance of asset income (the variance minimizing allocation sets the $s(i)$ equal).

In the full competitive equilibrium, consumption is constant over time while earnings and wages, are i.i.d.

III. Variable Labor Supply

A. The Spot Market Equilibrium

We now modify the model so that the production function is given by

$$f(\ell_t) = x_t \ell_t,$$

where ℓ_t is employment, and the worker's utility function is also a function of labor supplies (which equals total hours less leisure). For simplicity we assume that the utility function is separable in leisure and consumption. To calculate explicit solutions we also assume that utility is quadratic in consumption and leisure

$$u(c_t,\ \ell_t) = \alpha c_t - \frac{1}{2}c_t^2 - \frac{1}{2}\ell^2.$$

In this economy the worker maximizes the present discounted expected utility

$$E\Sigma\beta^t u(c_t,\ \ell_t)$$

subject to a constraint that depends on the credit arrangements to which the worker has access. The firm maximizes the present discounted value of profits

$$E\sum_{t=0}^{\infty}\beta^t(x_t\ell_t - w_t\ell_t).$$

Of course, the constraint that consumption must equal production is imposed as well:

$$\sum_{t=0}^{\infty}\beta^t(c_t - x_t\ell_t) = 0.$$

An inequality constraint could be imposed here, but this seems not to add any real generality since the constraint would always be binding in sensible solutions.

In spot market equilibrium the budget constraint in period t is

$$c_t = w_t\ell_t.$$

Equilibrium in the spot market for labor will require that

$$w_t = x_t.$$

Labor supply, or employment, is found by solving the first order conditions in each period:

$$u_{1t}x_t + u_{2t} = 0.$$

In the quadratic example this gives

$$x_t(\alpha - x_t\ell_t) - \ell_t = 0,$$

or

$$\ell_t = \alpha x_t[1 + x_t^2]^{-1}.$$

In this equilibrium the wage rate follows the same i.i.d. stochastic process as technology, employment is i.i.d. but with the less variance than technology, and consumption is also i.i.d. with less variance that technology. What is happening is that the consumer-worker is absorbing the effects of technology shocks in his consumption of both consumption and leisure, reducing the effect of the shock on each separately.

B. Bonds

By analogy with the previous section, the next case includes a bond market but no contingent securities markets. Unfortunately, this case is a little difficult, although some progress can be made. Consumption in period t is given by

$$c_t = x_t\ell_t - \beta s_t + s_{t+1},$$

where equilibrium conditions in the labor and bond markets have been imposed. The worker maximizes

$$V(s_{t-1}) = u(c_{t1}\ell_t) + \beta EV((s_t)$$

with respect to s_t and ℓ_t. The first order conditions are

$$- \beta u_{1t} + \beta EV_{1t+1} = 0 \text{ and,}$$

$$x_t u_{1t} + u_{2t} = 0.$$

The first equation implies that the marginal utility of consumption is a martingale. In the case of quadratic utility, consumption will therefore be a martingale process. The first order conditions in the quadratic case are (after some simplification):

$$x_t\ell_t - \beta s_t + s_{t-1} = E(x_{t+1}\ell_{t+1} - \beta s_{t+1} + s_t) \text{ and,}$$
$$\ell_t = x_t(x_t\ell_t - \beta s_t + s_{t-1}).$$

I have not made much progress toward solving these equations for the optimal ℓ_t and s_t policies (apart from finding the nasty solution $\ell_t = s_t = 0$ for all t). It seems unlikely, however, that the optimal ℓ_t is linear in x_t.

C. The Full Contingent Securities Equilibrium

Recall the discrete distribution of x specified above and recall the definition of the contingent securities $s_t(i)$. Equilibrium in the securities market leads to securities prices

$$q_t(i) = \beta p_i$$

and equilibrium in the labor market implies

$$w_t = x_t.$$

Consequently, the budget constraint is

$$c_t = x_t \ell_t - \beta \Sigma p_i s_t(i) + \Sigma D_t(i) s_{t-1}(i)$$

and the worker maximizes

$$V(\Sigma D_t(i) s_{t-1}(i)) = u(c_t, \ell_t) + \beta E V(\Sigma D_{t+1}(i) s_t(i)).$$

The first order conditions are

$$- \beta p_i u_{1t} + \beta E D_{t+1}(i) u_{1t+1} = 0 \text{ and,}$$
$$x_t u_{1t} + u_{2t} = 0.$$

The first system of equations can be solved by choosing investments so that consumption is constant across time and across states of the world. The last equation implies, in the quadratic case, that labor supply is proportional to productivity. Investments are chosen so that

$$cx(i)^2 + s(i) = \text{constant}.$$

In this equilibrium the wage rate is i.i.d. and consumption is constant. Employment is proportional to productivity, hence more volatile than predicted by the spot market model, due, I think, to the absence of income effects. Earned income is proportional to x_t^2.

IV. The Rigid Wage Equilibrium

The fixed employment equilibria have been treated above. When the wage rate w is fixed over time, the equilibrium in the case of fixed employment is trivial, namely:

$$c_t = w_t = Ex_t.$$

The situation is slightly more complicated when labor supply is variable. Here, unless the firm can induce the workers to supply extra labor in high productivity periods in exchange for supplying less labor in low productivity periods, real losses in efficiency occur. Of course, the usual way to induce variations in labor supply is with variations in the wage. In the contract equilibrium studied below the worker allows the firm to determine employment, as a known function of productivity. Without a mechanism of this sort the fixed wage equilibrium implies a fixed level of employment at

$$\ell_t = \ell = \alpha Ex_t \, [1 + (Ex_t)^2]^{-1} \, ,$$

so the wage, earnings, and employment are identical across time. This result, in contrast to some of the previous results, depends heavily on the assumption of constant returns to scale in production.

V. Contract Equilibrium

A. Fixed Labor

Consider the contract equilibrium with fixed labor supply. While the form of the optimal contract in this model is fairly clear (constant consumption), it is useful to go through the mechanics of constructing the optimal contract. Define a contract as a sequence of functions $\{c_t(x)\}$ giving consumption in period t as a function of productivity in that period. A contract is feasible if

$$E \sum_{t=0}^{\infty} \beta t(x_t - c_t(x)) = 0.$$

A contract is optimal if it is feasible and it maximizes $E \sum_{t=0}^{\infty} \beta^t u(c_t(x))$.

The first result is that we need only consider contracts of the form $c_t(x) = c(x)$ for all t; that is, the function giving consumption as a function of productivity is constant over time. This follows from the stationarity of the policy function in problems of this type (infinite horizon, i.i.d. random variables), but note that no proof is supplied at this point.

To solve for the optimal contract, suppose $c(x)$ is analytic and write

$$c(x) = \sum_{j=0}^{\infty} \gamma_j x^j.$$

The optimal contract can now be found by solving the constrained utility maximization problem for the optimal values of the coefficients γ_j. The

Lagrangian function for this problem is:

$$L = \sum_{t=0}^{\infty} \beta^t u \left(\sum_{j=0}^{\infty} \gamma_j x^j \right) + \lambda \left(\sum_{t=0}^{\infty} \beta^t \left(x_t - \sum_{j=0}^{\infty} \gamma_j x_t^j \right) \right).$$

The first order conditions for the γ_j are:

$$\sum_{t=0}^{\infty} \beta^t u_t' x^j - \gamma \sum_{t=0}^{\infty} x_t^j = 0 \qquad j = 0, \ldots, \infty.$$

These equations are satisfied by $u_t' = \lambda$, for all t, which implies constant consumption. Hence the optimal contract has

$$\gamma_0 = y'^{-1}(\lambda)$$
$$\gamma_j = 0, \qquad j = 1, \ldots, \infty$$

This result does not require quadratic utility.

In contract equilibrium the worker's consumption and earned income are constants. Note that the real allocation, consumption, is the same as in the full competitive equilibrium with complete contingent securities.

B. Variable Labor

A contract in the economy with variable labor supply is a pair of functions $(c(s), \ell(x))$, giving consumption and labor supply as functions of the random variable x. An equilibrium contract is a pair of functions $(c^*(x), \ell^*(x))$, that maximize the worker's expected utility subject to the budget constraint imposed by the production technology. note that we are not considering time-dependent functions in view of the result that they are unnecessary. We will restrict attention to analytic functions and write:

$$c(x) = \sum_{j=0}^{\infty} \gamma_j x^j \text{ and,}$$
$$\ell(x) = \sum_{j=0}^{\infty} \delta_j x^j.$$

The Lagrangian function is

$$L = E \sum_{t=0}^{\infty} \beta^t u \left(\sum_{j=0}^{\infty} \gamma_j x^j, \sum_{t=0}^{\infty} \delta_j x^j \right)$$
$$- \lambda \left[E \sum_{t=0}^{\infty} \beta^t \left(\sum_{j=0}^{\infty} \gamma_j x^j - \sum_{j=0}^{\infty} \delta_j x^{j+1} \right) \right]$$

and the first order conditions for the γ_j and δ_j are

$$E \sum_{t=0}^{\infty} \beta^t u_{1t} x^j - \lambda E \sum_{t=0}^{\infty} \beta^t x^j = 0 \qquad j = 0, \dots \text{ and,}$$

$$E \sum_{t=0}^{\infty} \beta^t u_{2t} x^j + \lambda E \sum_{t=0}^{\infty} \beta^t x^{j+1} = 0 \qquad j = 0, \dots$$

The first of these systems of equations is solved by $u_{1t} = \lambda$ for all t, which can be obtained by choosing:

$$\gamma_0 = u_{1t}^{-1}(\lambda) \text{ and,}$$
$$\gamma_j = 0 \qquad j = 1, \dots,$$

so the optimal contract fixes consumption at a constant, as expected due to the separability of the utility function. The second set of equations is solved by setting

$$u_{2t} = -\lambda x_t.$$

In the quadratic utility case this means $\ell_t = \lambda x_t$, so the optimal contract is obtained by setting:

$$\delta_1 = \lambda \text{ and,}$$
$$\delta_j = 0 \qquad j \neq 1.$$

Thus, the contract equilibrium stabilizes consumption and, in the quadratic case, sets labor proportional to x, marginal productivity. Note that this is not the ordinary labor supply function for this utility function.

VI. Conclusion

The models studied in this chapter are very abstract and obviously do not capture all the interesting features of real economies. The models are nevertheless useful for making some important points. First, contract equilibrium and competitive equilibrium with complete contingent securities markets are both Pareto optimal and indeed they lead to the same allocations of "real" variables—employment, consumption, and output. Second, it is these real allocations that must be compared in order to make welfare or efficiency comparisons across economies. Third, the path of earned income over time is not informative about welfare or efficiency in the presence of asset markets or contractual arrangements in the labor market.

The first point, that contractual agreements should lead to the same allocations as complete competitive equilibrium, was conjectured by Barro [1977] in response to the macro modelling technique of introducing long-term contracts to provide rigidity in adjustment of economic variables.

Table 2–1. Implications of the Different Organizations

	Fixed Employment				Variable Employment			
	Spot Equilibrium	Bonds	Contingent Securities	Contracts	Spot Equilibrium	Bonds	Contingent Securities	Contracts
Consumption	i.i.d	Martingale	Constant	Constant	i.i.d.	Martingale	Constant	Constant
Employment	---	---	---	---	i.i.d.	i.i.d.	i.i.d.[a]	i.i.d.[a]
Wages	i.i.d.	i.i.d.	i.i.d.	Constant[b]	i.i.d.	i.i.d.	i.i.d.	i.i.d.[b]
ρ Wages, employment					+	+	+	−[b]
ρ Consumption, employment					+	+	0	0
ρ Consumption, wages	+	+	0	0	+	+	0	0

[a]More variance than the other cases.
[b]Wages calculated as consumption/employment.

Wright [1985] established the equivalence of competitive and contract equilibrium formally in the context of an overlapping generations model. The simple logic behind this point is that agents will not enter into binding agreements when they would prefer the competitive quilibrium allocations. Consequently, agents must be indifferent between the competitive and contract equilibrium allocations. The optimality of competitive equilibrium then implies optimality of the contract equilibrium as well. In many settings, as here, uniqueness of the competitive equilibrium implies that the allocations in the contract and competitive equilibria must be identical.

Interest in real allocations leads to the conclusions that employment functions and demand functions are the interesting things to study in an effort to compare economies in welfare terms. Output is also an interesting economic variable, though more difficult to interpret. By studying employment functions it may be possible to get some insight into the time path of leisure consumption in the economy.[6] By studying demand functions we hope to get some information about the time path of consumption.

Wage equations, on the other hand, are very hard to interpret in the presence of contractual arrangements in the labor market. If the firm is acting, as the worker's agent, to stabilize consumption, perhaps to save the worker from transaction costs (including time costs) of entering securities markets, then the hourly compensation need not be closely related to consumption when employment is variable. Indeed, these arrangements can easily lead to a negative relationship between hourly compensation and productivity. Consequently, wage equations may not be informative about productivity or about welfare.

Table 2−1 gives a partial summary of the implications of the institutional organizations studied for the dynamics of labor market variables. Since consumption is constant at the optimal equilibrium (occuring in the contract and in the complete contingent securities cases), the correlation between consumption and employment, and the correlation betwen consumption and wages are zero. The correlation between wages and employment is positive, and wages are sero. The correlation between wages and employment is positive, and wages are zero. The correlation between wages and employment is positive in the competitive equilibrium and negative in the contract equilibrium. Since workers are indifferent between these organizations, it is reasonable that an economy could have some industries with different organizations. Consequently, the correlation between wages and employment in the aggregate is not informative about welfare or efficiency.

Notes

1. Azariadis [1975] and Baily [1974] introduced the notion of modelling long-term contracts as a means of transferring risk from workers to less risk averse firms. Empirical work has lagged well behind the development of the theory of contracts in the labor market, but see Abowd and Card [1983] and Kiefer [1984].

2. See Hart [1983].

3. Two technical issues can be dealt with here. First, since we are interested in equilibrium dynamics, we ignore "start up" problems. Second, we ignore the solution in which the consumer accumulates an infinite amount of debt.

4. Hall [1978] obtains the martingale property for the marginal utility of consumption, notes the implication for the consumption process in the quadratic utility case, and explores the empirical implications of the theory.

5. Fischer [1977] and Phelps and Taylor [1977].

6. Altonji and Ham [1985] study the temporal, geographic, and industrial variability of employment in Canada in this book. This analysis, together with assumptions about the optimizing behavior of economic agents, may lead to insight on the process of technology shocks (assumed in the stylized models above to be i.i.d.).

References

Abowd, J.M. and D. Card. 1983. "Intertemporal Substitution in the Presence of Long Term Contracts." Paper 166. Industrial Relations Section, Princeton University.

Altonji, J.C. and J.C. Ham. 1985. "Employment Variation in Canada: The Role of External, National, Regional and Industrial Factors." Working Paper.

Azariadis, C. 1975. "Implicit Contracts and Underemployment Equilibria." *Journal of Political Economy* 83: 1183–1202.

Baily, M.N. 1974. "Wages and Employment under Uncertain Demand." *Review of Economics and Statistics* 41: 37–50.

Barro, R.J. 1977. "Long-Term Contracting, Sticky Prices, and Monetary Policy." *Journal of monetary Economics* 3: 305–316.

Fisher, S. 1977. "Long-Term Contracts, Rational Expectations and the Optimal Money Supply Rule." *Journal of Political Economy* 85: 191–205.

Gordon, R.J. 1982. "Why U.S. Wage and Employment Behavior Differs from that in Britain and Japan." *Economic Journal* 92 (December): 13–44.

Hall, R. 1975. "The Rigidity of Wages and the Persistence of Unemployment." *Brookings Papers on Economic Activity* 2: 301–335.

Hall, R. 1978. "Stochastic Implications of the Life Cycle-Permanent Income Hypothesis: Theory and Evidence." *Journal of Political Economy* 86 (December): 971–988.

Hall, R. 1980. "Employment Fluctuations and Wage Rigidity." *Brookings Papers on Economic Activity* 1: 91–123.

Hart, O.D. 1983. "Optimal Labor Contracts under Asymmetric Information: An Introduction." *Review of Economics and Statistics* LXV: 3–35.

Kiefer, N.M. 1984. "Employment Contracts, Job Search Theory, and an Empirical Model of Labor Turnover." Working Paper, Department of Economics, Cornell University.

Phelps, E.S. and J.B. Taylor. 1977. "Stabilizing Power of Monetary Policy under Rational Price Expectations." *Journal of Political Economy* 85: 163–190.

Wright, R. 1983. "Labor Markets and Labor Contracts in a Dynamic General Equilibrium Model." Revised March 1985.

II OBSERVED DISLOCATION: INTERNATIONAL COMPARISONS

3 WAGE FLEXIBILITY IN THE UNITED STATES AND JAPAN

Masanori Hashimoto and John Raisian

I. Introduction

One of the most mystifying economic phenomena of our time, according to Robert J. Gordon, is the rigidity of wages in the United States [Gordon, 1981].[1] In apparent contrast to the United States' wage rigidity situation is the Japanese situation where long-term employment prevails, wages are seemingly quite flexible, and layoffs occur rarely. Indeed, Gordon finds that the United States exhibits more rigid wages and more flexible employment than either Japan or Great Britain, and that Japan has the most flexible

Hashimoto's research was conducted while he was at the University of Washington and a National Fellow at the Hoover Institution, and was supported in part by the U.S. Department of Labor Contract #41usc252c3. Many useful comments were offered by the participants at the conference. In particular, we wish to thank Joe Altonji, John Ham, Daniel Hamermesh, Nick Kiefer, Kazuo Koike, Duane Leigh, and Ronald Oaxaca for their helpful remarks. We apologize if we have missed other names. We are grateful to Peter Chinloy and Ernst Stromsdorfer for organizing such an interesting conference. We acknowledge the able research assistance by Barbara Brugman, Ken Emery, Eanswythe Leicester, Junji Shiba, Prapan Tianwattanatada, Charlotte Toney, and William Welch.

wages of the three countries examined. Gordon's findings are based on aggregate data for these countries.

The purpose of this chapter is towfold. First, we use the Panel Study of Income Dynamics (PSID) for the United States to investigate the possibility that the commonly used measures of wage rigidity based on aggregate data overstate the extent of wage rigidity. Although notable economists have documented the existence of wage rigidity in the United States (for example, Hall [1980] and Gordon [1982], there are issues for consideration that remain unsettled. We also investigate differences in wage flexibility across experience, race, sex, and education categories. The basic finding is that wages in the United States are more flexible than one might have thought based on the aggregate data. Second, we investigate the extent of wage flexibility in Japan and find United States wages to be less flexible than wages in Japan. We investigate the extent of wage flexibility and long-term employment in Japan, and evaluate the role of bonus payments that are thought to contribute to wage flexibility. In particular, we examine whether the relationships between the magnitude of bonus payments and their determinants have changed with the structural changes experienced by the Japanese economy in recent years.

II. Wage Flexibility in the United States

A. The Degree of Wage Rigidity in Aggregate Time Series

Employment and aggregate hours worked exhibit much more pronounced movements over business cycles than nominal or real wages when focusing on aggregate United States magnitudes. To show this pattern, we report in table 3−1 regressions of the logarithm of various labor force magnitudes on a time trend and the overall civilian unemployment rate. A one percentage point rise in the unemployment rate is associated with a 1.4% decline in employment and a 2.4% decline in aggregate hours worked, indicating procyclical movements in these series. In contrast, nominal and real wages, as well as compensation, are found not to vary appreciably, or statistically, over the business cycle. Only the real average hourly wage shows some procyclical movement: a one percentage point increase in the unemployment rate is associate with a 0.8% decline in the real hourly wage aggregate. However, the wage aggregate adjusted by the United States Bureau of Labor Statistics (BLS) for overtime premiums and interindustry employment shifts is not sensitive to the business cycle. (See the two rows for adjusted average hourly wages in table 3−1.)

Table 3−1.   Trends and Cyclical Variability in Aggregate United States Labor
Force Magnitudes (1967−84)

Variable	Annual Trend (percent)	Cyclical Coefficient* (percent)
Employment-to-population ratio	0.6	−1.4
Total hours worked index	2.3	−2.4
Average hourly wage— nominal	7.0	−0.2
Adjusted average hourly wage—nominal	7.1	0.2
Hourly compensation index— nominal	7.7	0.2
Average hourly wage— real	−0.1	· −0.8
Adjusted average hourly wage—Real ~ *takes out overtime et* ≥0.1		0.1
Hourly compensation index— Real	0.5	0.2

Source: Economic Report of the President, 1985, tables B−32, B−33, B−38, and B−40.
*The cyclical coefficient represents the percentage change in the variable under consideration associated with a one percentage point increase in the overall civilian unemployment rate.
Note: The employment/population ratio is relevant for the civilian non-institutional population; the total hours worked index is for all persons in the nonfarm business sector (based on establishment data); average hourly wages are for private nonagricultural employment; the adjusted hourly wage refers to computations made to net out overtime and interindustry employment shifts; the hourly compensation index is for all persons in the nonfarm business sector (based on establishment data); nominal figures refer to magnitudes in current dollars and real figures refer to magnitudes in constant dollars.

The evidence of wage rigidity presented in table 3−1 relies on aggregate data. These data underestimate the degree of wage flexibility for individual workers, however. One reason is that low wage workers are more likely to lose their jobs during recessions than high wage workers. As a result, low wage workers become less represented in the aggregate wage and employment statistics during recessions as compared to prosperous times.[2] Any procyclical fluctuations in the wages of those who remain employed throughout a cyclical disturbance become obscured in the aggregate data by the exit of low wage workers during bad times and their entry during good times.[3] Another reason that aggregate data underestimate the degree of wage flexibility is that contractions in labor demand are not evenly dispersed throughout the economy during a recessionary period. Given the existence of skill specificity, mobility costs, and implicit contracts, the pressure by the market to reduce wages is not even throughout the economy. Instead, it is concentrated in those sectors most affected by the overall contraction. Consequently, computation of overall wage aggregates could easily underestimate the degree of individual wage flexibility where demand contractions are pronounced. These considerations suggest that longitudinal micro data on individual workers provide more reliable evidence about the underlying pressures on wages over the course of cyclical activity.

To investigate the extent of wage rigidity in detail, we draw a sample from the PSID for the period 1967–79 that consists of heads of household below 65 years of age, who are employed (but not self-employed) in non-agricultural industries (excluding the military). To be included in this sample, these household heads must have worked during the course of a year. Wages earned from working extra jobs are eliminated from the labor income and the hours worked aggregates for each individual. The PSID data contain both a random sample and a sample of low income families. We confine our analysis to the random sample in order to limit potential contamination of any conclusions that are drawn from the empirical results.

Aggregate nominal and real hourly earnings series are displayed in table 3–2. To compare with the PSID series, the table includes hourly earnings of private nonagricultural workers published by the BLS. The average hourly wages for the PSID data are calculated in the same way that the BLS magnitudes are computed—total annual earnings of all persons in the sample divided by total hours worked of all persons in the sample.[4] In the PSID sample, earnings and hours worked magnitudes are drawn only from the main jobs of household heads who are not older than age 64. Otherwise, the series should be comparable. Using information attributable to only the main job purges wage variability that can occur as a result of shifts in hours worked across jobs for multiple job holders. It is not surprising to find that hourly wages of household heads are greater than overall hourly wages as presented in the BLS series. However, the simple correlation coefficients between the BLS and PSID series are 0.999 for nominal wages and 0.817 for real wages, suggesting that the series move in close relation to each other.

As is readily apparent, the time series of wages presented in table 3–2 shows an upward trend, especially the nominal wage series. While our purpose is to investigate wage variability, we are not interested in the variability associated with regular trend movements. To assess the extent of cyclical wage variability in the aggregate data (abstracting from trend), regressions of logarithm of wages on a time trend and the overall unemployment rate are again estimated. Resulting estimates are contained in table

Table 3−2.   United States Average Hourly Earnings Series

	Nominal Earnings		Real Earnings	
Year	BLS	PSID	BLS	PSID
1967	2.68	3.64	2.68	3.64
1968	2.85	3.86	2.73	3.70
1969	3.04	4.10	2.77	3.73
1970	3.23	4.42	2.78	3.80
1971	3.45	4.57	2.84	3.77
1972	3.70	4.87	2.95	3.88
1973	3.94	5.18	2.96	3.89
1974	4.24	5.65	2.93	3.83
1975	4.53	6.10	2.81	3.78
1976	4.86	6.63	2.85	3.89
1977	5.25	7.21	2.89	3.97
1978	5.69	7.75	2.91	3.96
1979	6.16	8.43	2.83	3.88

Source: Economic Report of the President, 1985, table B−38 and the PSID data base.
Notes: BLS earnings are for private nonagricultural workers. PSID earnings are for workers who are household heads not over age 64, not self-employed, not from the low-income portion of the PSID sample, and not in the agricultural or military sectors; income generated from secondary jobs is also excluded. Nominal hourly earnings are calculated as the ratio of aggregate earnings to aggregate hours for the BLS series, the time frame for measuring earnings is a survey week; whereas, for the PSID series, the time frame is an entire year. Real hourly earnings are nominal earnings deflated by the CPI.

3−3. For both the BLS and PSID series, nominal wages are trending upward by 7.1 to 7.2% per year over the sample period. Real wages are trending upward at a rate of between 0.5 and 0.6% per year for the two series. Both nominal and real wages are observed to be procyclical in that increases in the unemployment rate are associated with wage decreases. A one percentage point increase in the overall unemployment rate is associated with a 0.1% decline in the real hourly wage in the BLS series and a 0.2% decline in the real hourly wage in the PSID series. The comparable figures for the nominal wage series are 0.7 and 0.8%, respectively. Thus, the PSID series exhibits a somewhat more procyclical pattern, though none of the numbers is particularly large and certainly the differences between the BLS and PSID cyclical estimates are not statistically significant. Despite the differences in samples, the aggregate wage series are very similar in terms of trend and cyclical movements, even though there are clearly differences in wage levels between the two series.

Although the procyclical pattern is not very pronounced in the aggregate

Table 3–3. Trend and Cyclical Coefficient Estimates in Aggregate United States Wage Equations (1967–79)

Wage Measure	Nominal Wages			Real Wages		
	Trend	Cycle	Standard Error of Estimate	Trend	Cycle	Standard Error of Estimate
BLS	.0708	−.0067	.0092	.0050	−.0010	.0266
	(.0010)	(.0026)		(.0029)	(.0074)	
PSID	.0722	−.0080	.0231	.0062	−.0019	.0149
	(.0025)	(.0064)		(.0016)	(.0041)	
PSID—job maintainers	.0742	−.0081	.0141	.0082	−.0022	.0217
	(.0015)	(.0039)		(.0024)	(.0060)	
PSID—reported wage rate	.1017	−.0317	.0622	.0276	−.0336	.0480
	(.0068)	(.0194)		(.0052)	(.0150)	

Notes: Samples for the BLS and PSID wage magnitudes are described in the notes that accompany the previous tables. Job maintainers refer to observations on household heads who experienced no unemployment or who did not change jobs during the course of a year. The reported wage magnitude refers to a sample of household heads who report a straight-time hourly wage rate. This sample covers the period 1970–80 and consists of a subset of the PSID sample that pertains to average hourly earnings over the course of a whole year. Magnitudes in parentheses are standard errors pertaining to the coefficient estimates. The dependent variables are all in log form.

series, we check whether the pattern is solely attributable to individuals who experience some unemployment or change jobs. Observations that are indicative of those circumstances are deleted from the sample, leaving a sample of job maintainers.[5] As is evident in table 3−3, this sample yields an aggregate series that has a somewhat higher real wage growth and a somewhat higher procyclical pattern, though not different statistically. But the interesting point is that the aggregate wage series for job maintainers exhibits the same cyclical pattern as the whole sample. Those experiencing unemployment or switching jobs evidently are not totally responsible for observed cyclical wage movements.

A distinct contrast is available using the PSID data between the average hourly wages series and a reported wage rate series. In the early part of a calendar year heads of households are asked about their earnings for the previous calendar year and their current straight-time hourly wage rate, if appropriate. Whereas the sample period for the average hourly wage series is 1967−79, reported wage rates are available for the period 1970−80.[6] Findings indicate that a one percentage point increase in the overall unemployment rate is associated with a 3.2% decline in the aggregate nominal wage rate and a 3.4% decline in the real wage rate. These are substantially greater declines than observed for the average hourly wage series. Furthermore, they are greater than the percentage declines in employment and total hours worked protrayed in Table 3−1. The same increase in the unemployment rate is associated with a 1.4 and 2.4% reduction in employment and hours worked, respectively.

It was not immediately apparent why the aggregate series using reported wage rates exhibits a greater procyclical pattern. There are at least two underlying conceptual differences between the overall PSID series and the reported wages series. First, the reported wage is a straight-time wage rate, whereas the average hourly wage includes overtime premiums. Since overtime premiums tend to be procyclical, however, this consideration suggests that the reported wage may be less cyclically sensitive, contrary to what is observed. Second, the implicit weighting of wages is different in the two series. In the average hourly wage series, wages are weighted by annual hours worked. There is no counterpart in the reported wage series; every stated wage received an equal weight.

In general, one finds that low wage workers experience greater layoff propensities during a downturn, but that high wage workers experience somewhat greater reductions in weekly hours worked, abstracting from layoffs. Available research suggests that the layoff effect dominates the weekly hours effect (see Raisian [1983]). Consequently, this would cause either series to exhibit greater wage rigidity than in a situation where this composition effect is controlled for. In the average hourly wage series, individuals are less likely to disappear from the sample since wages and hours worked cover an entire year. Low wage workers receive lower weights, but few will receive zero weights. On the other hand, the reported wage series, which gives zero weights to workers laid off, will not capture as many workers experiencing layoff given that it represents a sample of wages at an instant in time. Thus, it is unclear how the differential weighting affects the cyclical movements in the two aggregate wage series.

It is possible that there is a sample selection issue involved—individuals who report their hourly wage happen to experience greater cyclical wage variability relative to the fuller PSID sample. As an approximate test, we can look at sample size characteristics to discern this possibility. The number of observations in the reported wage sample is 60% of the number in the PSID average hourly wage sample. Some reduction is expected because the reported wage is not available for the first two periods of the 13-year data period. Furthermore, a wage rate is not reported if a person is unemployed or out of the labor force at the time of the survey, even though the person reports positive earnings for the previous year and is included in the fuller PSID sample. Suppose that this reduction in sample size were accompanied by no reduction in the number of individuals surveyed, that is, observations per person fall with no change in the number of respondents. In this case, one would be reluctant to assert that cyclically sensitive people are being selected. On the other hand, if the number of individuals that report a wage rate were 60% of the number in the fuller PSID sample, one would be more confident that the differential cyclical result attributable to person-specific sample selection. As it turns out, the number of individuals in the reported wage sample is 82% of the fuller sample, indicating that some person-specific selectivity explains the differential cyclical finding.

Another piece of evidence is available. For the reported wage sample, we can estimate the cyclical effect by using average hourly wage magnitudes rather than reported wage rates. If the cyclical results in this sample are similar to the results for the overal PSID sample, one can infer that the difference is due to the definitions of the wage measures. If, instead, they are similar to the results for the reported wage sample, one infers the sample selection differences. Using the average hourly wage measures for the reported wage sample, we find that a one percentage point rise in the unemployment rate is associated with a 2.5% decline in nominal average hourly wages and a 2.2% decline in real average hourly wages. These estimates are much closer to those obtained using the wage rate than for those from the overall PSID sample. Consequently, we are confident that most of the differences in results between the overall average hourly wage and reported wage samples is attributable to the fact that individuals in the reported wage sample are more affected by business cycle fluctuations. This finding substantiates our premise that aggregation can mask much of the underlying cyclical wage variability. It is interesting to note that 52% of the overall PSID sample observations are blue-collar workers and 65% of the reported wage sample are blue-collar workers. This is the most notable characteristic that distinguishes the samples. One may infer from this evidence that blue collar workers are more likely to report hourly wages and that this group's wages are more cyclically sensitive.

B. Measures of Within-Individual Wage Flexibility

We contend that aggregate time series on hourly wages masks a great deal of cyclical wage variability experienced by individual workers, even on a collective basis. As evidence, we present estimates generated from the following two simplistic regression specifications:

$$1n \ w_t = a_1 + b_1 t + v_t \qquad (3-1)$$

$$1n \ w_t = a_2 + b_2 t + c_2 u_t + e_t, \qquad (3-2)$$

where $1n \ w_t$ refers to the natural logarithm of the chosen wage magnitude for time period t, u_t is the overall unemployment rate at time t, the a's are constant terms, the b's are trend coefficients, c is a cyclical coefficient, and v and e are disturbance terms. These regressions are estimated for each of the four aggregate series as well as for each individual separately using each of the three PSID samples.[7]

A measure of the variability in trend-adjusted wages is given by the standard error of the estimate associated with regression $(3-1)$, denoted as s_v. This estimate is generated for each of the aggregate series and is presented in column 1 of table $3-4$. With respect to real wages, the estimates range from .0144 for the overall PSID sample to .0578 for the PSID reported wage sample. That is, for the overall PSID sample, one standard deviation in trend-adjusted wages amounts to 1.44% of the trend-adjusted mean. A trend-adjusted standard error is also estimated separately for every individual in each of the PSID sample.[8] Averages of these individual standard errors are presented in column 2 of table $3-4$.[9] For the overall PSID sample, the typical (i.e., average) standard error of the estimte for real wages is .2046, or 14 times the same standard error estimated for the aggregate series. Thus, a typical individual's wage variability is much greater than the variability exhibited within the aggregate series. This observation

Table 3–4.   Wage Variability for Aggregate and Individual Time Series

Wage Measure	Trend-Adjusted Standard Error		Standard Error Attributable to Cyclical Disturbances	
	Aggregate	Average for Individuals	Aggregate	Average for Individuals
Nominal Wages				
BLS	.0114	---	.0026	---
PSID	.0237	.2026	.0017	.0217
PSID—job maintainers	.0161	.1352	.0027	.0160
PSID—reported wage rate	.0678	.1081	.0092	.0195
Real wages				
BLS	.0254	---	.0000	---
PSID	.0144	.2046	.0002	.0216
PSID—job maintainers	.0209	.1373	.0002	.0159
PSID—reported wage rate	.0578	.1121	.0125	.0202

Notes: For the aggregate series, the trend-adjusted standard error amounts to the standard error of the estimate for the regression of log wages on a time trend; the standard error attributable to cyclical disturbances is formally calculated as the trend-adjusted standard error minus the product of the relevant standard error presented in table 3–3 and a normalizing factor equal to the square root of $\{(N-3)/(N-2)\}$, where N denotes the number of years in the regression. The normalizing factor prevents the cyclical standard error from becoming negative due to the degrees-of-freedom consideration. Conceptually, it represents the variability in trend-adjusted wages attributable to cyclical disturbances. Regressions of log wages on a time trend as well as a time trend and the overall unemployment rate were estimated for every household head in the sample. Weighted averages of the above standard errors were calculated across individuals with the weights being the number of time periods observed for an individual.

holds true for each of the PSID samples and for both nominal and real trend-adjusted wages.

Observing that a typical individual experiences greater wage variability than is indicated in an aggregate wage series, however, does not signify that the greater variability is attributable mainly to cyclical phenomena rather than to pure random influences. To clarify this point, the trend-adjusted standard error of the estimate can be decomposed into two components: one that is attributable to overall cyclical disturbances, with the other being a random component, as follows:

$$s_v = s_u + s_e', \qquad (3-3)$$

where

$$s_e' = s_e \{(n-3)/(n-2)\}^{1/2}, \qquad (3-4)$$

and s_e is the standard error of the estimate for regression (3–2). The latter standard error, s_e, is renormalized so that the two standard errors are deflated by the same number of degrees of freedom. Failure to do this could result in a situation where $s_v < s_e$ and $s_u < 0$, a situation that is not intuitively pleasing. Renormalization ensures that $s_v > s_e'$ and $s_u = s_v - s_e' > 0$.

Components of the trend-adjusted standard errors attributable to cyclical disturbances, s_u, can be computed for each of the aggregate series as well as for each of the individual series. Averages of the s_u's are then computed across individuals for each of the PSID samples. With respect to real wages, a typical individual in the overall PSID sample has a cyclical standard error amounting to .0216 compared to virtually zero for the BLS and overall PSID aggregate series—indicative of much greater cyclical wage variability at the individual level. Furthermore, the individual cyclical standard error of .0216 is greater than the whole trend-adjusted standard error, s_v, for the aggregate series that amounts of .0144. Clearly, the aggregate series underestimates the degree of cyclical wage variability experienced by the typical individual. For each of the PSID samples and for both nominal and real wage measures, the individual cyclical standard error exceeds the aggregate counterpart by a significant margin. Thus, it is clear that using aggregate wage series attributes as a benchmark leads to an understatement of the degree of wage flexibility in the United States.

C. Demographic Differences in Wage Flexibility

Individual trend-adjusted standard errors, both overall and the cyclical component, s_v and s_e', respectively, are easily tabulated for different demographic groups—namely, sex, race, education, and experience level.[10] Averages are then computed so as to determine whether standard errors for typical individuals vary across demographic groups. These tabulations for real wages in each of the PSID samples are presented in table 3–5.[11] Women who are heads of household experience greater wage variability than male heads.[12] Furthermore, women do exhibit somewhat greater cyclical wage variability, though the contrast is statistically significantly only for the reported wage sample. Whereas the cyclical standard error is 11.5% greater for women in the overall PSID sample, it is 34.7% greater in the

Table 3−5. Real Trend-Adjusted Decompositions for PSID Samples

	PSID		PSID—Job Maintainers		PSID—Reported Wage Rate	
Group	Total	Cyclical	Total	Cyclical	Total	Cyclical
Total	.2046	.2016	.1373	.0159	.1121	.0202
Male	.1977	.0209	.1335	.0155	.1091	.0190
Female	.2319*	.0233	.1590*	.0182	.1210*	.0256*
White	.1980	.0210	.1333	.0156	.1094	.0202
Black	.2516*	.0225	.1772*	.0181	.1221	.0179
Other	.1993	.0280	.1281	.0160	.1176	.0225
Education						
0 Years	.2126	.0169	.2113	.0157	.1009	.0200
8 Years	.2062	.0197	.1455*	.0158	.1077	.0149
12 Years	.2030	.0211	.1332*	.0159	.1110	.0192
16 Years	.1998	.0226	.1346*	.0160	.1144	.0280
Experience						
0 Years	.2795	.0386	.1575	.0273	.1332	.0346
10 Years	.2212*	.0260*	.1426*	.0196*	.1221*	.0237*
20 Years	.1854*	.0179*	.1342*	.0149*	.1110*	.0168*
30 Years	.1722*	.0143*	.1321*	.0132*	.0999*	.0137*
40 Years	.1815*	.0152*	.1364*	.0145*	.0888*	.0144*
50 Years	.2134*	.0206*	.1471	.0189*	.0777*	.0191*

Notes: The above magnitudes are weighted average standard errors for each of the PSID samples and for each of the specified groups (weighted by the number of observations per person). "Total" refers to the trend adjusted standard error and "cyclical" refers to the standard error attributable to the cyclical disturbances. Asterisks beside the standard error indicate a statistically significant difference between that standard error and the first standard error presented within each grouping.

reported wage sample

Blacks are found to exhibit greater trend-adjusted wage variability than whites. This is not surprising given the empirical literature that contrasts earnings by race. We find, however, that variability attributable to cyclical disturbances is not significantly different between blacks and whites, at least not for household heads. In the overall PSID sample, blacks do exhibit cyclical standard errors that are 7.1% greater than whites (though not significantly different). However, in the reported wage sample, blacks have cyclical standard errors that are 12.8% *lower* than whites (also not significantly different). The stylized fact is that black employment is much more affected by cyclical shocks than white employment. In contrast, our findings indicate that that cyclical wage flexibility is rather similar for blacks and whites.

The degree of trend-adjusted wage flexibility, both overall and the cyclical component, is not found to vary appreciably by educational attainment in either the overall PSID or reported wage sample. On the other hand, wage variability does differ appreciably for individuals having differing levels of potential labor market experience—defined as an individual's age minus years of education minus six. For the overall PSID sample, both the overall and cyclical standard errors exhibit U-shaped patterns with respect to potential experience levels; individuals with the lowest and highest amounts of experience have the greatest wage variability. For the reported wage sample, results are similar except that overall standard errors decline with experience throughout. In either sample, the degree of cyclical wage flexibility for individuals with no experience is more than 2.5 times greater than for individuals with 30 years of experience.

Years of education and experience are commonly used as indicators of skill levels held by individuals. However, one does not know a priori what amount of the skills are general versus firm-specific. If the magnitudes of general and specific skills are not correlated with each other, then increasing education and experience levels are suggestive of increasing general skills, and the commonly assumed physical-human capital complementarity argument suggests moderate cyclical volatility in the demand for labor inputs having greater skill levels. In this case, more educated or experienced individals are prone to less cyclical wage variability. This pattern is evident in our results for experience, though not for education.

If general and specific skill magnitudes are positively correlated with each other, however, increases in education or experience indicate greater amounts of both general and specific skills on average. In this situation, there is an opposite response that can occur as a result of a short-term demand contraction. Labor inputs with greater amounts of specific skills have greater incentive to ensure their jobs status so as to receive future returns on their previous investments in specific skills. (See our discussion on Japanese bonus payments below.) This suggests an effect counter to the general skill argument, in that more educated or experienced individuals will offer greater wage concessions during a cyclical decline to ensure job stability. The net effect of the general and specific skill arguments is indeterminate, however. If the positive correlation assumption holds true, the empirical results suggest that in the case of education the net effect is zero, and in the case of experience the general human capital effect is dominant.

III. Wage Flexibility and Bonus Payments in Japan

Wages are quite flexible in Japan, as Gordon [1982] has pointed out. Flexibility is evident in all components of earnings—base, contract, bonus, and total earnings. Indeed, although bonuses are an important source of labor cost flexibility, they are by no means the sole source. The wage base itself is quite flexible: it is renegotiated every year during the Spring Offensive (Shunto), thereby providing labor cost flexibility in the Japanese economy (see Gordon [1982]).

This point is demonstrated with the aid of table 3−6, where we present time-series evidence on the flexibility in the base, contract (base plus overtime), bonus, and total earnings (contract plus bonus) by firm size and occupation. In the Basic Survey of Wage Structure (Chingin Kozo Kihon Tokei Chosa), the distinction between blue and while collar occupations is available only for a few industries. In particular, it is not available for all industries combined, and we focus on the manufacturing industry here. The figures in table 3−6 are the standard errors attributable to cyclical distur-

Table 3−6. Cyclical Variability in Male Earnings (1967−82) for Japanese Manufacturing Industries by Firm Size and Occupation

| Variability in Earnings | Firm Size (Employment) | | | | | | | |
| | (10+) | | (10−99) | | (100−999) | | (1000+) | |
	Blue	White	Blue	White	Blue	White	Blue	White
Nominal								
Base	.097	.096	.086	.094	.105	.094	.091	.097
Contract	.095	.092	.084	.092	.102	.092	.080	.088
Bonus	.102	.087	.099	.091	.106	.089	.073	.082
Total	.100	.092	.088	.093	.105	.093	.086	.089
Real								
Base	.043	.049	.043	.053	.044	.047	.037	.046
Contract	.049	.054	.049	.055	.051	.051	.039	.050
Bonus	.050	.057	.059	.069	.052	.054	.024	.046
Total	.051	.056	.050	.058	.052	.053	.039	.051
Average Ratio								
Bonus/Total	.188	.241	.150	.180	.192	.237	.211	.265

Source: Basic Survey of Wage Structure (Chingin Kozo Kihon Tokei Chosa).
Notes: Contract earnings are base plus overtime earnings and other contractually determined payments, and total earnings are contract plus bonus earnings. Variability is measured by the standard error attributable to cyclical disturbances as in table 3−4. Blue means blue collar (production) and white, white collar (nonproduction) workers. Real values are obtained by deflating nominal values by CPI (1965 = 100).

bances calculated as s_u in equation (3−3), just as in the United States measures reported in table 3−4. The only difference between the Japanese and the U.S. measures is that the cyclical variable in the underlying Japanese regressions (see equation (3−2)) is the gross national expenditure rather than the unemployment rate as in the U.S. regressions. The Japanese unemployment rate series is judged to be an inappropriate cyclical variable for our purpose, for it exhibits only modest fluctuations during the time period under consideration.

Comparison of this table with table 3−4 (column 3) strongly suggests that wages are much more flexible in Japan than in the United States, thereby endorsing Gordon's findings. The reader is cautioned, however, in comparing the United States and Japanese estimates because the Japanese data refer only to manufacturing while the U.S. data refer to all industries. The purpose of table 3−6 is not so much to provide a United States-Japan comparison as to demonstrate that all components of earnings vary considerably over the business cycle and that the extent of variability differs by occupation and firm size.

According to the last row of table 3−6, the bonus-total earnings ratio averaged over the 1967−82 period is higher for white than for blue collar workers, and is higher for workers in larger firms. During the period under study, blue collar workers in large firms received 21% of total earnings in bonuses while the figure for white collar workers was 26%. The importance of bonus payments is obvious even in small firms: blue collar workers received 15%, and white collar workers 18% of total earnings in bonuses.

Bonus payments fluctuate considerably over the business cycle, often more than other components of earnings. Variability in both base and contract earnings is vividly demonstrated in table 3−6. In real terms, white collar workers tend to experience slightly greater variability than blue collar workers, though in nominal terms the pattern is often reversed. For example, in firms employing more than ten workers, the real base wage varies by 4.3% for blue collar workers and 4.9% for white collar workers, but the nominal base wage varies by 9.7% for blue and 9.6% for white collar workers. Workers in larger firms tend to experience less variability in real earnings, though the medium-size (100−999) group is often a pattern breaker. In general, the variability in total earnings is only slightly larger than in contract earnings, implying that the covariance between the annual percent change in contact earning ($dlnC$) and the absolute change in the ratio of bonus to contract earnings ($d(B/C)$) is negative. The negative covariance in turn implies that the average annual percent change in bonus earnings is smaller than in contract earnings. An important message of table 3−6 is that the bonus is not the sole source of wage flexibility, as the base

Table 3−7.   Bonus Payments as a Percent of Annual Total Cash Earnings in Selected Years, 1951−81

	Workers in All Industries Size of Employment			Workers in Manufacturing Industries Size of Employment		
	5+	*5−29*	*30+*	*5+*	*5−29*	*30+*
1951	na	na	13.6	na	na	12.5
1955	na	na	14.4	na	na	12.6
1959	16.5	11.0	18.0	15.8	7.3	17.5
1963	19.9	14.4	21.3	19.0	11.4	20.6
1967	20.9	15.3	22.4	20.1	12.7	21.5
1971	23.1	17.4	24.8	22.9	15.2	24.5
1979	23.8	18.4	26.1	23.1	15.8	25.0
1981	23.9	17.7	26.4	23.5	15.2	25.5

Source: Year Book of Labor Statistics, various issues.
Notes: Bonus payments are based on the official data on special payments of which the bulk is bonus payments.

wage itself exhibits a great deal of volatility with aggregate economic conditions.

The payment of bonuses is widespread in Japan. Not only is it a common practice but the magnitudes are appreciable relative to total wages. Yet, the bonus issue has received much less attention in the literature than the "lifetime" employment practice, often cited as a symbol of unique industrial relations in Japan. We consider bonuses to be a key feature in the Japanese long-term employment phenomenon, and as this phenomenon is transformed, so will be the practice of bonus payments. Typically, bonuses are paid twice a year, once in July, when the Japanese celebrate *obon* (the occasion for the visitation by the spirits of the deceased) and again in December, when they get ready to welcome the new year. These payments are made not only to white collar but to blue collar workers as well (see table 3−6). The bonus is a common component of worker earnings, attested to by the fact that Japanese official statistics report special payments, of which bonus payments are the most significant component, in their earnings data.[13]

Table 3−7 indicates that bonus payments are a significant share of the annual cash earnings of Japanese workers. For example, in 1981 for all industries combined, workers received, depending on firm size, between 17.7 and 26.4% of their earnings in bonuses. As we observed in table 3−6, the share of bonus payments in total earnings is related to firm size. It is worth noting that the share of bonuses has tended to increase during the last

30 years, though in firms employing 5 to 29 workers it went down between 1979 and 1981.

A. Long-Term Employment in Japan

Since the bonus is viewed here as an integral part of the long-term employment phenomenon in Japan, we begin with a brief discussion of the phenomenon. Many of the workers are hired immediately after graduation

Table 3−8.   Probabilities for Retaining the Same Job for Fifteen Years by Sex: Japan and the United States

		Japan			
	In 1962				
Age	*Tenure*	*% of Population*		*Probabilities (1962−77)*	
		Males	*Females*	*Males*	*Females*
15−19 yrs	0−5 yrs	33.5	37.0	.364	.037
20−24	0−5	51.7	40.7	.451	.082
	5+	14.4	9.1	.653	.092
25−34	0−5	27.4	9.1	.427	.281
	5+	42.3	9.8	.730	.528
35−39	0−5	15.7	8.4	.377	.327
	5+	49.4	8.0	.759	.788

		United States			
	In 1963				
Age	*Tenure*	*% of Population*		*Probabilities (1963−78)*	
		Males	*Females*	*Males*	*Females*
14−19 yrs	0−5 yrs	25.1	19.6	.056	.011
20−24	0−5	64.7	38.2	.130	.050
	5+	5.1	1.8	.300	.242
25−34	0−5	54.3	23.9	.222	.125
	5+	32.9	8.1	.473	.383
35−44	0−5	34.9	24.5	.244	.189
	5+	54.3	15.8	.545	.427
45−49	0−5	28.8	21.1	.172	.172
	5+	59.3	23.6	.401	.276

Source: Basic Survey of Employment Structure (Shugyo Kozo Kihon Chosa), for Japan; *Special Labor Force Reports*, various issues, for the United States.

Table 3–9.   Percent of Employed Males by Tenure and Firm Size: Japan and the United States

Tenure	Japan (1979)					United States (1979)				
	All (1)	Tiny (2)	Small (3)	Medium (4)	Large (5)	All (1)	Tiny (2)	Small (3)	Medium (4)	Large (5)
Less than 1 yr.	7.9	10.4	9.7	7.7	3.8	19.4	29.7	22.3	16.0	11.2
1–4	21.5	24.8	22.2	21.6	13.5	30.6	37.7	37.1	32.2	24.4
5–9	22.2	20.4	22.4	23.9	21.8	19.4	16.0	18.5	21.3	21.7
10–14	17.7	16.4	16.6	18.9	19.1	11.7	7.6	8.9	12.6	15.4
15–19	11.9	9.1	10.0	12.3	16.2	6.5	3.9	5.2	7.3	8.4
20+	18.8	18.7	16.0	15.7	25.6	12.4	5.0	7.9	10.5	18.8
Median (years)	8.2	8.0	8.0	8.1	12.0	4	2	3	5	7
Eventual tenure years	25.0	23.6	22.4	23.6	30.8	15.6	9.6	12.2	15.4	20.6

Source: Calculated from the *Basic Survey of Employment (Japan)*, 1979, and the *Current Population Survey (United States)*, 1979. This table is reproduced from Hashimoto and Raisian [1985].

Notes:

Employed males in private industries.

Tiny means 1–9 for Japan and 1–25 for the United States, Small means 10–99 for Japan and 26–99 for United States, Medium means 100–999, and Large means 1,000+ for both countries. Eventual tenure is calculated as twice the mean tenure.

and expect to stay with a single employer throughout their working lives. It should be noted, however, that the "lifetime" employment practice applies primarily to male regular workers. The majority of female workers, as well as male temporary or casual workers, are excluded from the practice. Also, long-term employment is most evident in large firms, though in this respect many small firms try to emulate large firms, as we will discuss shortly. To be sure, the United States labor market manifests some degree of long-term employment as well [Hall, 1982]. Nonetheless, employment duration is considerably longer in Japan than in the United States.

Tables 3−8 and 3−9 are used to highlight Japanese U.S. contrasts in job tenure. Table 3−8 gives the estimates of the probability that a typical worker retains the same job for 15 years or more. In this table, we use the ratio of workers in a particular tenure-age category to population rather than to employed persons to allow for mobility between labor force and nonlabor force activities as well as among different employers. The probability estimates are calculated as follows: in 1962, 33.5% of the Japanese male population aged 15−19 years were in the 0−5 years tenure category. Fifteen years later, in 1977, only 12.2% percent of the male poplation 30−34 years of age were in the 15−20 year tenure category (not reported in the table to save space). Therefore, the probability that a typical male 15−19 years of age with 0−5 years of tenure in 1962 was still working for the same employer in 1977 is calculated to be .364 (12.2/33.5) or, in percentage terms, 36.4%. The comparable figure for the United States is 5.6%. There is no denying the fact that Japanese males have a much higher probability of staying with the same job for 15 years. In both countries, the probability of holding the same job for 15 years tends to be lower for women than for men, and it tends to be higher for Japanese than for American women, though these patterns are by no means without exception.

Table 3−9 presents distributions of employed males by years of tenure for four different firm-size categories for Japan and the United States. Eventual tenure is calculated by doubling the mean tenure of current jobs, a procedure commonly used to estimate the eventual duration of current unemployment spells. (See, for instance, Salant [1977] and Akerlof and Main [1981]). Both percent distribution and the estimated eventual tenure indicate that employment duration is longer in Japan than in the United Sates. There is also a clear tendency for workers in larger firms to have longer tenures; interestingly, this tendency is more pronounced in the United States than in Japan.

One reason for firm-size differences in job tenure could be the higher failure rates of small firms, resulting in a greater number of involuntary discharges than in large firms. However, there is evidence indicating that the proportion of job leavers due to involuntary discharge, which presumably includes the case of business failures, is, if anything, highest in the largest firms and lowest in the smallest firms [Cole, 1979]. Therefore, there must be more to firm-size differences in employment tenure than just the differential failure rates. (See Hashimoto and Raisian [1985] for detailed discussions on this point.) Note also that employment tenure is quite high even in tiny and small firms in Japan. This finding indicates that lifetime employment may not be confined to large firms. Indeed, some recent studies indicate that there exists a significant degree of "paternalism" among small scale Japanese employers [De Vos and Wagatsuma, 1973; Cole, 1979]. As paternalism often refers to employer pratices of providing various fringe benefits, including bonuses, the findings of these researchers suggest aht long-term employment may not be totally irrelevant for small firms in Japan.

B. A Hypothesis of Wage Flexibility

The incentive to introduce wage flexibility in employment contracts has been discussed earlier (see Hashimoto and Yu [1980]). In particular, it was argued that the lower the transaction costs between the employer and the employee, the more will be invested in firm-specific human capital. Wage flexibility promotes employment stability, thereby reducing the possibility of wealth loss associated with a fixed wage contract. Wealth loss occurs when returns from previous investments in firm-specific capital cannot be captured due to an "inefficient" employment separation. Separation may be ineffic- ient because, once specific capital is invested, quit and dismissal decisions are based on different criteria and, more importantly, because these criteria differ from the jointly optimal criterion. The parties try to minimize the wealth loss by choosing the sharing ratio for the return to firm-specific investment by determing who may initiate a separation and by introducing some flexibility in the wage contract[14] [Hashimoto, 1979, 1981; Hashimoto and Yu, 1980].

A model incorporating these considerations yields predictions regarding the flexibility of wages in general and the importance of bonus payments in particular as they relate to such variables as firm size, tenure, and educational attainment. These variables are likely to be positive indicators of the profitability of investments in firm-specific human capital. Unfortunately, the available data permit only a limited scope for multivariate analysis of the flexibility in base wages, and so our investigation has been focused on the importance of bonus payments. Bonus payments in Japan may be viewed as the employee share in the quasi-rents accruing to firm-specific human capital.[15] Past regression analyses of 1970 cross-section differences in the bonus-earninges ratio, for example, revealed that tenure, education, and firm size have significant positive effects on the bonus-earnings ratio [Hashimoto, 1979].[16]

C. New Evidence

The Japanese economy has undergone substantial changes since 1970. The double digit rate of economic growth in the 1960s gave way to a rather modest growth rate after the oil shock of the early 1970s. Indeed, it is sometimes said that the celebrated nenko employment system may be on its way out, that such a system can be sustained only when the economy is expanding rapidly. Whether the long-term employment system and associated phenomena will be transformed, or even eliminated, is an empirical question. Although it is too early to know, the available evidence suggests, popular opinion to the contrary, that some key features of Japanese employment practices remain intact. For example, employment tenures remain long in the late 1970s (cf. table 3−8), and earnings-tenure profiles are quite steeply sloped, more steeply than for the United States [Hashimoto and Raisian, 1985]. In view of these considerations, it is of interest to know whether the relationship between bonus payments and the various explanatory variables has changed over the years. We now turn to this issue.

Table 3−10 reports results of a regression specification similar to the one reported in Hashimoto [1979] for selected years between 1967 and 1981. The underlying data are available from published reports on the *Basic Survey of Wage Structure* (Chingin Kozo Kihon Chosa). This data source contains detailed information on contract earnings, bonus payments, tenure, and hours of work for cells grouped by industry, education, age, sex, and firm size. Since the variables are cell means, regressions are estimated by weighting each observation by the square root of the number of respondents in the cell.

The regressions are of the following form:

$$\ln RB = a + b(TEN) + c(PREV\ EXP) + d(EDC) + e(FMSZ) + f(IND) + v,$$

where a through f are regression coefficients to be estimated, $\ln RB$ is the logarithm of the bonus-earnings ratio, TEN is years of tenure, $PREV\ EXP$ is years worked before joining the current firm (calculated as age minus tenure minus years of schooling minus six), EDC, $FMSZ$, and IND are the dummy variables, respectively, for years of education, firm size, and

Table 3–10. Regressions of Log of Bonus-Earnings Ratio: Japanese Men for Selected Years (t-Values in Parentheses)

	1967	1970	1974	1976	1980	1981
Constant	-2.248	-2.013	-1.838	-1.880	-.875	-1.872
	(-75.4)	(-63.3)	(-75.7)	(-73.6)	(-66.9)	(-68.0)
Firm-size dummy						
Medium	.394	.265	.190	.318	.247	.226
	(14.7)	(10.3)	(9.8)	(16.3)	(12.3)	(11.6)
Large	.594	.346	.274	.454	.341	.323
	(19.5)	(12.1)	(12.6)	(20.0)	(14.3)	(14.0)
Education dummy						
Low	.236	.206	.189	.179	.164	.161
	(9.6)	(8.8)	(10.1)	(9.4)	(8.0)	(8.1)
Medium	.397	.345	.206	.339	.321	.335
	(5.0)	(4.3)	(4.1)	(5.9)	(5.7)	(6.4)
High	.415	.356	.299	.309	.315	.314
	(9.6)	(9.4)	(11.6)	(11.8)	(11.7)	(12.2)
Tenure	.033	.036	.029	.026	.031	.031
	(13.8)	(17.2)	(19.9)	(17.1)	(20.4)	(22.4)
Previous experience	.000	-.000	-.000	-.000	-.003	-.003
	(.1)	(-1.7)	(-1.4)	(-.5)	(-2.5)	(-2.4)

Source: Basic Survey of Wage Structure (Chingin Kozo Kihon Tokei Chosa), various issues.
Note: Firm-size dummy is relative to small firms (less than 100 employees). Medium refers to firms with 100–999 employees, large to firms with 1,000+ employees. Education dummy is relative to elementary schooling. Low means middle school, medium means high school, and high means university. These regressions hold constant eight industry dummy variables: construction, manufacture, trade, finance-insurance, real estate, transportation-communication, utilities, and service.

industry, and v is the disturbance term. For *EDC*, low means 12 years, medium means 14, and high means 16 or more years of education. The default value is less than 12 years. Small firms are those employing 10 to 99 workers, medium firms between 100 and 999 inclusive, and large firms, 1,000 or more workers. There are nine industry categories with the default category being mining. The main difference between this regression specification and the previous one [Hashimoto, 1979] is that the variable, *PREV EXP*, is explicitly introduced rather than relying on the age variable to capture the effect of years of previous experience.

Although the nominal values of the estimated coefficients vary from year to year, there is remarkable similarity in the general pattern of the relevant coefficients across different years. Thus, in every year under study, workers in larger firms have a greater bonus-earnings ratio; this is also true for those with higher levels of educational attainment. The coefficients for the industry dummy variables (not reported to save space) also exhibit similar patterns over the years.

The coefficient estimates for the tenure variable show an interesting pattern over time. The tenure coefficient may be viewed loosely as representing the "seniority" effects. If long-term employment has been diminishing in importance, one would expect to find the seniority effects weakened over time. As it turns out, the coefficient is somewhat smaller in 1974 and 1976 than in earlier years, but the recent trend seems to be for it to increase.[17] The mid-1970s were hard times for Japan's economy, which was suffering from the effects of high petroleum prices and general inflation. During these difficult times, many employers induced their older workers to retire early. (See the related discussion by Koike in this book.) It is not surprising, therefore, to find the tenure coefficient to be smaller in the mid-1970s than in other years. What is important is that the apparent weakening of the tenure effects evidently were temporary, and that they seem to be recovering their strength.

Years of previous experience have a negative impact on the bonus ratio in all years except 1967. This is reasonable. In Japan, workers with many years of previous experience are likely to be *chuto saiyosha*, half-way employees, who do not enjoy the usual privileges accorded to those who are hired right after school by the present employer. As for the industry differences (not reported in the table to save space), construction has the lowest bonus-earnings ratio in all the years examined, while finance and insurance have the highest.

By and large, the regressions reported in table 3–10 suggest that the predicted pattern of the regression coefficients persists over many years, underscoring the general validity of the specific human capital hypothesis regarding bonus payments.

IV. Summary and Conclusion

Our findings suggest that wages in the United States are more sensitive to cyclical phenomena than the usual portrayal based on evidence generated from aggregate time series data. Wages are generally more flexible in Japan than the United States, and the flexibility is evident in all three components of total earnings: base, contract, and bonus earnings. Moreover, inspite of the slowdown in the growth rate of the Japanese economy after early 1970s, the Japanese labor market appears to have retained many of its key features through the early 1980s.

The evidence of wage variability over business cycles in both the United States and Japan in noteworthy, especially in view of the implicit contract theories, that were developed to explain the existence of wage rigidity. Our finding does not necessarily contradict the existence of implicit contracting, however. Contracts can have procyclical conditional features. We interpret the existence in Japan of flexible wages as representative of these features. The bond between an employer and employee remains stronger for Japanese workers than for American workers. Not only is tenure longer for the typical Japanese worker, but the degree of cyclical wage variability, taking into account the role of bonus payments, is much more pronounced, enhancing the prospects for long-lasting employment relationships.

Notes

1. Gordon focuses on nominal wage rigidity, whereas we examine both nominal and real wage rigidity. His study suggest that wage rigidity is characteristic of the post-World War II U.S. economy; he observes that wages were relatively flexible during the period 1892–1940.

2. There are offsetting factors to be considered as well. First, overtime hours are reduced during the recessions. Since wages for overtime hours are usually higher than straight-time wages, the reduction in overtime hours has the partial effect of overstating the extent of wage concessions during a cyclical downturn. Second, high wage workers are somewhat more likely to reduce work hours without separating from the firm than low wage workers (see Raisian [1983]). Thus, this composition effect has the partial effect of increasing the observed procyclical pattern in aggregate average hourly wages.

3. As we were working on this study we came across Stockman's [1983] paper that deals with this source of aggregation.

4. There are 21,261 observations in our PSID sample and 3,688 separate household heads.

5. Formally, a job change is identified as a situation where tenure is less than 18 months. A

sample of 12,562 observations remains, composed of 2,670 individuals.

6. The question was not asked on the first two annual surveys. The survey year is one year ahead of the year for which full earnings and hours worked information is available. This sample is composed of 12,835 observations on 3,034 different household heads.

7. For the four aggregate series, regression results for specification 2 are presented in table 3–3. We could have disaggregated the unemployment rate variable also, for example, by geographic and industrial location. However, our main interest is to exhibit the extent of aggregation bias that exists over the course of overall business cycles. The use of an aggregate indicator within the regressions for each individual serves this purpose well. Disaggregation of the unemployment rate variable is expected to increase the measured extent of wage variability due to specific demand shocks by industry or region.

8. To generate a nonzero standard error of the estimate requires that an individual have at least four observations during the sample period. It was decided to proceed with these estimates only if an individual had at least five observations for the reported wage series. This eliminated 18% of the observations from the oveall PSID sample, 26% of the observations from the PSID job-maintainer sample, and 22% of the observations from the reported wage sample.

9. Specifically, a weighted average is computed, weighted by the number of observations available for the individual.

10. Admittedly, it would also be interesting to know how individual wage flexibility varies by characteristics such as tenure group, union status, and industrial classification. However, it is not convenient to supply these estimates using the statistical framework utilized in this study. Changes in these variables often occur for an individual over the course of time. This would almost certainly influence an individual's trend-adjusted standard error independent of the effect of the characteristic per se. Consequently, we do not address these factors in this study.

11. Tabulations for nominal wage magnitudes do not offer contrasts that are qualitatively different than the real wage tabulations.

12. Because our sample is restricted to household heads, women are less represented than the labor force composition would suggest. Approximately 15% of our sample is composed of women.

13. Special payments also include payments given to employees upon their marriage, arrival of a new baby, etc.

14. It can be shown that, under an innocuous assumption, that a long-term contract confers greater benefits than other types of contracts when specific capital is involved. See Hashimoto and Yu [1980].

15. We should mention that Peter Rupert at the University of Rochester is pursuing an alternative view that bonus payments serve as an income-smoothing vehicle. See Rupert [1984].

16. In addition, using time series data, the bonus-earnings ratio was found to be positively correlated with worker skill levels and overall demand conditions.

17. The F tests indicate that the tenure coefficient varies over the years 1970 through 1981, but does not differ when compared in pairwise fashion between 1974 and 1976. The differences in the tenure coefficient between 1970 and 1974 as well as between 1976 and 1981 are statistically significant, however.

References

Akerlof, George A. and Brian G. Main. 1981. "An Experience-Weighted Measure of Employment and Unemployment Duration." *American Economic Review* 71

(December): 1003–1011.

Azariadis, Costas. 1975. "Implicit Contracts and Underemployment Equilibria." *Journal of Political Economy* 83 (January): 1183–1202.

Baily, Martin N. 1974. "Wages and Employment under Uncertain Demand." *Review of Economic Studies* 41 (January): 37–50.

Cole, Robert J. 1982. *Work, Mobility, and Participation.* Berkeley: University of California Press.

De Vos, George and Hiroshi Wagatsuma. 1973. "The Entrepreneurial Mentality of Low-Class Urban Japanese in Manufacturing Industries." In George De Vos (ed.), *Socialization for Achievement: Essays in the Cultural Psychology of the Japanese.* Berkeley: University of California Press, pp. 201–219.

Gordon, Donald. 1974. "A Neo-Classical Theory of Keynesian Unemployment." *Economic Inquiry* 12 (December): 431–451.

Gordon, Robert J. 1982. "Why U.S. Wage and Employment Behavior Differs from That in Britain and Japan." *Economic Journal* 92 (December): 13–44.

Hall, Robert E. 1975. "The Rigidity of Wages and the Persistence of Unemployment" *Brookings Papers on Economic Activity* 2: 3012–3335.

—————. 1980. "Employment Fluctuations and Wage Rigidity." *Brookings Papers on Economic Activity* 1: 91–123.

—————. 1982. "The Importance of Lifetime Jobs in the U.S. Economy." *American Economic Review* 72 (September): 716–724.

Hall, Robert E. and David M. Lilien. 1979. "Efficient Wage Bargains under Uncertain Supply and Demand." *American Economic Review* 69 (December): 868–879.

Hashimoto, Masanori. 1979. "Bonus Payments, On-the-Job Training and Lifetime Employment in Japan." *Journal of political Economy* 87 (October): 1086–1104.

—————. 1981. "Firm-Specific Human Capital as a Shared Investment." *American Economic Review* 71 (June): 475–482.

Hashimoto, Masanori and Ben T. Yu. 1980. "Specific Capital, Employment Contracts and Wage Rigidity." *The Bell Journal of Economics* 11 (Autumn): 536–549.

Hashimoto, Masanori and John Raisian. 1985. "Employment Tenure and Earnings Profiles in Japan." *American Economic Review* 75 (September): 721–735.

Koike, Kazuo. 1985. "Japanese Redundancy: The Impact of Key Labor Market Institutions on the Economic Flexibility of the Japanese Economy." (in this book).

Raisian, John. 1983. "Contracts, Job Experience and Cyclical Labor Adjustments." *Journal of Labor Economics* 1 (April): 152–170.

Rupert, Peter. 1984. "The Flexibility of Wages and Bonuses in Japan." Draft chapter, Doctoral dissertation, Department of Economics, University of Rochester (in progress).

Salant, Stephen W. 1977. "Search Theory and Duration Data: A Theory of Sorts."

Quarterly Journal of Economics 91 (February): 39−57.
Stockman, Alan. 1983. "Aggregation Bias and the Cyclical Behavior of Real Wages." Unpublished manuscript, University of Rochester.
Summers, Lawrence H. 1980. "Comments." *Brookings Papers on Economic Activity* 1: 133−139.

4 THE IMPACT OF INTERNATIONAL TRADE SHOCKS ON WAGE ADJUSTMENTS IN CANADA

Jean-Michel Cousineau

I. Introduction

Recent studies of comparative international wage adjustments reveal some particularly interesting facts. We find, for instance, that the various OECD countries exhibit different wage behavior for the same national or international economic conditions.

Considering the impact of wage adjustments on the other major economic variables—employment and inflation—it happens that macro-economic stabilization policies that are desirable within each country concerned differ from one country to another, with consequent harmonization problems at the international level. Grubb and associates [1983] state that in 1976–77, at the very time when the United States asked its commercial partners for an active monetary policy, these partners resisted and failed to understand the American position.

I wish to thank Mr. Jacques Robert, University of Montreal, for his comments and research and technical assistance I also wish to thank Robert Lacroix and Yves Rabeau from the University of Montreal, Department of Economics, for many very useful discussions. Finally, I am indebted to Gregory Duncan for his useful suggestions and critique at the conference.

61

Given the rigidity of real wages in certain European countries, such as Germany, they could see very few advantages in carrying out such a policy. If real wages are rigid, this means that any price increase stimulated by monetary policy is automatically absorbed by wages. Since real wages remain unchanged, the impact on employment gain is minimal compared to the inflation increase.

In the United States the situation is quite different. Since nominal wages are rigid, monetary stimulation has the effect of stimulating inflation more than wages. With lowered real wages, employment tends to rise.

The question of real versus nominal wage rigidity has therefore become very important in the wage adjustment literature. At one extreme, we have such countries as Germany and the United States, respectively characterized by strong real and nominal wage rigidity. At the other extreme, we find Japan, with its strong wage flexibility. Canada is located between these two extremes.

Wages in Japan are four times more variable than employment. In the United States, employment is nearly three times more variable than wages. Canada is approximately halfway between these two extremes with a one-to-one ratio.[1]

In Canada, the question of relative wage rigidity has been thoroughly discussed. The duration of collective agreements, their desynchronization over time, the phenomenon of wage spillovers, and ex-post adjustments to inflation (partial wage indexation and ex-post catchup with inflation) are some of the many arguments used to explain these rigidities. Gordon [1982] discussed at length the institutional and sociocultural differences between the United States and Japan—such as bonus systems and sychronized negotiations each spring in Japan. No study specifically examined the fact that wages are less rigid in Canada than in the United States.

This study analyzes the impact of international trade shocks on wage adjustments in Canada and suggests that the degree of openness, and particularly the industrial structure, of Canada has the effect of increasing the relative flexibility of its wage adjustments. When we speak about international trade shocks, we mean in particular the oil shocks in 1973 and 1979, the various phases of expansion and recession of the American economy and their effects on Canadian exports, the fluctuations of Canadian currency and those of world prices for natural resources and manufactured products.

In such a context, the problem is essentially reduced to two questions. First, do international trade shocks affect wage adjustments in Canada? Second, how are wage adjustments affected?

Section II deals with the first question and uses what is available as a standard model for studying the impact of international inflationary shocks for a small open economy. Section III deals with the second question and suggests some new micro-econometric approaches to the study of the impact of international trade shocks on wage adjustments in Canada.

In section II, we will deal with the problem using the Scandinavian model, that is, by dividing Canadian markets into markets exposed to international competition and markets sheltered from it. International trade shocks will be specifically introduced into an aggregated wage equation of the exposed sector of the Canadian manufacturing industry. The spillover effects from these wages on those of the sheltered sector will then be taken into consideraton.

In section III, we broaden our discussion to include a more sensitive sector in terms of contact point between the Canadian and international markets; that is, the export-oriented natural resource sector such as wood, paper, pulp, aluminium, iron, natural gas, and oil. Our approach will be micro-econometric—wage changes in each individual bargaining unit are the focus of interest—and will explicitly integrate those factors that contribute to rigidity and flexibility in the wage determination process in Canada. At this stage our data base contains a large and unique sample of 2,684 individual collective bargaining agreements that were signed in the primary and manufacturing sector of Canada from 1967 to 1984. These data can improve the quality of empirical tests of spillover effects, since spillover effects are observed directly rather than being inferred from industry or economy-wide aggregates. The conclusion will discuss the implications of our results for Canadian public policy.

II. The Exposed Sheltered Dichotomy

One way to directly analyze the impact of international trade shocks on wage adjustments in Canada is to divide the Canadian economy into an exposed and a sheltered sector. Such a dichotomy has been successfully used in Scandinavian models [Aukrust, 1977; Edgren, Faxen, and Ohdner, 1973] and in their applications to the Canadian economy [Decaluwe, 1984; Dussault and Lacroix, 1983].

The first advantage of using this approach is that Canada fulfill the conditions of the model. With a population of 25 million and 30% of its gross national product (GNP) coming from its export sales, Canada can be considered a small open economy. The second advantage is that this model can identify interfaces between Canadian industries and world markets. A third advantage is that the impact of international trade shocks on these interfaces (the exposed sector) can be estimated, as well as the diffusion of this impact to the rest of the economy (the sheltered sector). A fourth advantage is that this theoretical approach lends itself to a number of verifiable empirical predictions. The Scandinavian models are summarized in the following discussion.

A. Theory

First, it is assumed that the exposed sector firms have no influence on the selling price of their products, which is strictly dictated by the world market over which they have no control. Second, the value-added share of wage is assumed to remain constant in the long run.

These premises rest essentially on observations that, first, national export industries only represent a small share of the world markets and, second, in the long run, the value-added share of wages effectively tends to remain relatively stable over time for the various industries.

In such a model, product prices correspond to the maximum price that the firm can obtain for its products, while the price of inputs other than labor is the minimum price that it must pay for the other factors of production. The difference between the maximum price for the product and the minimum price for inputs other than labor is therefore the residual that is available for wages. In such a context, the nominal wage changes become a positive function of the price changes of products but a reverse function of the price changes of inputs other than labor.[2]

In the case of the sheltered sector, firms operate differently. Not only because they can occupy a larger share of the market but also because the trend they create for wages is reflected by or reflects that of their competitors, they can more readily use the price mechanism to stabilize the relative value-added share of wages. Consequently, they can directly absorb or reflect the wage dynamics of the exposed sector of the economy.

The international trade shock transfer mechanism therefore passes from the world markets to the exposed sector, and then from the exposed sector to the sheltered sector of the economy.

It is in this context that we have adopted the exposed/sheltered sector dichotomy to discover whether the international trade shocks observed during the '70s and early '80s had any effect on Canadian wage adjustments made during the same period. The following section provides the detailed specification of the empirical model used to test our hypotheses.

B. Empirical Model

The empirical model includes two endogenous variables: the rate of change of nominal wage rates in the exposed sector (WEXP), and the rate of change of nominal wage rates in the sheltered sector (WSH) of the Canadian manufacturing industry.

In both cases, it is the quarterly average of the average annual percentage change in the nominal wage rate negotiated during the 1967I–1984I period (77 observations).[3] The criterion of distinction between exposed and sheltered sectors is that used by Decaluwe [1984] and Dussault and Lacroix [1983]. Essentially, it consists of drawing a dividing line at the level where imports or exports reach a threshold of 25% of the gross domestic product (GDP) per industry. As shown in table 4–1, eight industries are considered exposed, while nine are considered sheltered.[4]

The independent variables used to "explain" the rate of change of nominal wage rates in either sector include three components: (1) standard explanatory variables such as an excess demand variable (quarterly job vacancy rate index = help wanted index standardized for the labor force = JVI^2) and anticipated inflation (the inflation rate lagged by two quarters = $p^2)^5$; (2) control variables for the frequency of escalator clauses (% collective agreements indexed during quarter = $INDEX$) and the effect of the income and price control policy in Canada during the period 1975 IV–1978 II (variable = 0 before the controls, progressively increased to 1 during the

Table 4–1.   Canadian Manufacturing Industry—Exposed and Sheltered Sectors

Exposed Sector: Imports or Exports > 25% of GNP for Each Industry	Sheltered Sector: Imports or Exports < 25% of GNP for Each Industry
1. Textiles	1. Food and drink
2. Wood	2. Tobacco
3. Paper and related activities	3. Rubber
4. Metal manufacturing	4. Leather
5. Machinery	5. Clothes and garments
6. Transportation equipment	6. Furniture
7. Electrical products	7. Metal products
8. Chemical products	8. Nonmetallic products
	9. Oil and coal

Source: Decaluwe [1984] and Dussault and Lacroix [1983].

period of controls and later returning to 0); and (3) external trade shock variables such as GNP'_{US}: the percent deviation of United States real GNP from its long-term trend (major American recessions and expansions); OIL: the deviations of the Canadian oil price changes from the current inflation rate (oil shocks reflecting both input and output prices); PM: the annual rate of change of industry selling price index in the corresponding American manufacturing industries (price of products), and XR: the rate of change of the Canadian currency expressed in U.S. dollars. Each of these variables was lagged by two quarters.

Given the predictions of our theory, we had to specify different equations for each sector. Thus the sheltered sector wage equation includes the same components as the exposed sector wage equation with the exception that external trade shock variables have been removed and replaced by the rate of change of nominal wage rates in the exposed sector. Under these conditions, the tested model is as follows:

$$WEXP = a_0 + a_1JVI^2 + a_2p^2 + a_3INDEX + a_4C + a_5GNP'_{US}$$
$$+ a_6OIL + a_7PM + a_8XR \qquad (4-1)$$

$$WSH = b_0 + b_1JVI^2 + b_2p^5 + b_3INDEX + b_4C + b_5WEXP \qquad (4-2)$$

The expected signs are a_1, b_1, a_2, b_2, a_5, a_7, and $b_5 > 0$, and a_3, b_3, a_4, b_4, $a_8 < 0$. No particular sign is expected for a_6 since oil prices are both an input and an output price (Canada is a net exporter of oil).[6]

C. Estimated Results

Estimated results obtained with the ordinary least squares method read as follows:

$$
\begin{aligned}
WEXP = 4.58 \quad &+ 6.2JVI^2 + .038p^2 - .17C - 4.36INDEX \\
(10.59) \quad &(4.39) \quad\;\; (4.66) \quad (.04) \quad (3.54)
\end{aligned}
$$

$$
\begin{aligned}
&+ 27.19GNP'_{US} - .0640IL + .226PM \\
&\;(3.22) \qquad\qquad (1.82) \qquad (3.02)
\end{aligned}
$$

$$
\begin{aligned}
&- .316XR - .17JVI^2DUR \\
&\;(5.23) \qquad (3.54) \hspace{5cm} (4-1)'
\end{aligned}
$$

$$
\begin{aligned}
WSH = 1.54 \quad &+ 2.9JVI^2 + .012p^2 - 3.27INDEX - 1.74C \\
(3.19) \quad &(2.54) \quad\;\; (2.66) \quad\;\; (3.10) \qquad\quad (2.61)
\end{aligned}
$$

$$
\begin{aligned}
&+ .905WEXP - .12JVI^2DUR \\
&\;(12.90) \qquad\quad (2.87)
\end{aligned}
$$

$$\bar{R}^2 = .847 \qquad D\text{-}W = 1.648 \qquad NOBS = 77$$
The absolute value of the t-statistics appear under the coefficients.   (4–2)'

Equation (4–1)' clearly supports the hypothesis that international trade shocks have a significant impact on wage adjustments in Canada. With a +27.19 coefficient on the GNP'_{US} variable, the American recession at the beginning of the '80s would have had the effect of reducing the rate of change of money wages in the exposed sector of the Canadian manufacturing sector by some three percentage points, just as the expansion of the early '70s may have contributed to accelerating the growth of Canadian wages in the mid-'70s. This phenomenon can clearly help explain the greater variability of Canadian wages compared to American wages. Figure 4–1 shows that the gap between maximum and minimum wage growth rates is 6.5 percentage points in the United States, against 13.5 percentage points in Canada.

The impact of the 1973 and 1979 oil shocks on wage increases in Canada is not clear. Given the sign of the coefficient of the OIL variable, the price of oil used in the production process may have reduced, other things being equal, the capacity to pay off industries exposed to international competition and may have created downward pressures on the wage growth rate. However, this effect is weak and seems to have little significant impact on nominal wage changes, considering in particular the autocorrelation problems indicated in the Durbin-Watson statistic.[7]

Finally, American price movements and exchange rate fluctuations seem to be partly absorbed by wages in the exposed sector of the Canadian manufacturing industry. A joint test on both variables ($PM\text{-}XR$) supports the hypothesis of similar coefficients (.30).

In summary, we conclude that the empirical results clearly indicate that the Canadian manufacturing industrial sector exposed to foreign (mostly America) competition is particularly sensitive to international economic conditions.[8]

On the other hand, it would also appear that the sheltered sector wage equation supports the Scandinavian hypothesis that the sheltered/exposed wage has an elasticity of one. In fact, the coefficient obtained on $WEXP$ is not significantly different from one. This result is consistent with the work of our predecessors [Decaluwe, 1984; Dussault and Lacroix, 1983], who used quite different specifications and data, but concluded that the sheltered/exposed wage elasticity was not significantly different from one.

The following section deals with the impact of such international trade shocks on wage adjustments in the primary and secondary sectors of the Canadian economy.

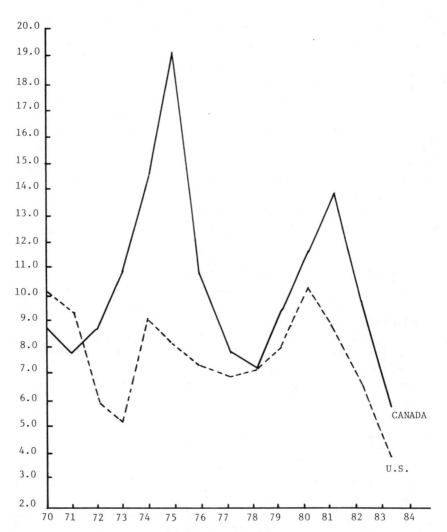

Figure 4−1.   Nominal Wage Growth Rates in Canada and the United States—1970−1984. Source: Riddell (1983) and *Revue Economique* (1984).

III. Integration of the Natural Resource Sector

As mentioned before, the natural resource sector represents a large part of the Canadian export market, which can be subdivided into three major

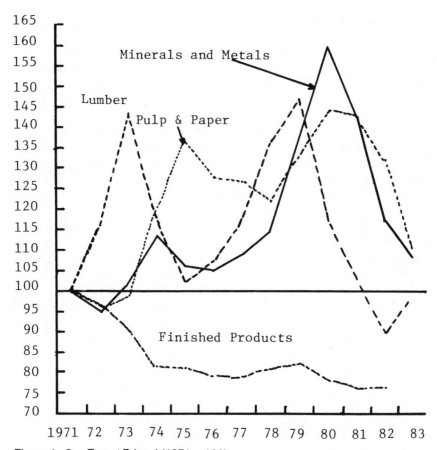

Figure 4–2.   Export Prices* (1971 = 100)
*Prices as an implicit index of Gross National Expenditure.
Source: Department of Finance.

components: (1) agriculture and basic food products, 20.2%; (2) natural resources and basic products related to these resources, 42%; and (3) automotive vehicles, approximately 20%.[9] The major industries associated with the natural resource sector are forestry, mining (iron, copper, zinc, nickel, asbestos, oil, gas, etc.), wood products, primary metals, nonmetal mineral products, and oil and coal primary products. As shown in figure 4–2, several of these products are subject to strong price fluctuations over time. It is therefore important to know, first, how wages adjust to such fluctuations in demand for these products; and then, how such adjustments are transferred to the rest of Canadian industry.

A. Theoretical Model

The general specification of the model assumes that the supply of labor for a firm is both a function of inflation and relative wages, that is, wages prevailing in competing firms. Therefore, the opportunity cost for the worker is linked both to his wage prospects elsewhere and the leisure he can enjoy by removing his supply of labor if the real wage changes.

First, inasmuch as the alternative wage varies from a certain amount, pressure is applied to the employer to grant similar wage increases. Excess demand in the labor market will also affect such a threat. Consequently, it is expected that excess demand and the wage agreements recently signed in the same industry and in the same region will affect the wage agreements negotiated at the level of the firm.

Second, concerning the wage-price relationship, it must be emphasized that bargaining units can adjust to inflation in various ways. If there is no implicit long-term contract[10] with periodical renegotiations between employers and employees, and if the inflation level is stable and easily forecast, ex-ante adjustments might prove desirable. With implicit contracts and uncertain economic conditions, it may be desirable to proceed with ex-post adjustments. It is then expected that employers and employees first agree on a certain contract that will provide a certain adjustment for anticipated inflation. If this adjustment has not taken place or has exceeded expectations because of errors in forecasting inflation, a correction mechanism may be at work when the agreement is renewed. Consequently, adjustments to inflation can be expected to take place through a partial indexation clause,[11] or through a catchup adjustment based on the gap between past wage and price increases.[12]

Given this basic model, we are now in a position to consider explicitly the mechanisms of absorption and then of transmission of international trade shocks. These must first go through the incidence of input and output price changes on the natural resources sector wage agreements (absorption) to then be transmitted to the other bargaining units through a regional and interindustrial wage spillover effect. In order to catch such spillover effects, the natural resource sector becomes a critical leading industry affecting the rest of the economy. Thus the primary and secondary sectors of Canadian industry have been subdivided into four groups: (1) a subgroup of natural resource sector bargaining units located in the regions with high concentrations of resource industries; (2) a subgroup of natural resource sector bargaining units located in regions with low concentrations of natural resources industries; (3) a subgroup of nonnatural resource sector bargaining units located in regions with high natural resource concentrations; and

(4), a subgroup of nonnatural resource sector bargaining units located in regions having low natural resource concentrations.

It is expected that natural resource industries are particularly affected by international trade shocks and that the other industries or regions are more or less sensitive to such leading industries.

In this context, our task was to assess the specific impact of wage changes negotiated in resource industries on other industries of the same region.

The empirical specification of the model appears as follows:

$$W_j = a_{j_0} + a_{j_1} JVI + a_{j_2} W_i + a_{j_3} W_r + a_{j_4} W_R + a_{j_5} OP_6$$

$$+ a_j IP_7 + a_j INDEXP_8 + a_j R \qquad (4-3)$$

where W_j = is the average annual rate of change in the base wage rate negotiated under agreement k belonging to subdivision j.

j_1 = resource industries in a concentrated resource region (75% and more of bargaining units in the region belong to the natural resouce sector).

j_2 = resource industries located in a low concentration resource region (less than 75% of bargaining units in the region belong to the natural resource sector).

j_3 = nonnatural resource industries located in concentrated resource regions (25% or more of bargaining units in the region belong to the natural resource sector).

j_4 = nonnatural resource industries located in low concentration resource regions (less than 25% of bargaining units in the region belong to the natural resource sector.)[13]

JVI = Help Wanted Index (HWI) standardized for the labor force (LF):

$$JVI = HWI. \frac{LF1969}{LF_t} \text{ where } t = t \text{ quarter}$$

W_i = Average rate of change of base wage rate negotiated in the 12 previous collective agreements in the same industry (industrial spillover effect).

W_r = Average rate of change of base wage rate negotiated in the 12 previous collective agreements in the same region (all industries, 39 regions) (regional spillover effect).

W_R = Average percentage change in the base wage rate negotiated in the natural resource sector weighted for the relative importance of such agreements in the region (specific resource sector effect on the region).

OP = Average pecentage change of the selling price of products (13 natural resource product prices or the industrial selling price index associated with the sector of activities other than natural resource)—average over the previous four quarters (output price).

IP = Average percentage change of the selling price of natural resources weighted for their importance in the cost of inputs other than labor (from the 1977 input-output matrix)—average for the previous four quarters (input price).

$INDEXP$ = Rate of inflation prevailing at the time the indexation clause appeared in the collective agreement, 0 other-wise.

R = Difference between the average annual rate in inflation and the average annual percentage change in the base wage rate achieved in the previous agreement (catchup).

The model's expectations are that, in the natural resource industries JVI, OP, and IP are the dominant variables to explain wage behavior and that, in relative terms, the wage spillover variables will not be as large. If such industries are exposed industries, they must depend more on the economic conditions of the industry and much less on wage variations achieved elsewhere.

On the other hand, in equation (4–3), JVI, OP, and IP play a less determining role, and the regional (W_r) and industrial (W_i) wage spillover variables play a major role. In these industries and regions, which are more sheltered from international competition on the natural resource market, the wage determination process will depend much more on this type of wage spillover.

Finally, it is expected that the resource sector wage spillover will have a distinct impact on other industries of the same regions but that impact is expected to be much less pronounced in off-resource regions. The signs of these expectations are as follows: (1) a_{11}, a_{15}, and $a_{16} > a_{41}$, a_{45} and a_{46}, respectively; (2) a_{42} and $a_{43} < a_{12}$ and a_{13}, respectively; and (3) a_{24} and $a_{34} < a_{44}$.

Estimated results are presented in table 4–2.

As expected, resource sector bargaining units in resource regions appear as wage-flexible units. Their major wage determination factors are JVI, Output Prices, OP, and Input Prices, IP (see equation (4.3a)). Compared to

Table 4–2. Estimated Results (MCO)

	a_{j1} JVI	a_{j5} OP	a_{j6} IP	a_{j2} W_i	a_{j3} W_r	a_{j4} W_R	a_{j7} INDEXP	a_{j8} R	$R^2/\bar{R}^{-2}$
(4.3a) Resources in resource regions	.054 (6.67)	.076 (6.53)	−.18 (4.97)	.27 (4.00)	.26 (1.10)	.13 (1.10)	−.21 (4.77)	.37 (8.65)	.517 / .507
(4.3b) Resources in non-resource regions	.032 (4.05)	.022 (1.84)	−.09 (3.09)	.44 (6.11)	.14 (1.64)	.08 (.98)	−.12 (3.11)	.50 (12.02)	.518 / .511
(4.3c) Nonresources in resource regions	.027 (3.13)	.124 (3.22)	−.10 (1.34)	.44 (6.62)	.33 (3.39)	.35 (3.99)	−.27 (6.23)	.25 (5.03)	.528 / .520
(4.3d) Nonresources in nonresource regions	.027 (6.71)	.024 (1.76)	−.02 (.61)	.42 (9.20)	.44 (8.87)	−.05 (.73)	−.19 (8.39)	.28 (11.73)	.550 / .547

*The constant term is not given; the absolute value of the t-statistics are given in parentheses under the coefficients.

nonresource sector bargaining units in nonresource regions in equation (4.3d), the JVI, OP, and IP coefficients are, respectively, .54 versus .027, .076 versus 0.24, and $-.18$ versus $-.02$. For the nonresources industries in nonresources regions, OP and IP coefficients are not significant at the 5% level.

As can readily be seen, the wage spillover effects are much larger in equation (4.3d) than in equation (4.3a). In the first case W_i and W_r coefficients are .42 and .44, respectively. In the second, they are .27 and .26, respectively. In the first case, this means that an acceleration of one percentage point in the rate of change of nominal wages for the industry and region on the whole implies, other things being equal, an acceleration of .86 percentage points in the rate of nominal wage changes of the following agreements. Such a result confirms the presence of strong nominal wage rigidities for this large subgroup of collective agreements in Canada.

Finally, we find that the resource sector wage spillover effects spread to resource regions. In equation (4.3c), the W_R coefficient is .35, which, added to the W_r coefficient, means that 68% of the wage variability observed in the wage agreement of the resource sector is reflected in the wage agreements settled in these regions, whatever the sector. This specific effect seems to disappear once it reaches nonresource regions. In such cases, the W_R coefficients lose their significance, which means that natural resource spillover effects are diluted through the general wage spillover effect.

These results, therefore, give a rather faithful image of the way in which the world natural resource markets affect Canadian labor markets. First of all, they affect Canadian resource industries, that in turn affect the region's wages. Finally, they are transferred, but in a much more diluted manner, to the other regions and to the other industries, through the standard or general wage spillover process.

One may note an apparent source of wage rigidity in the resource sector. At their highest value, the wage-price elasticities do not exceed .75% for the output price variable, and $-.18\%$ for the input price variables. Note, however, that the prices' variations under consideration are substantial and that they may cause large relative wage changes due particularly to the fact that what are output prices for some are input prices for others.

Finally, it is important to indicate that the major factor affecting natural resource sector wage behavior is the level of excess demand. Even though the JVI variable is a global variable of excess demand for the oveall economy, its coefficient is exactly twice as large in equation (4.3a) as that in equation (4.3d). The average coefficient for an economy is, therefore, clearly dependent on the weight of industries more sensitive to fluctuations in labor demand. This should not be a surprise given the constraints that face the natural resource sector. This analysis clearly shows that such is the case for other sectors located in resource-oriented regions but not for off-resource regions.

IV. Conclusion

This study has assessed the impact of international trade shocks on wage adjustments in Canada. Two questions are pertinent: first, do international trade shocks affect wage adjustments in Canada?; and second, if so, in what way? The first question can be answered in the affirmative. The exposed/sheltered dichotomy supports the hypothesis that the various phases of the American economy have important effects on wage behavior in the Canadian manufacturing sector. Oil price fluctuations have ambiguous effects since oil price is both an output price and an input price. American selling prices, just as Canadian currency fluctuations expressed in American dollars, appear to be partly absorbed by the wage variation rates.

To the second question, we can respond that the natural resource and related basic product sector is an important interface between Canadian industries and world markets. The labor markets associated with these industries face considerable pressures on labor demand and input and output prices. Such pressures clearly affect the wage adjustment process in these industries, which in turn affects the wage adjustment in the regions where natural resources are concentrated. Fifteen out of 39 regions contain 33% of all collective agreements.

The economic policy implications of these results are that the relative degree of flexibility or variability of wages in Canada may be greater than that of the United Staes due to three factors: (1) the degree of openness of the Canadian economy; (2) the relative importance of the natural resource markets; and (3) the span of economic fluctuations that characterize the labor markets associated with these markets.[14] The same macro-economic stabilization policies and international trade shocks will therefore have a different impact depending upon the economy—United States or Canada—under consideration.

At the regional level, it seems that interprovincial policy conflicts could appear within the Canadian economy, since the various provinces of Canada are facing different conditions regarding their respective degrees of openness to international trade and resource concentration. Such results can, therefore, have implications for the regional macro-economic stabilization policies in Canada.

Whether it is desirable to have more wage flexibility in Canada, it should be emphasized that increased wage flexibility can hardly be taken into consideration for the natural resource sector of the Canadian industry and regions involved. Private agreements do not necessarily appear suboptimal from a social point of view if one takes into account the flexibility observed and the disadvantages that could be caused by more wage variability in markets characterized by considerable upheavals.[15]

In addition to these considerations, the fact remains that Canadian wage behavior is affected by major sources of nominal and real wage rigidity. Variables W_i and W_r (spillover effects) are generally significant in all equations and cause large nominal wage rigidities, while the variable R (the catch-up effect) is one of the most significant variables in the model and involves a certain degree of real wage rigidity. These reasons, together with the effect of the long duration of collective agreements in Canada and United States,[16] are sufficient to explain a good part of the similarities of the Canadian and U.S. wage adjustment process. Our data show that upward adjustments appear long after the 1972−73 expansion, just as downward adjustments were delayed for several quarters with respect to the 1981 recession (see figure 4−1).

If there is to be more flexibility in wage behavior in Canada, measures should be taken in the off-resource industries located in off-resource regions (more than 45% of all collective agreements).

Auxiliary regressions with an interaction term between the JVI and the duration of collective agreements (available upon request), show that a shortening of collective agreements would have the effect of improving the flexibility of wage agreements. The wage-JVI adjustment coefficient can be increased by as much as 50% with a decrease of one year in the duration of collective agreements. Taking into account the importance and visibility of unionized labor in public administration, health and education in Canada, the governments should perhaps set a good example. If wage policies were to be determined on an *annual basis*, for instance, during the presentation of the annual budget, the various governments could facilitate the flexibility of wage adjustments on the various labor markets in Canada. This policy would introduce costs for a bargaining unit to settle for a different time period given the risks of undesired relative wage changes. Finally, one should equally consider whether such policies should also be used as a complementary management tool consistent with general macroeconomic stabilization policies. If this is the case, that means that governmental wage policies should not necessarily aim at giving what the private sector gives, but instead at what macro-economic stabilization policies target.

Notes

1. In Canada, for instance, the unemployment variable coefficient in a Phillips model was −.64 and significant. In Japan, it was −8.09 and significant. In the United States, it was only −.24 and not significant.

2. In the long run, the Scandinavian model also predicts that productivity gains will be proportionally shared among the various factors of production (equal percent increases).

3. The data are from the Labor Canada data base. They include all collective agreements covering 200 employees or more filed with the Federal Department of Labor.

4. During our preliminary research on this question, we were unable to find exposed sector equivalents in American industries. We must add that Decaluwe has also tried to take into account, in the exposed sector, industries whose domestic price elasticity in relation to international prices differed significantly from zero and/or was more than .5. This, however, did not affect the classification (see Decaluwe [1984, p. 166]. An interesting suggestion came from Daniel Hamermesh who suggested that the wage observations be weighted by the relative importance of external trade for each observation.

5. These variables are squared to capture the nonlinearity in the ratios of gross wage rate of excess demand and anticipated inflation measurements. For more details, see Cousineau and Lacroix [1977].

6. A JVI^2 interaction term was tested in order to take into account JVI decreasing effect with the length of collective agreements (expected sign: < 0). As indicated in the result presentation, this specification was fairly successful. A three-stage least squares analysis was applied to the full model, including simultaneity effects; there was little difference in results in terms of the dominant effect of the exposed sector on the sheltered sector.

7. Various autocorrelation corrective tests have proved unsuccessful.

8. The excess demand variable has the expected sign, while adjustments for inflation vary according to the rate of inflation observed but remain less than one (.38 at 5%, .76 à 10% inflation) for inflation values lower than 13%. These results tend to support the hypothesis that economic conditions in Canada allow for a certain flexibility of real and nominal wages. One may not also that wage adjustments tend to be more rapid when collective agreements are shorter (see the coefficient on JVI^2 DUR). As indicated in our conclusion, tests based on micro-economic data also support this hypothesis on the basis of individual data.

9. Source: OECD [1984] and Finance Canada [1984].

10. An implicit contract implies durability of relations between employers and employees through various phases of the economy and the possibility of periodic readjustments.

11. For a study of conditions and factors explaining the incidence of escalator clauses in Canada, see Cousineau and Lacroix [1981] and Cousineau, Lacroix, and Bilodeau [1983], respectively.

12. This adjustment can by symmetrical, i.e., can act upward, as in the mid '70s, or downward, as in the early '80s.

13. Source: Unpublished Labor Canada data on wage agreements covering 200 employees or more signed during the 1967−1984 period, except for the wage and price control subperiod (October 1975 to April 1978). For j = 1, there were 419 observations; for j = 2, 540; for j = 3, 525; and for j = 4, 1230.

14. To counteract these factors, Canada is more unionized than the United States.

15. Optimal agreements at the private level can be suboptimal at the social level if they introduce wage rigidities which destabilize employment.

16. For more details on this effect, see Riddell [1983].

References

Artus, Jacques R. 1984. "The Disequilibrium Real Wage Hypothesis." *IMFSP* 249–302.

Aukrust, O. 1977. "Inflation on the Open Economy—A Norwegian Model." In L.D. Krause and W. Salant.

Auld, D.A.L., L.M. Christofides, R. Swidinsky, and D.A. Wilton. 1979. "Facteurs déterminants des ententes salariales négociées au Canada." *Commission de la lutte contre l'inflation*, Ottawa.

Branson, William H., and Julio J. Rotemberg. 1980. "International Adjustment with Wage Rigidity." *European Economic Review* 13:309–332.

Cousineau, J.M., and R. Lacroix. 1977. "La détermination des salaries dans le monde des grandes conventions collectives: une analyse des secteurs privé et public." *Economic Council of Canada*, Ottawa.

Cousineau, J.M., and R. Lacroix. 1978. "L'impact de la politique canadienne de contrôle des prix et des revenus sur les ententes salariales." *Analyse de Politiques/ Canadian Public Policy* I:88–100.

Cousineau, J.M., and R. Lacroix. 1981. *L'indexation des salaires*. Monograph No. 10, Ecole de relations industrielles, Université de Montréal.

Cousineau, J.M., R. Lacroix and Danielle Bilodeau. 1983. "The Determination of Escalator Clauses in Collective Agreements." *The Review of Economics and Statistics* LXV (May): 196–202.

Decaluwe, Bernard. 1984. "Le modèle scandinave et l'économie canadienne." *L'Actualité Economique* 60: 164–179.

Dussault, François, and R. Lacroix. 1982. "Les modèles scandinaves et la détermination des ententes salariales des industries manufacturières canadiennes: une analyse microéconomique." *Canadian Journal of Economics* XI: 395–404.

Finances Canada. 1984. *Revue économique*. August. Ottawa.

Gordon, Robert J. 1982. "Why U.S. Wage and Employment Behavior Differs from That in Britain and Japan." *Economic Journal* 92 (March):13–44.

Grubb, Dennis, Richard Jackman, and Richard Layard. 1983. "Wage Rigidity and Unemployment in OECD Countries." *European Economic Review* 21: 11–39.

Krause, L.B., and W.S. Salant. 1977. *Worldwide Inflation: Theory and Recent Experience*. Washington, DC: Brookings Institution.

OECD. 1984. "Canada 1983–84." *Etudes Economiques*. July.

Rabeau, Yves. 1983. "Les services et l'inflation: le cas canadien." *Revue d'économie politique* 93:421–436.

Riddell, W. Craig (1983), "The Responsiveness of Wage Settlements in Canada and Economic Policy." *Canadian Public Policy* I, 9–23.

Sacks, Jeffrey D. 1979. "Wages, Profits and Macroeconomic Adjustment: A Comparative Study." *Brookings Papers on Economic Activity* 2:269–318.

Sacks, Jeffrey D. 1980. "Wages, Flexible Exchange Rates, and Macroeconomic Policy." *Quarterly Journal of Economics* 94 (June): 731–747.

5 JAPANESE REDUNDANCY: THE IMPACT OF KEY LABOR MARKET INSTITUTIONS ON THE ECONOMIC FLEXIBILITY OF THE JAPANESE ECONOMY

Kazuo Koike

I. Introduction

This chapter attempts to explain the impact of key labor market institutions on the Japanese economy. The approach is different from previous writing on this topic, and it utilizes data in a comparative perspective with the United States.

The popular argument takes as its starting point institutions peculiar to the Japanese economy, such as permanent employment, harmonious industrial relations, and enterprise unionism. Permanent employment naturally lessens adjustment in employment, while harmonious industrial relations tend to invite flexibility in wage changes. With the guarantee of permanent employment, workers can adopt a long-term view that encourages them to invest more in the area of human capital development and consequently promotes an increased competitiveness of the economy. In short, the peculiar institutional setting plays a central role in producing rigidity in

---

The author is extremely thankful for the valuable comments of Professor H. Miyazaki. Because of his comments, subsection V-E has been added.

employment as well as flexibility in wages and hence in promoting efficiency of the economy in general.

In contrast to this popular argument, the explanation presented in this chapter focuses above all on a vital aspect that, I believe, has been neglected: the quality of employment in redundancy, that is, the character- istics of workers who are to be made redundant. The extent to which those whose redundancy is costly[1] are laid off would be a crucial factor in calculating the cost of employment adjustment to an industrial society. Even though the quantity of employment adjustment may be equal, the extent of damage done to the industrial society differs greatly depending on who is made redundant. This framework is discussed in section II.

Within our framework, two major variations in institutions emerge that differ completely from those of the popular argument. One is the reverse role of seniority in the practice of redundancy, the issue examined in section III. Strict seniority prevails in the United States, particularly in the unionized sector while, on the contrary, Japan does not have any established seniority rules or practices relating to redundancy. Section IV analyzes the second difference in institutional arrangements, that is, the ratio of internal production to total production. In the United States, large firms tend to produce more components of the final product within their own firm, using their own employees, whereas their Japanese counterparts rely more on external components suppliers. In other words, the function of these independent suppliers is integrated within the large firms in the United States.

By considering these differences jointly, a vital difference in employment adjustment patterns becomes clear. In the United States layoffs are con- ducted in the reverse of seniority, and consequently, the workers in those departments that produce the same components as the suppliers to the Japanese counterpart firms are the first to be laid off. In contrast, those U.S. workers who are engaged in the same work as the employees of large Japanese firms are the last to be laid off. This implies that the U.S. workers with longer seniority have more of a buffer against layoff relative to their Japanese counterparts. Conversely, in Japan, since both the large firms and the parts suppliers are independent companies, each must take the burden of employment adjustment separately in the case of redundancy. Moreover, in both sets of firms, with no seniority practice in redundancy existing, costly workers are the most vulnerable when the firm must resort to a policy of redundancy. This suggests that the Japanese capability to adjust to a large decrease in output would be less than in the United States. Because Japan focuses her redundancy measures upon costly workers, there is the possi- bility that social tensions will easily exceed the limit, even with the smallest unemployment. If redundancy exceeds this limit, serious industrial disputes lasting for more than six months may occur, just like the cases in the 1950s.

It may then be asked: if there is little difference in the guarantee of employment for costly workers between the United States and Japanese cases, or even if the guarantee is greater for the United States workers, what are the reasons for the gap in workers' behavior in investing in human capital? Section IV deals with this problem. The most important reason would be whether there are sufficient incentives for the workers to invest. Japanese incentives are twofold: first, a challenging career or a series of jobs is arranged that partly overlaps with those of engineers; second, compensation given to production workers is also white-collarized both in the level of wages as well as in the age-wage profile. Both result in higher levels of compensation than those commonly attributed to production workers in terms of work and wages.

The final section develops major policy implications for the United States and Japan. For the United States, no drastic change in the way of employment adjustment is necessary because it has been efficient so far, but effective incentives to encourage workers to invest in human capital formation should be established. A system similar to the Japanese case can be transferred because it is not based on Japan's specific culture.[2] For Japan, conversely, a loose seniority in redundancy, partly following the U.S. pattern, is required to lessen the cost of redundancy, while incentives for human capital formation can be promoted further.

II. Costs of Redundancy

A. Costs Incurred Through Disuse of Skills

The costs of unemployment have often been disscussed. They include primarily the real costs due to unemployment, such as the decrease in output and the decrease in income of the unemployed, as well as decreases in tax revenue to the government and increases in government expenditure for unemployment benefits. Nonpecuniary costs, such as a rise in mortality or deterioration in health, can also be taken into account. To these well-established arguments, the framework presented here adds two features: one is to focus on workers' skills, and the other is to pay due attention to the costs incurred even after the state of unemployment is over, the cost of misusing skills in subsequent jobs.

The cost of unemployment to the unemployed individual is, first of all, that he cannot utilize his skills during unemployment. I call it the cost incurred through "disusing skills." The higher the level of skill and the longer the period of unemployment, the greater the cost becomes. Why do I stress such a self-evident fact? Why do I prefer to state it not in terms of "foregone income" but in terms of workers' skills? It is solely because I wish to emphasize and clarify the Japanese features of redundancy practice, and to present a new general framework to analyze this issue. Japanese redundancy is, as mentioned elsewhere,[3] likely to affect those workers in their late 40s and 50s, that is, those with long service. But workers with long service are apt to have high levels of skill, resulting in a large redundancy cost.

Although the idea presented here is extremely simple, it is unlikely that similar concepts are clearly developed in the existing literature. The reason why this has rarely been discussed is due to the type of redundancy practiced in the United States and Europe that may have created stereotyped views of redundancy. In the United States, redundancy measures are conducted according to the reverse to seniority strictly applied to labor union members and informally to the unorganized sector. Whether it is *strictly* according to seniority is not important; rather, it is enough to know that redundancy measures tend to focus on workers with the shorter term of service. Since it is so clear and so widespread in the United States and the United Kingdom that redundancy measures focus on short-term workers, there is no reason to build a framework to deal with redundancy affecting workers with high skill levels. Even in other European countries that lack institutionalized seniority rules like the United States and the United Kingdom, there is a tendency to make young workers redundant relatively more frequently, and consequently a short-term phenomenon appears.

Again, the question may be raised, why is it necessary to focus on workers' skills when similar issues have been developed and subsumed under the concept of "foregone income"? Three reasons can be given for this. First, skills are more fundamental than income. Hence we can infer another important cost even after the period of unemployment is over. This cannot be grasped without a clear understanding of the importance of "workers' skills" as a concept. Second, there long has been theoretical argument concerning the gap betweeen "skill levels" and "wage levels," particularly in post-war Japan. Although we know that we must depend on income figures as operational indicators, it is still crucial to pay due attention to the possibility of a gap. Third, it is not necessarily clear that a discussion of 'foregone income' consciously includes the concept of 'workers' skills.' A word of caution: I do not deny all the foregoing arguments. Rather, I retain most of them, but add this viewpoint.

B. Costs Incurred Through Misuse of Skills

The unemployed cannot be unemployed permanently but must obtain another job to maintain their daily lives. I do not consider those unemployed who retire from the labor market. When a worker cannot, in the next job, fully utilize the skills that he/she has acquired in his/her former jobs, I call this the cost incurred through misusing skills.

Discussions of the above cost have rarely appeared in articles and books so far. This does not, however, imply that scholars have never been aware of this cost. Retraining the unemployed is one of the popular issues discussed. It is likely that they think this cost is not important because most redundancy measures apply to those workers with low skills, as noted above. Contrarily, this cost becomes distinctly evident in the practice of Japanese redundancy. In contemporary Japan, redundancy measures are apt to concentrate upon those workers with high skills. High skills are a product of specific occupational experience. In addition, the occupational classification that is made redundant in some companies may provide few additional vacancies for recruitment in other companies. Thus, the highly skilled unemployed are compelled to find their next employment in other occupations, which results in the cost of misused skills. Moreover, if there is any firm-specificity at all in the character of the skills, it is inevitable that a loss or misuse of skills will result, even when the worker finds his/her next job in the same occupation. In contrast to this, if the tendency is for those workers with low skills to be made redundant, then the loss through misuse of skills becomes small. This is the main reason why this variable has been neglected in the West, since redundancy tends to concentrate on those workers with low skills in the West, as stated above.

All the statements above are concerned with costs relating to the individual worker or unemployed person. The costs to the national economy and to the individual company may differ from those to the worker. In the case of the economy, the cost of misused skills can be calculated in accordance with those incurred by the individual worker. The cost of disused skills can vary from that of misused skills. No change is needed for calculating the cost of disused skills, that is, the higher the skill, the larger the cost becomes. But the second aspect concerning the length of the period of unemployment, that is, the longer the period, the larger the cost becomes, cannot stand for the whole economy. Given the quantity of unemployment as a constant, then the problem of the period of unemployment must to be analyzed according to the following two situations: (1) a longer period of unemployment with a smaller number of unemployed, or (2) a shorter period of unemployment with a larger number of unemployed. It is not clear which is more beneficial, the first or the second. For individual companies, the costs of the disuse and misuse of skills become obscure. To the individual company, there is little cost incurred by disusing skills; when a recession comes, it is more profitable for the company to lay off surplus workers rather than to retain them. Even the cost of misused skills cannot be very large. When business recovers, the benefits of rehiring those who have worked before is not large, if the company promotes incumbents to fill the vacancies and recruits workers with low skills to the lowest grade jobs. Here, my focus is on individual workers and the whole economy, not on individual companies. In other words, I constrain attention to the level and specificity of skills of the unemployed.

III. No Seniority[4]

A. Redundancy Is Not Rare

It has been often said that large Japanese firms have rarely conducted redundancy measures in response to declines in demand and that, instead, they depend on other measures such as internal transfers from declining departments to growing ones, layoffs of temporary workers, and reduction of their orders to suppliers. Figure 5−1 largely confirms this. It is based on questionaires to individual firms surveying their adjustment measures to decrease employment. Internal transfers, temporary layoffs, and recruitment cutbacks are distinctly more frequent in large firms than in small firms. And the ratio of firms that conducted redundancy measures is as small as 2% to 3% in large firms, but reaches nearly 4% for small firms. At first glance, this low figure for large firms seems enough to support the common perception of "permanent employment." It must be considered, however, that these figures relate to short-term responses. Once a recession lasts longer, say, for one year, which is not exceptional, these measures that try to avoid redundancy become less effective.

Extremely valuable statistics exist on the diffusion of redundancy measures by size of firm, covering a period of three and a half years, from January 1975 to June 1978, the period just after the first oil shock. Table 5−1 tells, first, that even in large firms with 1,000 or more employees, nearly 20% of the establishments have conducted redundancy measures, and that this figure differs little from that of small firms. This result is completely different from what has been commonly described. The figure 20% is far from negligible, so that no one can say redundancy is exceptional, even for large firms in Japan, and the small gap between large firms and small firms is in

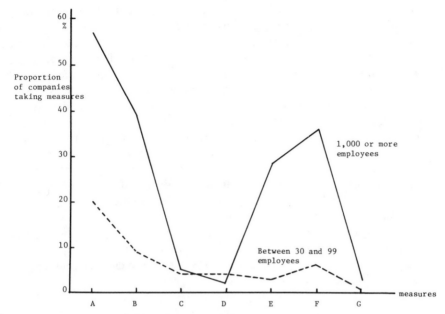

Figure 5−1. Employment Regulation Measures: The Percentage of Establishments Taking Measures by Company Size, in Manufacturing and Distribution Companies, November 1977. A = total employment measures taken; B = cutbacks in recruitment; C = temporary workers made redundant; D = regular workers made redundant; E = transfers; F = overtime cutbacks; G = temporary layoffs. Source: Rōdōshō (Ministry of Labor) *"Rōdō Keizai Dōkō Chōsa"* (Labor Market Survey).

Table 5−1. Diffusion of Redundancy Measures: The Percentage of Establishments Conducting Redundancy Measuring During the Period January 1975 to June 1978, by Size of Manufacturing Establishment

	Percentage of Establishments Conducting Redundancy Measures
Total	19.4
1,000	20.3
300−999	30.7
100−299	29.5
30−99	26.1
5−29	16.9

Source: Ministry of Labor, *Koyō Hendō Sōgō Chōsa* (Survey on Changes in Employment), 1979.

striking contrast to the popular argument that employees in large firms enjoy "permanent employment" even during recessions.

One question still remains; the data in table 5−1 indicate only the percentage of establishments that have conducted redundancy measures but do not show the degree of redundancy, that is, what percentage of employees were made redundant. Fortunately, these data include estimates of the average number of workers made redundant for the period per establishment. Table 5−2 shows these as well as transfers, by size of firm, as well as the extent of decrease in output. Since the proportion of the establishments using redundancy measures is around 20%, we have to multiply the figures by five in order to estimate the number of workers redundant per establishment actually making dismissals. Then, we see that nearly 15% of employees in an establishment with 1,000 and more employees were made redundant during this period, as opposed to 20% to 30% for small firms. Even the figure "15%" for large firms is far from the popular conception that Japanese large firms maintain permanent employment. Because there are no equivalent statistics in the West, no comparative studies are possible at the moment.

B. Deficits over Two Terms Invite Redundancy Measures

When do large firms conduct redundancy measures? Do they dismiss workers only in extremely hard times, so that no effective option other than

Table 5−2. Size of Redundancy: The Average Number of Workers Made Redundant, and Transfer per Manufacturing Establishment, by Size of Establishment and by Change in Output, during the period January 1975 to June 1978

Number of Workers	Output Level	Redundancy	Transfer
1,000−	120−149	28	66
	100−119	13	58
	− 99	32	113
30−99	120−149	4	1
	100−119	5	0
	− 99	6	1

Source: See table 5−1.
Note: "Output level" is the index of output level in June 1978, taking the January 1975 level as 100.

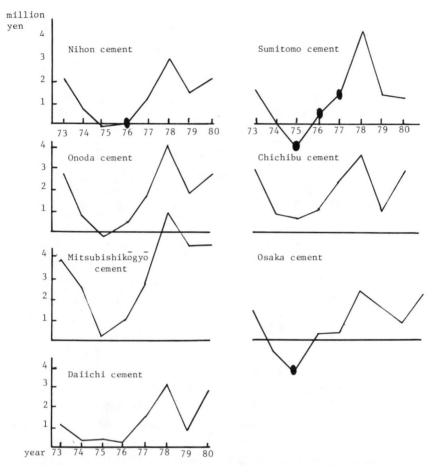

Figure 5—2.   The Relationship between Corporate Deficits and Redundancies:
Net Profit/Loss per Employee in Cement Companies—1973—1980. Note: The
years when redundancy occurred are dotted. Source: Koike (1983), p. 117.

redundancy is possible, or do they do so immediately after suffering
reductions in demand? According to the popular view, large Japanese firms
conduct redundancy measures as a last resort, if at all. Figure 5—2 describes
the amount of profit per employee compared to years when redundancy
occurred. These data are for large firms with labor unions in the cement
industry. The cement industry was selected because it suffers from frequent
reductions in output, and redundancy is so frequent as to be highly visible.[5]
In general, it appears that two years of deficit tend to invite redundancy

Table 5–3.   The Relationship Between Corporate Performance and Redundancies, Electric Machinery Companies: 1973–80

		More than 10,000	5,000 to 9,999	1,000 to 4,999	500 to 999	1 to 499
				Number of Employees		
Deficits in two or more periods	No redundancies	1	--	12	--	--
	Redundancies	--	--	4	--	--
Deficits in one period	No redundancies	--	--	9	3	--
	Redundancies	1	--	--	1	--
Low profitability	No redundancies	--	--	4	--	--
	Redundancies	--	--	3	1	--
Profitable	No redundancies	10	3	33	5	1
	Redundancies	--	--	--	--	--

Source: Rōdōshō, "*Shiryō Rōdō Undō-shi*" and Okurashō, "*Yūkashōken Hōkokusho.*"

measures. This statement is partly supported by table 5—3, which deals with the growing electrical machinery industry. A number of firms with deficits for one or two years, and even those with small profits, conducted redundancy measures, while no redundancy is seen in profitable companies. Similar results, even more striking, were obtained by Muramatsu in his study[6] of the machine tool industry in Japan, where nearly 70% of firms with deficits for two years conducted redundancy measures.

In short, we cannot say that Japanese large firms have dismissed workers only in extremely hard economic conditions. Rather they have done so when there were two continuous years of deficits.

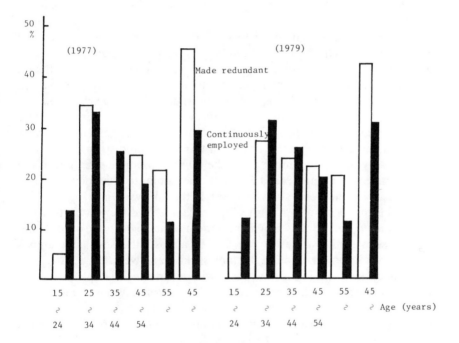

Figure 5—3.   Redundancies by Age of Worker, Males, 1977 and 1979, Percentage Distribution by Age. Those made redundant are the persons who have separated from a job since 1974 and whose reasons for separation are redundancies and bankruptcy, among the employed, the unemployed and nonparticipants in the labor market. Source: Rōdōshō (Ministry of Labor), Rōdōryoku Tokubetsu Chōsa (Special Report of Labor Force Survey).

C. Who Are To Be Redundant

Now, we return to the most crucial issue, who are to be made redundant? Figure 5—3 shows the age distribution of those who are made redundant, regardless of the size of firm. No figures by length of service are available. Age can, however, be a substitute for experience, and can suggest skill grades, although only approximately. From figure 5—3, it is clear that redundant workers are slightly older than those remaining employed. For both 1977 and 1979 for age groups older than 45 the percentage of the redundant group becomes larger than the employed group.

To investigate in more detail, we must depend on case records, no statistical sources being available. Fortunately, the Ministry of Labor has compiled documents of industrial disputes of importance in the *Documentary History of the Labor Movement*. In order to utilize this document, an outline of the Japanese practice of redundancy must be explained. Two periods can be identified in the history of industrial disputes after the second World War: one is the first half of the 1950s when redundancy, even in large firms, was not rare but rather frequent. The other is the period after the oil shock. In the first period, management in large firms usually proposed to advertise for "volunteers" to apply for "retirement," with a large premium of redundancy payment. Here, volunteers meant that no nomination of who was to be considered redundant was offered by management. Without exception, the Japanese labor unions in this first period strongly opposed this company offer to volunteers. In the severe economic situation of the '50s, management then declared the criteria pertaining to redundant persons. After this, even the weakest labor unions at the time went into long strikes, some being longer than six months. Strikes cannot be effective, particularly in a situation of recession, when management wants to decrease output, and this was so with the strikes in the '50s. In almost all cases, labor unions exhausted their power through the long strikes, and were forced to accept redundancy measures in the final phase without any negotiation concerning who was to be dismissed. In practice the criteria offered by managment were applied to most cases.

Table 5—4 shows the criteria in the six cases that are described in detail in *The Documentary History of the Labor Movement* for the period 1953—55, which mentions 36 cases of redundancy, most of them not being well documented on the issue of who was to be made redundant. The table indicates that there is a distinct tendency for those who are costly in redundancy to be dismissed, because the first-ranked criterion is "old age." Second, this suggests that the "performance" of workers is one of the important criteria, but there is always a tendency to managerial subjectivity

Table 5−4. Criteria for Layoffs, 1953 to 1955

	Number of Cases in Which the Criterion Was Stated (total = 6 cases)
Older worker:	
Over 45 yrs.	--
Over 50 yrs.	5
Absenteeism:	
Irregular attendance	4
Long absenteeism	4
Long leave	3
Often taking sick leave	6
Income reasons:	
Two salaried household members	3
Alternative income source	4
Performance:	
Inadequate performance	6
Frequent mistakes	2
Lacking cooperation	2
Contravening work regulation	2

Source: Rōdōshō, *"Shiryō Rōdō Undō-shi."*

or "vagueness" in the assessment of performance. Vagueness is enough to cause conflict between labor and management, since management is apt to dismiss those employees who are not loyal to management, in the name of bad performance. It is understandable that disputes of long duration occur in the first stage.

The lessons were carried over from the first period to the second. Management was careful not to resort to the nomination of candidates for redundancies, but maintained instead a system of advertizing for volunteers. The labor unions, unlike in the first period, did not reject the advertisement, but negotiated minutely concerning the conditions involved. Thus, reference as to who is to be made redundant becomes unclear. Of the 86 cases that are referred to as conducting redundancy measures in the *Documentary History* for the period of 1972−78, 15 cases mention the issue of who is to be made redundant. Even in these 15 cases, reference to the issue is naturally obscure because it only concerns criteria with which management tries to recommend workers to "retire." Table 5−5, classifying these obscure criteria, indicates the criterion, "old age, 50 and above," as being overwhelmingly crucial.

Table 5—5.   Guidelines for Voluntary Redundance, 1972—78

	Number of Cases in Which the Guideline Was Stated (total = 15 cases)
Older worker (over 50 yrs.)	13
Husband and wife in same company	4
Inadequate performance	3
Absenteeism	1

Source: See table 5—4.

In a smaller number of cases, criteria concerning performance are adopted that naturally cause conflict because of the potential for vagueness, as discussed above. Although Japanese industrial relations systems have been thought to conduct redundancy measures without strikes, the records available suggests that nearly one-fifth of the cases of large firms conducting redundancy experience strikes. Since 1960, statistics on industrial disputes by size of firm and on the cause of the strike are available. Another questionnaire survey of companies tells us the percentage of firms which conducted redundancy measures by size of firm. A combination of these two materials gives the above estimation.[7]

To sum up, two major features have been made clear. First, even large Japanese firms have conducted redundancy measures, and the incidence is not rare. Second, Japanese redundance is inclined to concentrate around those workers whose loss creates relatively large damage to themselves when they are dismissed. This is because Japan lacks a seniority practice, quite unlike the United States. This implies that Japanese redundancy can cause greater social tension for a comparatively small amount of redundance. This characteristic is strengthened by another institutional feature of crucial importance: that is, the high degree of dependency of large Japanese firms on their suppliers, or the difference in the extent of internal production, the theme of the next section.

IV. Low Degree of Internal Production

A. Small Shock Absorber

Another difference of prime importance in the institutional comparison between the United States and Japan concerns the extent of internal production. Compare, for example, Toyota and Ford. The number of employees is far larger in Ford than in Toyota, although the number of cars produced by each company per year does not differ much. This results in a large gap in apparent productivity. Average productivity per worker at Toyota appears to be four times greater. Needless to say, the actual differential in productivity cannot explain the full gap, but only a small part of it, say 10% to 20%. The most crucial cause of this large gap is the variation in the extent of internal production: Toyota depends far more on suppliers, most of which are independent companies, while Ford prefers to produce relatively more components within its own production complex.

Although there is no statistical evidence to confirm the difference in this ratio between the two countries, reference to another representative case is sufficient to show that Japanese large firms have lower levels of internal production than their U.S. counterparts. In 1976, the United States Steel Corporation produced 19 million tons of steel, with 166,000 employees, while Nippon Steel Corporation made 35 million tons of steel with 76,000 employees. This seemingly enormous gap in productivity can be partly explained by the variation in the production of other materials apart from iron and steel; 30% of the total output of United States Steel in that year was occupied by materials other than iron and steel, while the figure for Nippon Steel was less than 10%. Taking this into account, the gap is still too large to be due to this practical difference in productivity. Again, there is a variation in the extent of internal production; United States Steel conducts more tasks among its own employees, while Nippon Steel submits more work to those workers employed by other firms.

What are the implications of this institutional phenomenon of production for labor market adjustment? When we connect this difference to redundancy with or without seniority, then a result of crucial importance emerges: that is, the shock absorber in the labor market in the United States is greater than in Japan. This is the opposite of the popular conception.

Let us take the case of a 20% reduction in output and, accordingly, a reduction in labor demand in both Ford and Toyota. At a glance, Ford has a smaller shock absorber for employment adjustment because its ratio of internal to total production is high and, hence, it is surrounded by a smaller number of ancillary firms. As Ford follows strict seniority practice, however, the actual effects of redundancy are exactly the reverse. Since redundancy is strictly conducted in reverse of seniority, those workers who have worked in the lowest 20% of job grades are made redundant. Because they do not possess high grade skills, the costs of disuse and misuse of skills are relatively small. As a result, the experienced workers in the main production lines of Ford have such a degree of protection that it requires an enormous reduction of output for redundancy measures to reach them.

In large Japanese firms, the story is completely different. The workers who are doing jobs similar to those who are most vulnerable in redundancy in Ford are not employed by Toyota, but by suppliers of components. These Japanese suppliers are in most cases independent in terms of ownership as well as in their discretion to sell their products to other auto makers, although a small number of the largest parts-suppliers are owned by Toyota. Since most of them are not owned by Toyota, they are not compelled to function as shock absorbers for Toyota employees. Hence, both Toyota and the suppliers share the burden of employment adjustment. Here, Toyota itself is not appropriate as an example of employment adjustment. Except for the first half of the 1950s, Toyota has never experienced a large reduction in output, and even in Toyota, in the first half of the '50s, many were made redundant after a two-month strike. To sum up, although large firms can generally hold surplus labor within the company, if a depression in demand lasts for long, say for a year or so, the firm is compelled to conduct redundancy measures. And without any practice of seniority, the workers in the main lines of production are vulnerable in redundancy, lacking a sufficient shock absorber within the system to protect them.

B. Dual Structure?

Strong doubts will definitely be leveled against my assertion that the Japanese system has but a small shock absorber against redundancy. According to the popular argument, the low level of internal production is nothing more than the traditional Japanese feature of a dual structured economy. Because the number of suppliers producing the same products is considerable; and because firm size, and accordingly, the financial strength of the suppliers is self-evidently smaller than that of the large firms, it is natural that the bargaining position of the parts-suppliers is weak in relation to the large firms. Consequently, it is reasonable to assume that suppliers are compelled to take most of the burden of redundancy, letting the employees of large firms enjoy permanent employment.

No decisive statistical evidence is available, although an excellent study on the relationship between large auto makers and suppliers by Professor Asanuma most clearly illustrates this issue.[8] He reveals three features in the character of this relationship. First, the most visible feature is that the relation lasts long, at least for several years, during which time a basic car model is maintained. To minimize the cost of producing parts, a supplier naturally needs to have a certain level of output, because the marginal cost of making tools and jigs specifically for the components or the model will then become smaller per unit. Second, and more importantly, the large firm and the suppliers are noncompeting, producing different products; the suppliers produce those items which are not made by the large firm. The third and most imporatnt feature is that, based on these two previous features, the suppliers have developed their own technology independently from the large firm; the suppliers use their own staff of engineers to design parts. Once such a production relationship is established, it becomes difficult for the large firm to allocate redundancy mostly to the suppliers. On the other hand, there are many small suppliers that cannot develop such technology; they make parts of a general type. Detailed observations show that such suppliers of general items have no direct relationship with the large firm itself; instead, they mostly do business with the suppliers of the first rank, which have their own technology. Hence it is not common for the large firm to utilize these suppliers as shock absorbers.

Additional evidence can be obtained by examining their labor union organization. Suppliers with high technology are not the smallest firms, but employ hundreds of workers, and usually have labor unions that are affiliated with the Toyota Confederation of Japanese Auto Industry Federation of Labor Unions. This federation has nearly 350,000 members, approaching the membership of the Ford Confederation of the United Auto Workers. As is well known to informed people, the agent who conduct wage negotiations between the Ford Corporation and the United Auto Workers is actually this Ford Confederation, as is also the case with Toyota. Since the workers of the suppliers affiliate with the Toyota Confederation of Labor Unions, wages for similar grade of workers differ little between Toyota and the suppliers. Hence this cannot be called a dual structure.

The above statements do not deny the possibility that the burden of redundancy is distributed slightly more among the suppliers than to the large firm. This is because two or more suppliers still produce the same components. Hence there is a difference in bargaining power between the large firm and the suppliers. This is, however, far from the so-called dual structure paradigm, within which scholars attribute most redundancy to the suppliers.

V. Intellectual Skills

A. Unusual Operation

The above analysis raises a crucial question to challenge the popular argument, what is the basis for Japanese workers to invest in human capital development? According to the popular argument, because of the guarantee of employment provided through the peculiar institutional setting, such as "permanent employment," Japanese workers have rationally elevated their skills. Now that the presumption of permanent employment cannot be supported, even for large firms, we must search for the grounds upon which workers invest in skill formation, and even raise a further question, that is, whether Japanese workers have actually been eager to engage in skill formation.

It is extremely difficult to measure accurately how much investment in human capital has taken place, in particular when it is conducted in terms of on-the-job training, because it is difficult to identify the invisible costs and investments separately from the work itself. And it is on-the-job training through which Japanese workers have mainly invested in human capital. There are two common ways used for calculating this investment in human capital. One is to measure the amount of investment by the number of years dedicated to employment. The human capital acquired, however, can differ for a common job duration. This difference is crucial in explaining Japanese skill formation, as will be seen later. The other is to utilize "wages" as an expression of the skill grade acquired. Particularly in Japan, as elsewhere, long, heated discussion exists as to whether wages can indicate skill grades, leaving doubt that there is a large gap between the skill attained and the wage level. The method adopted here is to examine in detail the method by which workers conduct their jobs, employing intensive interviews with veteran workers on the shop floor.

When we examine the work on the shop floor carefully, we can identify major components of "work": one is the usual conduct of routine or repetitive work, and the other is any unusual operation to deal with non-routine work, such as changes in the process or product mix, and trouble shooting. People who look at production systems as visitors are apt to miss the latter and to conclude that little skill is necessary. Even in a repetitive and monotonous flow of mass production, however, changes and troubles occur more frequently than is generally believed. Minor changes in the production process as well as the product mix must be recognized along with changes in the labor mix. To give an example of this latter phenomenon, someone must take over the job of an absent member, the result of a change in the deployment of labor. If workers can deal with these changes efficiently, productivity definitely improves. Even more so, skill in dealing with troubles and defects in goods and parts can affect efficiency. To handle these problems with the smallest cost, workers are, first, required to find the parts with defects and to replace them as soon as possible. Second, and more importantly, it is crucial that the workers prevent the recurrence of such troubles. For this purpose, workers have to discover the cause of such defects and rectify it in order to eliminate further occurrences. In the optimum case, workers can predict any trouble from the smallest sign.

B. Integrated Systems

Industrial tasks demand highly intellectual skills. Production problems arise either in the structure of the products themselves or in the mechanism of the machinery that makes them. In order to reduce the cause of and to eliminate production problems, workers have to know the structure, function, and mechanism of machines and products. These requirements are shared with engineers and technicians so that they can be called intellectual skills. Actually in many industrialized countries, unusual operations are handled at least in part by technicians or even engineers. These I call "separated systems," in which usual operations and the unusual are conducted by different occupational groups.

In contrast, on the Japanese shop floor, the workers staffing production lines are in charge of both the usual and unusual operations. This I call an "integrated system": both operations are done by a single occupation or within a single career of a worker. The superiority of an integrated system is obvious, provided that the operators have intellectual skills. Compare the delay in calling technicians or engineers every time operators notice something unusual, with the case in which the operators along the line can deal with troubles immediately as they arise. The high investment of Japanese workers in human capital can thus be seen in this area of intellectual skill.

On-the-Job Training of a Wide Range. Unfortunately, no space is left to describe in detail the process by which Japanese workers acquire intellectual skills. In short, this consists mainly of on-the-job training of a wide range and, in addition, short, inserted periods of off-the-job training in between on-the-job training. On-the-job training of a wide range covers almost all major positions in any given workshop and extends the experience to other workshops that are closely related technologically. This wide range of experience affords better opportunities for workers to understand the mechanism of production. Short, inserted off-the-job training is different from the ordinary off-the-job training commonly given in the initial period after entry; rather, its feature is that it takes place between ongoing on-the-job training experienced during normal production. Every three to five years short courses of two to five days are arranged in classrooms or training centers either in the plant or outside. A part, but not all, of it contains the theory of work relevant to the shop floor. This affords the workers appropriate opportunities to theorize concerning their own experience and to polish up on intellectual skills.

D. Incentives

A final question remains: why do Japanese workers acquire intellectual skills? The answer lies in the system of well-arranged incentives, both of a monetary and nonmonetary nature. The monetary incentive is remuneration that is equivalent to that received by engineers, in both the level and the structure of wages. A natural result of this is that, among industrialized countries, Japan has the smallest differentials in wages by grade of education. The nonmonetary incentive is the challenging nature of the work itself, including unusual operations and self-development over a wide range of one's career. When operators are expected to conduct difficult work with appropriate remuneration, it is natural for most of them to accept the challenge. A word of caution: the small gap in wages by grade of education is not the product of so-called "Japanese culture," for it is of recent origin since World War II; the gap in the latter part of the 19th century was enormous.

E. Gap between the Short-Run and Long-Run Prospect

The above analysis of the character of skills raises a delicate question: why do Japanese large firms concentrate redundancy toward long-served workers who have the higher level of intellectual skills? According to the popular argument, the answer is simple: since workers skills differ little between Japan and other countries, the wage cost for Japanese large firms naturally becomes greater than the Western counterparts because of seniority wages in Japan. Given that the nature of skill turns out to be of the higher intellectual level, it is unreasonable for the large firms to concentrate redundancy for the long-served workers simply because of their long service.

Here, note that there is a gap between short-run and long-run equality between skill level and compensation. Suppose there is firm specificity to some extent in the character of workers' skill in contemporary large firms in Japan, and suppose a part of the cost of training is borne by the workers. And, presume that there is an equilibrium between the skills and compensation in the long run. Then, it is clear that the skill level in the latest part of the workers' career is slightly below the compensation level. If not, no equilibrium in the long run can be guaranteed, because the workers must collect a return in the latter part of their career, for the costs of training borne by them in the earlier stage of their career. It is this gap that makes the large firm impose redundancy mainly on the long-service workers, because it is a reasonable short-run policy. It is not reasonable, however, for the long run, so that, if the firms repeat such policy, naturally the workers resist the firms strongly. The companies that know this fact conduct redundancy in this manner because they feel that a given situation is a rare emergency case. According to the analysis given above, it is not rare for the large firms to conduct redundancy. If this is repeated, therefore, it is natural for the workers to realize the situation and to make industrial relations as militant as that in the day of the 1950s.

VI. Policy Implications

Major policy implications for the United States are clear, although the above discussion has not focused much on the United States. First, no drastic change in the way of employment adjustment is necessary because it has been efficient and of relatively low cost thus far; the least skilled workers are first to be laid off, which results in small costs to society. Second, and conversely, effective incentives to encourage workers to invest in human capital development should be established, both in monetary and nonmonetary terms. The nonmonetary incentive should be to develop and arrange slightly more promising careers for production workers by including a more challenging mix of jobs and responsibilities. For monetary incentives, lessening the gap between engineers and production workers would be crucial.

For Japan, the policy implications are the reverse of those of the United States. To deal with employment adjustment, Japan had better adopt a loose seniority practice in redundancy, partly following the U.S. pattern: that is, start redundancy with those workers whose service is of shorter duration, but not following strict seniority. As discussed above, the Japanese practice of redundancy tends to concentrate on those workers whose loss upon being dismissed is extremely high. Consequently, Japanese social tension becomes high with the smallest amount of redundancy or unemployment. This reduces the Japanese capability to adjust to economic changes, particularly for the situation of a decline in demand. To remedy this, the suggestion to follow partly the U.S. pattern is of crucial importance.

In human capital formation, Japan has done well, yet, there is room for more effort in arranging and enriching short, inserted off-the-job training. The content of these courses should allocate more time to theorizing about the work relevant to the jobs on the shop floor. Present courses are inclined toward quality control circles or company policy, though they themselves are meaningful.

Notes

1. If the damge to a worker is large when he is made redundant, he is designated a costly worker in redundancy. As stated later, the higher the skills of a worker, the larger the damage becomes.
2. Koike [1978].
3. Koike [1983].
4. This section depends heavily on Koike [1983].
5. Data sources are complicated. Company deficits were obtained from balance sheets published by the Ministry of Finance. The records of redundancy are derived from the *Documentary History of the Labor Movement* by the Ministry of Labor.
6. Muramatsu [1985].
7. Koike [1983, pp. 124–125].
8. Asanuma [1984a; 1984b].
9. Koike (forthcoming) describes this wide range of OJT in detail.

References

Asanuma Banri. 1984a. "Nihon ni okeru Buhin Torihiki no Kōzō—Jidōsha Sangyō no Jirei" (Contractual Framework for Parts Supply in the Japanese Automobile Industry). *Keizai Ronsō*. (March). An English translation will appear in forthcoming *Japanese Economic Studies*.

————. 1984b. "Jidōsha Sangyō ni okeru Buhin Torihiki no Kōzō—Chōsei to Kakushin teki Tekiyō no Mechanism" (The Transactional Structure of Parts-Supply in The Automobile Industry—Mechanism for Adjustments and Innovative Adaptation). *Kikan Gendai Keizai*. (Summer).

Koike, Kazuo. 1978. "Japan's Industrial Relations: Characteristic and Problems." *Japanese Economic Studies* 7 (Fall): 42–90.

Koike, Kazuo. 1983. "Kaiko kara mita Gendai Nihon no Rōshi Kankei" (Redundancy in Contemporary Japanese Industrial Relations). In Moriguchi, et al. (ed.), *Nihon Keizai no Kōzō Bunseki* (The Structure of the Japanese Economy). Tokyo: Sōbunsha.

————. *Japanese Workers Skill*. London: Macmillan (forthcoming).

Muramatsu, Kuramitsu. 1983. *Nihon no Rōdō Shijō Bunseki* (An Analysis of Japanese Labor Markets). Tokyo: Hokutō Shobō.

————. 1985. "Kaiko, Kigyō Rieki to Chingin" (Redundancy, Profit and Wages). Unpublished.

Rōdōshō (Ministry of Labor). *Shiryō Rōdō Undōshi* (Documentary History of the Labor Movement). Tokyo: Ministry of Labor. Yearly, since 1945.

Rōdōshō (Ministry of Labor). 1978. *Koyō Hendō Sōgō Chōsa* (Survey on Changes in Employment). Tokyo: Ministry of Labor.

6 THE IMPACT OF MEXICAN MIGRATION ON THE UNITED STATES AND MEXICAN ECONOMIES AND LABOR MARKETS

Juan Diez-Canedo Ruiz

Introduction

This study examines the phenomenon of undocumented Mexican migration to the United States. The United States faces an apparent imbalance between jobs and native workers in the lower strata of the labor market. Historically, certain jobs have usually been taken by new immigrants and refused by second generation migrants. This imbalance is similar to that faced by many Western European nations such as Germany and Switzerland, and appears to be characteristic of most developed countries. The development process entails upward mobility for the native labor force and, apparently, after a certain stage of this process, there is insufficient native labor to take the jobs located at the bottom of the labor market. Historically, these jobs have not disappeared and have been filled by immigrant labor.

European countries have dealt with the phenomenon by hiring migrant

This study was prepared for delivery at the Conference on Adjustments in Labor Markets, Santa Clara, CA, June 6–8, 1985. Thanks are due to Peter Chinloy and Ernst Stromsdorfer for their editorial assistance.

workers contracted specifically, and temporarily, for the purpose of closing the gaps between labor supplies and demands in certain areas. The United States has refused to implement similar policies except briefly and on a limited scale, as in the case of the Bracero program for Mexican workers and on even more restricted programs affecting Jamaican nationals. The existing gaps did not originate or disappear with the legislation, however, and have been continually filled by international migrants who are in most cases undocumented. The migrants are illegal in a technical sense, but in many cases their illegal pressence is overlooked because it helps satisfy existing economic needs.

The idea of establishing a category of temporary international migratory workers without citizenship rights, as in Germany or Switzerland, seems to be inadmissible in the United States. At the same time the right to acquire citizenship has been severely curtailed through reductions in the immigration quotas, while the need for migrant labor has not abated. The jobs are there and are being filled up with international migrants. The laborers are illegal, but the jobs are not. If apprehended, the illegal migrant laborers have virtually no rights, except to choose voluntary deportation, and consequently, they exist in a limbo located somewhere inside the secondary sector of the labor market. The apparent major supplier of these migrants, Mexico, faces the problems of a dual economy. It has a fast-growing modern sector coexisting with evident economic backwardness. This is complicated by rapid population growth in the rural areas and the "traditional" sector of the urban centers.

Heavy migration from the rural areas to the cities in Mexico and the inability of the modern economic sector in Mexico to absorb the tremendous growth in labor supply has resulted in a peculiar urban labor structure. The resulting structure of the economy reflects the contradictions of an improving modern sector and worsening conditions elsewhere. The rural sector is overcrowded, characterized by relatively low wages and a falling rate of labor productivity.

The other major outlet for the overcrowded rural sector is the United States. There seems to be a labor market complementarity between the United States and Mexico; a symbiotic relationship between workers searching for jobs in one country and jobs lacking workers in the other, operating fluidly but in a clandestine way.

In understanding this process one should see the issue of international labor migration as a transfer of resources. The international transfer of resources has been studied mostly in the context of financial transfer of capital from rich to poor countries. Foreign capital supplements low domestic savings and also helps finance imports. The objective is to supplement savings in order to optimally increase investment per worker.

International labor migration has been seen mostly as a sociological or demographic problem rather than an economic phenomenon. Few have argued that labor, like its economic complement, capital, flows across national boundaries, thereby obeying a fundamental economic calculus of cost and return. Transfers of capital from developed to underdeveloped countries do not generally meet with serious economic objections. Labor transfers do not receive the same reception. However, imports of labor should be seen as the mirror image of capital imports. It may be necessary for developed countries to supplement deficiencies of their low level, lower skilled workers in order to eliminate underutilization of resources because of bottlenecks in the labor market, and thus reach greater levels of national income. The gain in national income due to the value added of imported labor should compensate for the wages paid.

When interpreting these flows of labor as an equilibrating reaction to international disparities in factor prices, the evidence used to measure their importance to the United States and Mexican economies is highly imprecise. For instance, if one believes the conventional wisdom, which insists that there may be as many as 12 million illegal aliens in the United States, about 5 million of which are Mexican, then one would also have to realize the following:

1. If these estimates are accurate, it would mean that the number of Mexican undocumented workers in the United States is almost equal to the total "black and other" male labor force in the United States, 5.7 million in 1975.[1] It would also mean that it would be about as common to see a Mexican undocumented worker as a black male worker, and it would be much more common to see an illegal alien of any nationality than a black male worker. However, it is hard to believe that the above estimates are accurate, since no one seems to notice illegal aliens very much except in times of severe unemployment.

2. If 5 million Mexicans were working in the United States, then 20% to 25% of the 15- to 59-year-old Mexican labor force, or about 50% of the total 15-to-29 male labor force, would be working in the United States.

3. Finally, if one believes the current estimates of the amount of remittances sent by these workers to Mexico, of over $3.0 billion in 1975,[2] then one would also have to believe that remittances are as important to the Mexican economy as *total* merchandise exports, which were $3.0 billion in 1975.[3]

It will be shown below that the number of undocumented workers in the United States indeed seems to have been overestimated, as has the volume of remittances. It will also be shown that the fact that not everybody migrates to the United States does not reflect irrationality, but rather that constraints exist and the process of migration is more complicated than a simple calculus involving wage differentials and the probability of finding a job.

The ideas developed in this study are derived primarily from a series of interviews with illegal migrants in their home communities. In addition to the interview materials, quantitative data were collected on Mexican migrants' remittances through a sampling process.[4]

Undocumented Mexican migration (because it is perceived to be responsible for most of the illegal immigration into the United States) has received a great deal of the blame for unemployment in the United States, especially among youths.

Although it is possible that most of the illegal immigration into the United States may come from Mexico, it is also true that most of the existing estimates of illegal migration are obviously incorrect since they are based on apprehension statistics gathered by the U.S. Immigration and Naturalization Service (INS).

The undocumented migratory process is one that, due to its very nature, has proven to be unmeasurable. Therefore, a great deal of the debate in the literature pertaining to illegal aliens is centered around how many undocumented immigrants there are in the United States and where they come from. Most of what is "known" about illegal migrants in the United States comes from data on apprehensions.

Several attempts at estimation have been made, but only one deserves particular attention. Lancaster and Scheuren [1977] used capture-recapture techniques with a sample of the population, including illegal aliens (who were not identifiable as such) and an independent estimate or count of the population excluding illegal aliens. This data set was matched to Internal Revenue Service individual income tax records and Social Security Administration earnings and benefit data. This last estimate was then subtracted from the initial sample (Exact Match Study Data).[5] Their estimates, which varied widely, suggested that the value could be anything from 2.9 million to 5.7 million individuals in 1973; the best estimate was that there may be about 4.0 million illegal aliens in the United States. This study, although clearly the best, has not received as much publicity as the others that use apprehension statistics.

II. The Nature of Emigration from Rural Mexico

Economists have studied the question of geographical labor mobility following lines stated by J.R. Hicks: " . . . differences in net economic advantages, chiefly differences in wages are the main causes of migration."[6] Migration, indeed, seems to have followed economic opportunity. Available evidence indicates that wage differentials and job openings matter to the migratory flows and thus, in the long run, wages and employment opportunities should tend to equalize.

Econometric studies show complete unanimity on the positive effect of income on migration to a region, and near unanimity on the effect of income in the region of origin, which is normally negatively related to migratory flows.[7]

Among other variables that have been considered in econometric studies are: education, whose effect is ambiguous; urbanization, which, like destination, is positively related to migration (though it does not appear to be clear which effect it does have in the region of origin); and distance, whose effect—operating through cost and uncertainty—appears to be negative.

This analysis deals mainly with Mexican international migration from rural areas. However, it is necessary to analyze some specific qualitative differences to explain the fact that two distinct patterns of migration originate within the same villages.

Three patterns of migratory flows are studied: (1) internal migration (rural-urban); (2) international temporary migration to the United States from the rural areas; and (3) international temporary migration to the United States from the urban areas.

The first two patterns of migration coexist within the same villages. Migration to the United States from the rural areas might be thought to be more rational than internal migration, for the wage differential is higher, and labor demand in the United States for the relevant segment of the labor market seems to be much greater. However, internal migration to the informal sector of the domestic urban labor market is much more common.

The existing legal barriers to labor migration in the United States do not seem to be an important factor in deciding the pattern of migration. As shall be shown, this pattern is highly correlated with the prevailing land tenure institutions and the organization of production in rural Mexico.

Alongside the typical or traditional Mexican international migrant, mostly agricultural workers, unskilled, of a rural origin, non-English-speaking, and as revealed by interview materials and remittances data, there is another more sophisticated, skilled, English-speaking, visa-abuser similar to most of the non-Mexican undocumented workers. These workers are urban in origin, and seemingly prefer urban destinations in the United States. This may be viewed as a third type of migrant in contrast to the two rural migrants mentioned above.

A. Research Methodology

As was mentioned before, the main interest of this analysis is international Mexican migration to the United States. As noted above, there exists little information on this issue, and considerable disagreement on the numbers, importance, and, in general, the whole process of this migratory phenomenon. Given that this flow has been predominantly clandestine, it is necessary to exercise great caution in the collection and interpretation of the available evidence. Misuse and lack of care in the use of existing evidence has resulted in a poor understanding of the phenomenon.

The empirical evidence we were able to draw on for this work comes from diverse sources: (1) field research, that consisted of in-depth interviews with Mexican international migrants in their home communities; (2) anthropological and other community studies of Mexican villages, that, although never focused directly on the phenomenon under study, always incidentally mention the flows of international return migration; (3) data on remittances collected as suggested by (1) and (2), analyzed with the objective of evaluating the economic importance and distribution of the Mexican undocumented workers, both in Mexico and United States; and (4) census data that were used in order to verify at an aggregate level the general hypothesis advanced in this study. Although information on key variables is either not collected or is spread among a number of sources which cannot be linked, the available census data added another element that helped to round out the analysis.

B. General Characteristics of the Migrants: Who Migrates and Where

Mexicans who go to the United States as migrant workers from the Jalisco area have the following general characteristics:

1. They are male—the women go only when the whole family gets established legally in the United States—in the 18- to 35-year age group, although there are some up to 68 years old. The ones in the older age group were in all cases legal migrants.

2. They had little education, usually from three to six years.

3. Contrary to what some studies have found, migrants were not even close to the bottom of the income distribution in their home communities. Although they appeared to be landless *jornaleros*, they were not. In most cases they could be considered as underemployed family members in the middle to upper middle-class strata.[8] Those in the lowest classes, that include the landless *jornaleros*, could not afford the cost of migrating, which

included transportation to the border and money for being smuggled across the border, a sum amounting up to $250.

The underemployed (not surplus) family member had his family's backing and everyone benefited by this migration. Those staying behind did not really need him for labor, had one less mouth to feed, and had the prospect of receiving money from him. When the migrant returned he could use some of the money previously sent for a business project. According to this research, these family members are the ones that apparently have been mistakenly included in the illegal alien surveys as landless *jornaleros*. Although they are in fact landless, they did not usually work outside the family unit which, in turn, worked the land communally. The landless *jornaleros* are the ones at the bottom of the economic scale, being surplus laborers most of the year. Other studies[9] corroborate the fact that individuals at the bottom of the economic scale seldom migrate to the United States, although the same studies, in apparent confusion, name *jornaleros* as those who migrate mainly to the United States. Actually, the *jornaleros* seem to migrate on a permanent basis to the urban centers, if at all. This migration pattern was not possible to document in the rural communities included in the present study for obvious reasons (they were not there), but it is amply documented in many other studies.[10]

After analyzing the interview materials, the following was apparent:

1. When land or other means of rural livelihood allow families to live above the subsistence level, the prevailing migratory pattern will be of a temporary character to the United States.

2. When the family plots get overcrowded, and thus its members live at or close to subsistence, new or additional members will be forced to migrate permanently to the urban centers. Unless this distinction is made, the picture would be one of migration to urban centers (which show a marked excess supply of unskilled labor) paradoxically coexisting with an entirely different flow to the United States (with an apparent excess demand for this type of worker, and where the minimum wage is at least four times higher than the highest minimum in Mexico—$20 a day in the United States in 1977 versus a range of $5.95 to $3.16 a day in Mexico).

C. A Theoretical Explanation of the Possibility of Coexistence of Two Patterns of Migration from the Same Rural Villages

It was found that the two different types of migratory flows emerging from the rural areas were conditioned initially on the production arrangements prevailing in the place of origin. In this section a graphical analysis

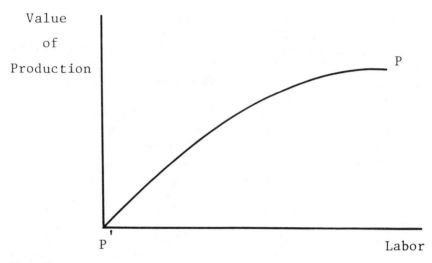

Figure 6–1.

considering the specific structure of Mexican agriculture is developed.

The Mexican agricultural sector is divided into two broad categories: *ejidos* and small private property.[11] The plots that have the greatest marketable surplus are seemingly the ones that have more than five hectares, while the *ejidos* are, in at least 83% of the cases, subsistence plots. In most cases these *ejidos* seem to be overcrowded, and their production is largely for home consumption. The plots of less than five hectares are, in at least 96% of the cases, at subsistence; 50% of the producers (mostly *ejidos* and small private property) produced only 4% of the product while 0.5% produced 32%.

The general picture that emerges is one of an apparently overcrowded sector with limited amounts of land and institutional restrictions on land sales.

Families living in subsistence plots are generally producing in a communal fashion. Families with income above subsistence may produce communally, in a "pure capitalistic" fashion, or communally while occasionally hiring some additional workers.

When family income was at subsistence, and one of its members left, this was usually a permanent move. He or she neither received from, nor contributed anything to, the family. That individual had to earn his or her subsistence wage (essentially biological subsistence) outside the family farm.

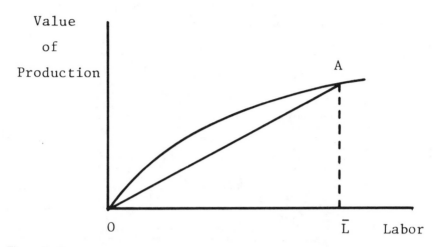

Figure 6-2.

In what follows it will be shown graphically how, when combining the existing institutional and production arrangements with the population pressure on land, the two patterns of immigration may be explained.

The curve P'P of figure 6-1 describes the production function of an individual farm. Underlying this curve are identifiable production processes with different input mixes and different outputs.

In figure 6-2, the slope of the line OA represents the average output per person in a farm when there are L family members. Every member of the family living on the farm gets the average product.

Most farms are subsistence farms and the prevailing average product or wage in the rural areas will be at subsistence.

In the rural areas, the demand for labor will be determined by the prevailing rural wages, which, to simplify, will be assumed to be at biological subsistence.

Capitalist families may be thought of as disembodied profitmaximizing managers of the land, and will produce at the optimal output, E (see figure 6-3). At this point, E, the prevailing rural wage will just equal the marginal product of labor, and a line with slope equal to the wage will be tangent to the production function. L* laborers will be demanded and a rent R will be obtained.

From figure 6-4, three different types of production units may be identified: (1) "capitalist" families; (2) families working the land communally (i.e., no hired labor with a marginal product of labor less than the prevailing rural wage), but whose average product is above subsistence; and (3)

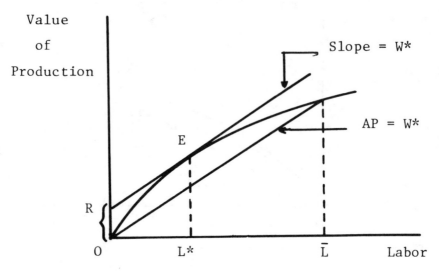

Figure 6−3.

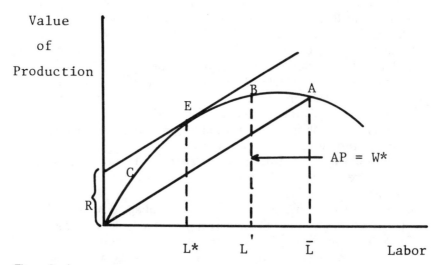

Figure 6−4.

families working the land communally, but whose average product is above subsistence.

A profit-maximizing capitalist will produce at point E of figure 6−4. At that point, he will need L* labor and will receive R as rent. It should be mentioned that if "subsistence" *ejidos* (with average product at subsistence) would be put up for sale (which cannot legally be done), demand for farm labor in the rural areas might be lessened, as labor is discharged until the marginal product of labor increases to the prevailing wage. ($\bar{L} - L^*$ would have to migrate.) In the same figure, it may be seen that some family units produce in a communal way, yet still hire some labor as long as family members provide less than L^* in labor, as at point C. At point B, members of these production units receive a total return that is higher than the subsistence wage, since they will have more than L^* and less then $\bar{L}$ members, they won't hire additional workers since the going wage would be less than their marginal product.

Families working the land communally, but whose average product is *at* subsistence, will be at point A. So, on one extreme we will have family plots worked communally with an average product or salary equal to subsistence. On the other extreme, there will be the large farms that produce in a capitalist fashion hiring labor at the going wage. In between them there will be found family farms worked communally, but where the average product is above subsistence. The case of the communal production unit working at subsistence levels can probably be identified with most of the *ejido* plots and the private *plots* of less than five hectares (which are very few, having 3.0% of the total arable land in 1970). In general, most plots are subsistence plots, and will be producing with the maximum number of people that still permit a subsistence average income. In the *ejido* case, the plots are small and the natural population growth in the rural areas is a very high 3.5% per year. Many of these plots are, consequently, in the condition where the average product is at the subsistence level or close by. When the families on these plots grow, or when some family member marries, an extra head may bring the whole family under subsistence. The majority of the rural population seems to be in this condition, since 70% of the rural population in 1970 was composed of the *ejidatarios* and their families, and they had a ratio of 3.4 hectares of arable land per *ejidatario*. For plots of less than five hectares the same ratio was 0.8, while this ratio for plots bigger than five hectares was 13.38.

These facts suggest that most people in the rural areas are living at a subsistence level, and therefore tend to confirm the hypothesis that prevailing rural income must be the average product on these plots.

"Capitalist" farms are the only ones that are going to demand labor in the agricultural sector at the going subsistence wage. The reader is reminded that the wage could not possibly be lower, because once one family member has to work outside the family and the ties with the family are cut, he or she receives no help from the family. Therefore, the minimum wage has to be at

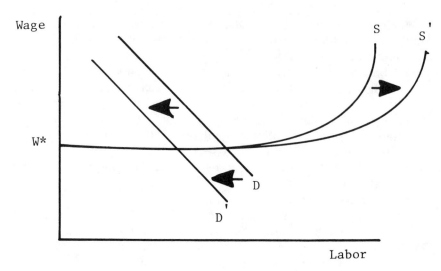

Figure 6-5.

least the subsistence wage.

Labor supply in the rural areas will be perfectly elastic at the going subsistence wage (see figure 6–5). There is a large pool of landless laborers that is composed of the workers who, due to population growth, are forced outside the family units, and there is an already existing stock of *jornaleros*. This implies that the relevant segment of the supply curve is the horizontal portion. Population growth will shift the curve to S' and extend the horizontal portion of the curve. The upward-sloping portion of the supply curve exists because, as the wage rate rises above the average product on the wealthier farms, additional farmers may be attracted into the rural labor market.

As mentioned above, the demand for labor in the rural areas will come from the "capitalist" farms. Population growth could also imply that capitalist families could grow above L* unless labor on such families migrated (figure 6–4), and thus the demand would shift to the left (figure 6–5) as capitalist farms become pure communal farms producing with an average product above the subsistence wage, but where the going wage will be less than their marginal product. Thus, they will not hire any additional labor.

Now, going back to our original problem, we need to know why there can be two different migratory patterns coming from the same areas.

Capitalist farms and families producing an average product above subsistence have the flexibility of producing, if necessary, with more people.

This flexibility does not exist in subsistence plots, in which, if more people are included or families grow, all the members' incomes will drop below subsistence.

Surplus *ejidatarios* can stay close by the family by working for some time at the prevailing subsistence wage on a capitalist farm, but their income is effectively independent of the *ejidos*. For an *ejido* family, the gain of having one family member working outside will be the increase in consumption per capita on the farm. However, the worker who was laboring close by will eventually have to migrate on a permanent basis to an urban center. When he or she marries, and a new family starts to grow, the worker will have to raise his or her subsistence supply price, i.e., one's price will no longer be one's own, but will have to reflect ones family's needs. The worker's new price will include the minimum subsistence income per capita of his or her family.

The local capitalist farmers are going to hire single *jornaleros* who have a lower subsistence requirement and supply price. The new family unit will be expelled from the original nucleus, and the only place where this new family's supply price could probably be matched will be in the cities. Wages in the lower tiers of the urban labor market will presumably allow the family to survive even if the family members have to work in such occupations as begging or sorting out salable objects from the municipal garbage dump. The jobs available to these migrants are in most cases definitely not very desirable, and this may be the reason they will postpone their migration to the urban areas until it is unavoidable.

Migration to the United States for these people, although probable, is not likely for several reasons. First, as noted above, it is very hard for them to get the necessary capital for the travel expenses that are involved in going to the United States. The forgone income, when traveling and when at subsistence, is fairly important. Another problem is that even if they go temporarily to the United States, since there is no possibility of buying any land at their place of origin due to legal restrictions, they will still have to get established elsewhere. They cannot leave their families and cannot take them to the United States. As a practical matter, the only solution is to migrate permanently to an urban center in Mexico.

The migratory perspective of family units who live above subsistence is altogether different. Since family members are relatively unskilled, many of the jobs that they may be able to get in the urban areas will probably pay wages below their supply price (average product forgone). So, there might even be a negative wage differential with respect to the cities, and thus, this alternative will not be even considered. On the other hand, temporary migration to the United States is very attractive to them. There is an obvious

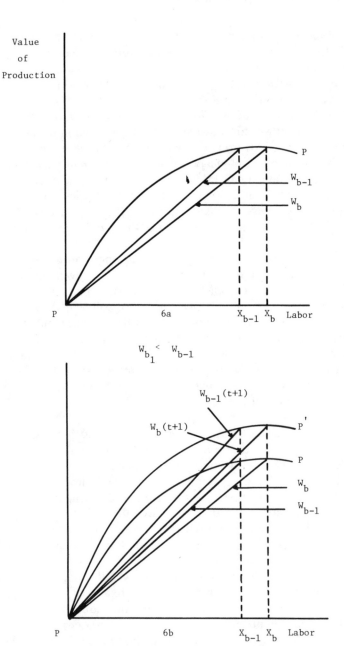

Figure 6—6.

positive wage differential, and the outlook for finding a job is very good as confirmed by past experience.

Suppose, in figure 6–6A, the X_b members of the family enterprise are working at a given moment and that one member decides to work for a time in the United States. At the moment he or she leaves, and assuming that he/she doesn't receive any money from the family after he/she leaves, the average wage will rise, making every remaining member better off. After he/she leaves, he/she will probably remit some additional money that can be used to further improve the family's position through immediate consumption, or, perhaps after the funds are invested in a water well or some other improvement to the land, increasing production possibilities. Here, as well as in the case of the subsistence plot, the average product rises when one family member leaves. The marginal productivity of that member is lost, but the gains in terms of per capita consumption of the rest of the family and the money remitted more than compensate the losses. As this is the case, when one member leaves, the remaining family members will be see their earnings increased from W_b to W_{b-1}. If the migrant remits money and the family puts it to a productive use, it will see its earnings further increased to (figure 6–6B) $W_{b-1, \; t+1}$. When he or she returns, everybody will be better off having their income increased to $W_{b, \; t+1}$. The worker can also start an independent business buying some land, and starting as a capitalist hiring labor at w^s, and his/her family will nevertheless be better off at W_{b-1}. Highly efficient capitalist farms hiring labor at the prevailing wage will have high rents and provide no incentive for its owners to work abroad, since they must manage the farm to collect their rents.

In summary, from the same general geographical areas two different migratory behaviors will occur. Both will be perfectly rational, one clearly more profitable, but foreclosed to poorer families without savings or mortgageable land.

It could be added that, afterwards, the migrants who had to go to the domestic urban areas will possibly take the option of migrating on a temporary basis to the United States, following the patterns that they observed in their towns, but could not follow at that time. So summarizing, when a family produces communally and one member leaves, independently of whether they are at subsistence, the marginal member cannot return to the family unit because he or she would push all the family below subsistence.

Since there is no income pooling, once a family member leaves the farm, the individual will have to earn at least a subsistence wage. Since there is an excess supply of labor, the going wage is going to be precisely the individual subsistence wage. When the families of these ejected, landless workers (*jornaleros*) grow, the *jornaleros*' supply price will have to reflect their families' increased needs. This price will be higher than the going wage (*individual* subsistence), and they will have to go to an urban center, the only place where their supply price can be matched. These people will not migrate to the United States, basically because when at biological subsistence, there is no possibility for acquiring the savings that are required for the migratory process to the United States, a move that entails a large period of income forgone and a relatively high migration cost.

When families are producing above subsistence, the outlook is altogether different. One important difference is that their average product is higher than the subsistence wage, and probably higher than the prevailing wage in the informal sector of the urban labor market. This means that, first, they are not pushed off the farm, and second, that there is no necessary incentive for them to migrate to the cities. These people thus have the possibility of saving, and they can take advantage of the basic economic incentives provided by a significant United States wage differential and an excess demand for their services. Afterwards, as capital is accumulated, they may return and produce on the land as capitalists, receiving rents higher than the prevailing wage for their services in the United States. Thus, their rationale for continuing to migrate temporarily will cease to exist.

D. Considerations Regarding the Place of Destination of Internal Labor Migration

Internal migration can hardly be understood from its economic point of view by assuming that it happens only because there is a positive wage differential between two given regions. Claims that the migrant weighs the wage differential alone, perhaps along with an unemployment rate, will give us an incomplete view. This view is hard to document for several reasons.

First, there is an empirical problem. Since the urban labor market in Mexico is segmented, with numerous dualities existing, it would be difficult for an unskilled rural migrant to determine what would be his or her possible wage. Wage data for unskilled labor refer to the legal minimum wage, which is supposed to be about the same in real terms for both the urban and the rural sectors.

However, this wage is not paid by many of the employers in either urban or rural areas. In the smallest firms of the manufacturing sector the mean wage lies well below the legal minimum. Reported wages are probably biased upward. (It is illegal to pay under the minimum, so firms probably over-report their wage bills in industrial census reports.)

The "modern sector," however, seems to be highly segmented, and generalizations about labor market conditions are hard to make. In the tertiary sector, and especially in its lower strata, where most of the rural unskilled migrants find jobs, there is much more disorganization. Here almost anything can be a job. Self-employment and child labor are very common, and to change occupations at this skill level is not difficult. An almost continuous spectrum of underemployment is the rule, while open unemployment is rare. The close-to-subsistence wages force every member of the family to bring home whatever one can. [12] In this sense, any increase in labor supply that results from immigration must result in increased employment (or underemployment) in the urban areas.

The prevailing wage in the "informal" sector of the urban labor market appears to be close to subsistence, although a little higher than the prevailing wage in the rural areas. In this sense, unemployment would mean starvation in a Malthusian sense, and thus, although the jobs may be almost anything, extreme unemployment is not possible.

For rural unskilled migrants the decision to migrate to an urban center will often mean working in the tertiary sector, under the circumstances mentioned above. They will go to the urban center where the probabilities of survival are best.

E. The Mexican Migrants in the United States Labor Market

As mentioned above, Mexican migration to the United States has a long history. The Mexican *bracero*, or migrant worker to the United States, is, as was mentioned before, an institution that has prevailed through history in some rural communities. Historically persistent is also the fact that once migrants cross the border they find little problem in finding a job on a farm or a gang where a limited knowledge of English on the part of one member will suffice.

The peculiarities of the migratory phenomenon have persisted over the decades. One of the risks involved in this process is the risk of deportation. Apparently the risk of deportation was relatively high at entry, but that was taken into consideration by migrants. They knew there was a high degree of uncertainty regarding the intensity of the deportation "campaigns," INS raids to respond to cyclical fluctuations in the supply of native labor, the type of job taken, and the economic cycles. [13] The risk of deportation has therefore been a persistent element in this phenomenon, but it has not deterred the flow.

Another element that has varied little during the different stages of this flow has been the possibility of finding a job. It could have been expected that, for instance, after the termination of the Bracero Program, finding a job should have been more difficult. This was definitely not the case, according to the field research I conducted.

According to the people who had both experiences (32% of the sample), things *improved*. During the Bracero Program, migrant workers were hired to work by a specific employer prior to going to the United States, and could not legally get another job. In contrast, as illegal workers, they had no problem finding a job. Moreover, if they did not like the job or could get better pay elsewhere, they could always move. The only problem was initially to cross the border, and that was not difficult. Migrants looking for agricultural jobs usually found them, either directly in the fields or in small towns. The usual procedure was to begin, early in the morning, to scout for groups of workers lining up for employment. They just joined the group and were employed in a matter of a day or two.

In considering the kind of jobs taken by illegals, the question of exploitation is often raised. Exploitation is a difficult thing to measure, but nobody interviewed in our sample of migrants felt that they were exploited because of their illegal status. In all cases their wages were at the U.S. federal minimum wage or above. Usually they tried to make as much as they could. They felt they were working like slaves but earning like kings.

"Exploitation" in their home villages was more obvious. Even though wages were very low due to an overall labor surplus and below the Mexican legal minimum, complaints were not voiced. Workers were afraid they might lose those jobs. These laborers were also the ones who normally would not migrate to the United States for the reasons discussed previously.

The destination chosen for work in the United States, for those who had a preference for agricultural jobs, or feared the winter,[14] was basically California. They typically migrated for six or seven months from March to August. Texas was also preferred because it was closer; but wages and working conditions there were less preferable. Those who planned to stay longer usually chose an industrial job in the areas of Chicago or Los Angles. It depended very much on their skills, past experiences, preferences or plain luck. The ones that migrated to the industrial areas were usually the more skilled and had more experience. They typically stayed at least one year and up to three years at the most. Their reasons for leaving were generally deportation, a strike, or family motives. They usually migrated or considered migrating three or four times, or were professional temporary migrants who went every year. This last group (18%) was composed mostly of legal migrants (14%), but included some who said they never had any problems even crossing the border, so they weren't worried at all about getting legal papers. This frequency of migration has been observed at least since the start of the Bracero Program, and reflects, to some degree, the professional *bracerismo* often mentioned in anthropological studies.

F. The Search for a Job

This aspect of the migratory process was not well understood by the migrants, for there were no rules of thumb. They simply got where they thought they wanted to go and, somehow, tried to contact someone who spoke Spanish. The latter usually offered a helping hand, either taking them directly to a job, or helping them leave their names in the job-wanted lists in different companies. These same people helped them find a place to stay and, in a short time, they were working.

Whenever they reached industrial centers, they tended to fill the so-called secondary labor market jobs. Due to the high turnover rates typically observed in that market, it is easy to find job openings. Such jobs are constantly being filled by these laborers. The job search process in the agricultural sector was, as described, also very quick.

G. The Issue of Illegality

The illegal status of part of the work force did not seem to matter either for the job search process or in labor relations. It did not seem to affect or modify in any way the internal labor market mechanisms.

Several reasons can be offered as an explanation. First, when someone is working illegally, his best-guarded secret is precisely that, so he is going to try very hard to hide that fact. Although fellow workers widely suspected that there were many illegals working in a factory, there was no certainty except with the occurence of an INS raid. When this happened it was common that some they had suspected were not illegals were, while some others, apparently above suspicion, were working without papers. The other reason is that the only thing that the employer needs to be "legal" is to hire those who have a social security card. A social security card is very easy to get, since machines exist that make a metal card for a quarter or so. In their home communities, they have a stock of cards that are constantly recycled.

In the industrial centers, therefore, the labor market—or more precisely the secondary labor market—was not illegal. No one was hired beccause he or she was illegal, for several reasons. First of all, as was mentioned before, nobody advertised this fact. Secondly, the employer probably preferred to be within the law; and thirdly, if the employer decided to lower wages, suspecting his employees were illegal, they would immediately quit that job and go somewhere else. After all, they were in the United States to make money, and wage rates were perfectly known among illegals. This was very clear in the agricultural jobs. If they knew the going wage was even five or ten cents an hour per box higher in the next orchard (if working on a piece rate basis) they would immediately move. This made wages about the same everywhere.

Labor relations were normal. Seniority was very important in the allocation of overtime, selection of work shifts, and in enhancing the probability of becoming a foreman. The individuals we interviewed were union members when required in all but two cases, and most workers joined the Teamsters Union, even though they claimed not to have made a voluntary choice.

In all cases, they paid income tax, which was retained by the employer, and, in our sample, no one received welfare. The reasons were twofold: first, they had very little information; and, second, they were afraid of being caught. Consequently, they appeared to contribute much more to social services than they used. This fact is documented in many other studies,[15] even though there have been claims that there is a considerable tax burden for each illegal worker.

In summary, the labor market structure for the illegal aliens seems to work very smoothly at two different levels. While English-speaking, skilled, visa-abusing Mexicans work in some areas, amazingly, somebody who cannot speak a word of English and can hardly read and write in Spanish, can find a job within a week in, say, Highland Park (a Chicago suburb) doing custodial work in a big hotel chain.

There is a labor market within a market in the United States. The fact that there are jobs that nobody other than the illegals wants has been explained by dual labor market theorists. But why is it that the illegal labor supply is taken for granted? How do the employers know that they are going to have this kind of labor available? After all, if the supply were uncertain, many firms or industries would not survive under current conditions of demand. Illegals seem to earn, in many cases, more than the minimum wage. They are highly mobile and react to wage differentials within the United States. It must be that some "mechanism," conditioned by history, is working.

III. Empirical Results (see Table 6−1)

California, Illinois, Texas, New York and Minnesota are the most important states for migrant destinations. California was chosen as a destination by migrants coming from 28 out of a total of 32 Mexican States. Most came from Guanajuato, Mexico City, and Zacatecas. Regardless of the origin of the migrant, the mean check sent from California was very similar, with an overall mean of $135, a small deviation, and 99% of the checks less than $500. It appears that the income received by migrants is very similar, and the remittances are therefore also very similar. These facts suggest that in California there is a high probability that illegals do cluster in specific areas or jobs, and therefore earn about the same amount of money. The illegal labor market is definitely a defined market in this state, which apparently is also heavily dependent on Mexican laborers.

Table 6−1. Remittances by American State (Origin) Bank X, 1975

State	Total Amount ($)	Mean ($)	% Under $500
Alabama	16,527	98	100
Arizona	304,945	175	95
Arkansas	274,785	1,636	88
California	11,666,342	135	99
Colorado	1,383,948	102	99
Connecticut	891,699	90	100
Delaware	4,200	100	100
Florida	923,811	638	91
Georgia	15,372	146	100
Hawaii	6,762	161	100
Idaho	204,724	222	91
Illinois	8,165,167	193	96
Indiana	179,341	259	91
Iowa	38,894	103	95
Kansas	141,162	129	98
Kentucky	61,919	491	83
Louisiana	68,852	364	78
Maryland	7,601	72	100
Massachusetts	16,485	87	100
Michigan	98,574	142	94
Minnesota	2,012,210	86	100
Mississippi	4,200	200	100
Missouri	574,185	977	93

Table 6–1 (*continued*)

State	Total Amount ($)	Mean ($)	% Under $500
Montana	8,010	64	100
North Carolina	27,300	260	80
Nebraska	17,850	213	100
Nevada	17,632	53	100
New Jersey	138,990	147	95
New Mexico	46,536	123	94
New York	3,550,062	348	92
Ohio	164,808	357	73
Oklahoma	63,711	233	92
Oregon	95,491	108	100
Pennsylvania	257,967	178	96
Rhode Island	7,511	179	100
Tennessee	6,804	81	100
Texas	3,922,051	209	97
Utah	65,541	240	85
Vermont	4,305	51	100
Virginia	36,708	135	100
Washington	242,362	160	94
Wisconsin	569,867	936	90
Virginia (UP)	483	12	100
0000[a]	1,341,790	145	98
????[b]	6,249,994	106	100
Total final	43,897,472	151	98

[a]0000—Money orders, origin unknown.
[b]????—Postal money orders, origin unknown.

People from 27 states of the Mexican Republic choose Illinois as their destination. Most of them come from Mexico City and the state of Guanajuato. The total mean check is $193 and the deviation, as expected, is much higher than the one found in California.

The next state in importance, Texas, received people from 27 states, with an average check of $209. Guanajuato, the Distrito Federal, San Luis Potosí, and Zacatecas are the most important source states.

New York is the fourth state in importance in terms of remittances. People from 22 Mexican states go to New York. The mean check is $348 and the dispersion is relatively high, with only 92% of the checks less than $500. An interesting result is that the most numerous group going to New York comes from Mexico City. The evidence from other studies does not point to New York as having Mexican illegals in important numbers. This is another indicator of how little is known of the relative importance of aliens of different nationalities in the United States labor market.

The state of Minnesota is fifth in importance as a destination for people, also from 27 states of Mexico. This state previously has never been found to be an important destination for Mexican illegals, probably because the INS has very few agents in this state. Minnesota's newspapers do not spend much time with the illegal alien issue, for although it exists, it is not thought to cause unemployment.

Three important differences with other studies were found in this survey. First, as was pointed out above, Mexico City appears to be among the most important source region of migrants to the United States. Second, New York is fourth in importance as a destination, after the traditional areas of California, Illinois, and Texas; finally, Minnesota ranks very close to Texas and New York.

These results may also reflect the fact that other studies indeed have important biases, having obtained their results only from samples of apprehended aliens.

The studies of illegal Mexican migration of INS statistics rarely report illegal aliens coming from Mexico City into New York or any other area. The probable causes are: first, there seems to be a considerable number of aliens of other nationalities working in or around New York, so Mexicans are not easily detected; and second, most of the INS policing is done along the Mexican border. The Mexicans that enter the country as "entrants without inspection" (EWI's) by swimming across the river or crossing the fence in the California area usually go to California, Texas, or Chicago. Therefore it is understandable that most apprehensions are of Mexican EWI's, while the stock of visa-abusers, Mexican or otherwise, is bound to be dramatically misrepresented.

C. Amount of Remittances

Using the sample of remittances, a total of $317,559,988 of remittances was obtained. This figure can be criticized on the ground that it is an underestimation. It can be argued that it does not include the amount of money brought back by the undocumented aliens. A "guesstimate" could have been obtained, but that approach was rejected for several reasons:

1. There is evidence that they avoid bringing much money with them. The Zazuetas [1977] found that when migrants brought money back, they

were abused by the authorities on both sides of the border.[16] In my survey I found that they tried not to bring much money, or if they had to, they brought a money order.

2. When they brought money back, it was in small amounts and was often spent for gifts, clothes, and travel expenses before crossing the border.

A figure that closely resembles the amount of remittances found in this study may be seen in the 1968 national survey on household incomes and expenditures.[17] This survey includes two tables with the following information: aid received by households, including remittances, gifts, and other sources of income. As a counterpart of this table we have transfers made from outside the family unit. Ideally, these two figures, transfers given and received should cancel out; however, they do not. There is a positive balance of $222,432,000 that might be attributed to *bracero* remittances[18]. If we accept this figure as a possible remittance figure for 1968, and the $317,559,998 figure found in this study for 1975, the annual percentage rate of growth would be 5.2%, which resembles the mean rate of growth of non-agricultural wages in the United States which was 6.8%.

D. Remittances and the Number of Illegals: Counting the Uncountables Once Again

It was mentioned above that illegal migration, due to its characteristics, has proven to be unmeasurable directly. What follows is an exercise that aims to assess the possible magnitude, and the ranges within which the number of undocumented Mexican aliens may fall, on the basis of data from this research.

Our procedure is to apply assumptions about the remittance behavior of Mexican migrants to data on total remittances. Reasonably reliable data on the remittance behavior of apprehended illegals have been collected by North and Houstoun [1976]. In that study, the authors found illegals captured in the Southwest were, as a group, making the largest average monthly remittances, followed by, respectively, Mexican illegals in general, Western hemisphere illegals, visa-abusers, and, remitting the least, Eastern hemisphere illegals (table 6−2).

Given assumptions about the incidence of payment (IP), and average remittance(AP), we shall further correct the average monthly payment reported for apprehended illegals by a correction factor (PR). Since this correction factor is less than one, this procedure has the effect of increasing the number of illegals *above* the levels implicit in the use of the raw North

Table 6–2.   Payments Made to Homeland Relatives and Wages of Selected Groups of Apprehended Illegal Alien Respondents

	Average Weekly Wage	Average Monthly Payments[a]	Percentage of Group Making Payments	Average Monthly Payments[b]	Total Number of Respondents
Region of origin:					
Mexican illegals	$106	$169	89	$129	481
Western hemisphere illegals (excluding Mexico)	127	116	72	76	237
Eastern hemisphere illegals	195	104	44	37	75
Entry technique:					
Entered without inspection[c]	108	162	87	124	555
Visa-abusers	150	115	63	63	238
Illegals in SW border counties	74	186	89	129	68
All apprehended respondents	120	151	79	105	793

Source: Linton & Company Illegal Alien Study, 1975. Taken from D. North and M. Houstoun, *The Characteristics and Role of Illegal Aliens in the U.S. Labor Market. An Exploratory Study.* Linton & Co., March 1976. p. 86.

[a] Average based on only those making such payments.
[b] Average based on all illegals, including those not paying.
[c] INS term for aliens who enter the U.S. without authorization.

and Houstoun results.

We expect *PR* to be less than one (*apprehended* illegals make larger average monthly payments than the general population of Mexican illegals) for three reasons. First, as noted by North and Houstoun, visa-abusers make smaller average monthly payments than those that enter without inspection. As is noted in the last chapter, the remittance data suggests a substantial undetected population of Mexican visa-abuser type illegals. Second, North and Houstoun found that aliens apprehended in the Southwest made greater monthly payments than other apprehended aliens, and Southwestern apprehensions probably overrepresent the true probability of finding a randomly selected Mexican alien in the Southwest. Third, North and Houstoun suggest some tendency on the part of apprehended aliens to exaggerate their remittances to families.

Definitions:

$$TRM = NI \times IP \times PR \times AP$$

with *TRM* = total remittances in a given month by illegal aliens

    NI   = number of illegals

    IP   = incidence of payments (% of illegals remitting money)

    PR   = average monthly remittance among *all* Mexican aliens as a proportion of average monthly remittance among *apprehended* Mexican aliens.

    AP   = average monthly payment per remitting illegal

That is, total remittances in a given month are equal to the number of aliens weighted by the incidence of payments, multiplied by the average remittances corrected for overreporting of monthly remittances among apprehended aliens. Solving for *NI* (number of illegals) we have:

$$NI = TRM/(IP \times PR \times AP).$$

Using the incidence of payments and the average monthly payments from the North and Houstoun study (page 86), the following estimates may be made:

1. Upper Bound—It is assumed that 44% of the Mexican illegals send money— a proposition similar to that reported by North and Houstoun for Eastern hemisphere illegals— and that they send the same average monthly remittance of $104. This is a conservative estimate, since Eastern hemisphere illegals are presumed to have a low average propensity to send money. To truly provide an upper bound, we assume that Mexican illegals sent only one-fifth of the average monthly remittance reported by apprehended Eastern hemisphere illegals.

    IP = .444   *AP* = 104   *PR* = .20

$$\$26,460,000 \div 9.15 = NI^u = 2.9 \text{ million}$$

2. Lower Bound—It is assumed now that all Mexican illegals behave like the Mexican illegals of the North and Houstoun study. Yet as was mentioned above, to accept as a standard that behavior of apprehended Mexican illegals implies introducing severe biases.

It is statistically incorrect to assume that because most apprehended illegals are Mexican, most illegals are Mexican. It is also untenable to assume that non-apprehended Mexican illegals are similar to apprehended Mexican illegals.

Again from table 6–2 we have:

$IP = .89$ $AP = 169$ $PR = .75$

$PR = .75$ amounts to assuming that the general population of Mexican illegals sends three quarters of the average monthly remittance reported by apprehended Mexicans.

$$\$26,460,000 + 112.8 = NI^L = 234,575$$

3. Middle Range—For this estimate it is assumed that Mexican illegals behave on average like their Western hemisphere counterparts, as reported in the North and Houstoun study. PR will be .4, or equivalently, all illegals sent 40% of the remittances sent by apprehended illegals.

$IP = .7$ $AP = 116$ $PR = .4$

$$\$26,460,000 \div 32.48 = MR = \$814,655$$

Thus, using the data of this research and on the basis of the evidence found by North and Houstoun, there could be a population of Mexican illegals working in the United States, in any given month in 1975, ranging from 243,575 up to 2.9 million. A more likely figure is around 815,000 workers.

D. Taking into Account Remittances Through Personal Checks

It could be argued that the remittance figure for illegal labor is underestimated because personal checks are also sent by illegals. This section analyzes the effect on the magnitudes of adding up the personal checks.

The personal checks sent from persons with Spanish surname to persons with the same characteristics added up to $216,894,980 for the year 1975 (on the basis of the methodology applied to postal money orders and money orders described in the previous section). Adding this sum to the illegal remittance estimation, a total remittance of $534,454,968 is obtained. That implies a monthly average of $44,537,914.

Upper Bound total PC and illegal—
$IP = .44$ $AP = 104$ $PR = .20$

$$\$44,537,914 \div 9.15 = NPC + I^u = 4,867,532$$

Lower Bound total PC and illegal—
$IP = .89$ $AP = 169$ $PR = .75$

$$\$44,537,914 \div 112.8 = NPC + I^L = 394,839$$

Middle Range total PC and illegal—
$IP = .7$ $AP = 116$ $PR = .4$

$$\$44,537,914 \div 32.48 = NPC + I^M = 1,371,241$$

E. Sensitivity Analysis

Assume that the remittances figure is equal to W. Cornelius's figure of "probably exceeding 3 billion dollars"[19] first, and then from W. Cornelius's other figure of "probably in excess of 2 billion per year"[20] ($NIC2$). This will be done on a monthly basis to avoid any seasonality problems and using again North and Houstoun's data on average payment and incidence. Three billion dollars implies a monthly average of $250,000,000, as opposed to my estimate of around $26 million a month.

Upper Bound—
$IP = .44$ $AP = 104$ $PR = .2$ $NICI^u = 26,322,404$

Lower Bound—
$IP = .89$ $AP = 169$ $PR = .75$ $NICI^L = 2,216,312$

Middle Range—
$IP = .7$ $AP = 116$ $PR = .4$ $NICI^M = 7,697,044$

Now, using the $2 billion estimate, average monthly remittances = $166,666,666.

Upper Bound—
$IP = .44$ $AP = 104$ $PR = .2$ $NIC2^u = 18,214,935$

Lower Bound—
$IP = .89$ $AP = 169$ $PR = .75$ $NIC2^L = 1,477,541$

Middle Range—
$IP = .7$ $AP = 116$ $PR = .4$ $NIC2^M = 5,131,368$

The total Mexican labor force estimated for the year 1975 is 16,334,000.

Clearly the upper bounds imply in one case, $NIC1^u$, almost 11 million more people in the labor force than the existing ones; while in the second case, $NIC2^u$, implies almost 2 million additional non-existing people. The lower bounds, with clearly exaggerated parameters, reflect acceptable levels.

For the middle range, $NIC1^M$ implies that almost 50% of the population 12 years and older [1975] is working in the United States illegally and in $NIC2^M$ that more than 30% of the labor force, as described above, is working in the United States in any given month.

Zacatecas and Guanajuato were considered to be states heavily dependent on remittances. The per capita money remittances in 1975 were $48.9 and $41.1, respectively. If the $3 and $2 billion estimates are considered, and the same distribution by state is used, some interesting results are obtained.

The $3 billion estimate would be equivalent to $53.0 per capita *on a national level* and, with the $2 billion estimate, of $35.3 per capita.

Using the $3 billion estimate and the distribution by state found in my study, Zacatecas would have to receive $462.06 per capita per year (every man, woman, and child). The comparative numbers for Guanajuato and Durango would be $388.4 and $97.0. If the $2 billion estimate is used, Zacatecas would have $308.0 per capita, Guanajuato $259.0, and Durango $64.6 per capita per year.

The per capita Gross National Product (GNP) for Mexico in 1975 was $1,360.08, while in Zacatecas it was $483.9, in Guanajuato $643.78, and in Durango $819.8.

This means that with the $3 billion estimate, 95.4% of Zacatecas per capita GNP, and 60.3% of Guanajuato per capita GNP, would be due to remittances. With the $2 billion plus estimate, at least 63.6% of Zacatecas per capita GNP and at least 40% of Guanajuato would be due to remittances.

In conclusion, the two estimates mentioned above would imply that almost all or nearly all the income generated in Zacatecas and Guanajuato would depend on illegal laborers. Thus, in a certain sense, Zacatecas should be considered another state of the union.

IV. Conclusions

With regard to the issue of international undocumented migration in general, and, specifically Mexican undocumented migration to the United States, there are little accurate data and considerable disagreement on the numbers, importance, and, in general, the whole process of this migratory phenomenon.

Since this flow is clandestine, it is necessary to exercise great caution in the collection and interpretation of the available evidence. Ths misuse and lack of care in the use of existing evidence has resulted in a faulty understanding of the phenomenon.

The cumulative effect of the different bits of evidence suggests that certain key features of the phenomenon, which we now recapitulate briefly, appear to be firmly established.

1. Different patterns of migration coexist within the same villages. One is of a permanent character to the domestic urban centers, and one is of a temporary character either to an urban center or to the United States. Migration to the United States could be thought to be more rational than internal migration, for the wage differential is higher and the labor demand for the relevant segment of the labor market much higher. However, internal migration to the informal sector of the urban market is more common. It is conditioned by the relative high fixed cost of immigration linked with low savings possibilities where individuals are living close to biological subsistence.

2. The pattern of migration followed is highly correlated with the prevailing land tenure institutions and organization of production. When land or other means of rural livelihood allow families to live above subsistenc, the prevailing migratory pattern will be of a temporary character to the United States. When family plots get overcrowded and members live at levels close to subsistence, new or additional members will be forced to migrate permanently to the urban centers. Unless this distinction is made, the picture is one of migration to an urban center with a market excess supply of labor paradoxically coexisting with other migration to the United States, where there is apparently an excess demand for this type of worker.

3. The supply price of international migrants may be higher than the prevailing wage in the informal sector of the urban centers, thus implying a negative wage differential. This pattern of migration will not then be considered by rural workers living above subsistence, while migration to the United States will be a rational move. The supply price of internal migrants is the subsistence wage, while the prevailing wage in the informal sector of the urban labor market seems to be slightly above subsistence. When families grow, some of their members will have to leave. They can work nearby at a capitalist farm earning the subsistence wage, but eventually they will have to move permanently to an urban center. This will happen when their (new) family grows and the supply price of the head of the new family unit increases in order to reflect the needs of all its members.

4. The remittances from temporary migrants represent, in some regions, an important source of capital. This capital provides villagers financial leverage, helps them get credit lines, represents the first stage for further

sustained development, and reduces the need for further migration.

5. The jobs taken by most Mexican international migrants are still apparently agricultural, although there is a growing percentage working in the urban centers.

6. The labor market in the United States industrial areas has within one of its segments a sort of "limbo" labor market, operating fluidly, although in a semi-clandestine way—clandestine because of the worker, but not because of the job. Most of the jobs are located within the secondary labor market. The incredibly short time span needed to find a job by a non-English-speaking alien (what could be thought of as an apparent severe handicap) suggests an excess demand for this type of worker.

7. Illegal aliens do not seem to affect labor relations a great deal. They are perhaps easier to manage and more productive than their native United States counterparts. In any other segment of the labor market except in the secondary, they would be severely handicapped when searching for a job. The secondary labor market, due to its characteristics, is the perfect economic sector for illegal aliens.

8. The number of undocumented workers in the United States has been severely overestimated. The numbers that have been used with greatest frequency are untenable from a scientific point of view and have hindered understanding of the phenomenon.

9. The migratory flow of temporary Mexican migrants to the United States and the evident demand existing for their services suggest a mutually beneficial relation for both countries.

Notes

1. U.S. Department of Labor, Bureau of Labor Statistics, *Handbook of Labor Statistics*, 1979, p. 31, table 3.

2. Wayne Cornelius. "La Migracion Ilegal Mexicana a los Estados Unidos: Conclusiones de Investigaciones Recientes, Implicaciones Politicas y Prioridades de Investigacion." *Foro Internacional* Enero-Marzo 1978.

3. World Bank *Special Study on the Mexican Economy 1979*, Vol. II, table 3.2.

4. The interviews were structured to cover certain basic questions, but were open-ended, since personal contact and considerable cooperation on the part of the migrants was essential to success. Since the universe of undocumented Mexican aliens is unknown, it is impossible to obtain a scientifically valid sample. One region was therefore selected somewhat arbitrarily. Consequently, the interview materials cannot support any generally valid conclusions, but do indicate gerneral patterns that were tested with additional information. The procedure followed was as follows: (1) first the field study was done; (2) the field study was complemented with information contained in anthropological and community studies of Mexican villages; (3) a sample of migrants' remittances was undertaken; (4) simple models of migrants' behavior were

tested with published data on migration and other variables related to the migratory processes.

5. Initially a sample of one day per week was selected at random. Afterwards, due to time and budget limitations, the sample was limited to one working day per month throughout the year 1975. The sample of remittances was weighted afterwards by the total number of working days at banking institutions in order to come up with a total monthly and annual figure for remittances. To obtain a national estimate of remittances, it was assumed that the total absorption of foreign currency at this particular bank in every state was representative of its total absorption of remittances. The bank's share of total absorption (liabilities) by state was obtained from unpublished data of the Bank of Mexico, and a total national estimate was calculated.

6. J.R. Hicks, *The Theory of Wages*, London: Macmillan, 1932, p. 76.

7. P. Krugman, and J. Bhagwati, "A Decision to Migrate: A Survey," MIT, mimeo, June 1975. See also reenwood M.J. "Research on Internal Migration in the U.S.: A Survey," Dec. 1975.

8. See also O. Lewis, *Tepoztlan*.

9. Wayne Cornelius, *ibid*.

10. This is an important distinction to be made as necessary for understanding the theoretical explanation of the phenomenon done in section 3. See for instance Abraham Iszaevich, *Modernizacion en una Comunidad del Valle de Oaxaca*.

11. The *ejido* is not private property. It is a plot of land (whose dimensions vary according to the use and the zone) handed to a community of peasants by the government. It cannot be sold, leased, or mortgaged. It is owned by the nation through a community of *ejidatarios*. The *ejido* is a small plot, not distant in many cases from "petty landholding." The small private property has been categorized for census and analysis purposes in two broad categories: private plots of less than five hectares, and private plots of more than five hectares.

12. Lisa Peattie, "Organization de los Marginales." In R. Ketzman and J.L. Reyna, *Fuerza de Trabajo y Movimientos Laborales en America Latina*. El Colegio de Mexico, 1979, p. 111.

13. Michael Piore, *Birds of Passage*, p. 173. Obviously the deportation risk exists since there is an immigration law, but the number of deportations has varied widely according to specific policies like "Operation Wetback," carried out in 1954, which resulted in over a million deported Mexicans.

14. See Luis Gonzalez, *Pueblo en Vilo*, p. 225.

15. See U.S. Department of Labor, "Illegal Aliens Study, Statistical Highlights," 1975. Memorandum (11/18/75) from William H. Kolberg to Secretary John H. Dunlop on Study by D.S. North to Linton and Co., issued as a press release. Also D. North and M. Houstoun, *The Characteristics and Role of Illegal Aliens in the U.S. Labor Market*.

16. Zazueta, Carlos, and Cesar Zazueta, 1977.

17. *La Distribution del Ingreso en Mexico*. Encuesta sobre los Ingresos y los Gastos de las Familias 1968. Banco de Mexico F.C.E. Mex. 1974.

18. Jesus Reyes Heroles, *Politica Fiscal y Distribution del Ingreso*. Tesis de Licenciatura. ITAM. 1976, p. 54.

19. The reader is reminded that although some illegals may send this money through this channel, no evidence for it was found in this study. The reader is also reminded that it could be argued in a similar way that the remittances will include personal checks plus money orders; however, illegal remittances were exclusively sent through postal and money orders, and were the ones taken into consideration in the previous section.

20. Wayne Cornelius, "La Migracion Ilegal Mexicana a los Estados Unidos: Conclusiones de Investigaciones Recientes, Implicaciones Politica y Prioridades de Investigacion." *Foro Internacional*. El Colegio de Mexico. Enero-Marzo, 1978. p. 415.

References

Cornelius, Wayne. 1978. "La Migracion Ilegal Mexicana a los Estados Unidos: Conclusiones de Investigaciones Recientes, Implicaciones Politicas y Prioridades de Investigacion." *Foro International* Enero-Marzo de 1978.

——————. 1978. "Mexican Migration to the U.S., Causes, Consequences and U.S. Responses." Cambridge, MA: Massachusetts Institute of Technology.

—————— and Juan Diez-Canedo. 1976. "Mexican Migration to the U.S. The View from Rural Sending Communities." Paper presented at the Conference on Mexico an the United States: The Next Ten Years. School of International Service, The American University, Washington, D.C., March 18–19.

Dillingham Commission. 1911. Report to the U.S. Immigration Commission, 61st Congress (42 volumes, Washington, D.C.).

Gonzalez, Luis. 1972. *Pueblo en Vilo*. El Colegio de Mexico, Mexico.

Greenwood, M.J. 1975. "Research on Internal Migration in the United States: A Survey." *Journal of Economic Literature* XIII (June): 397–433.

Handlin, Oscar. 1959. *Boston's Immigrants: A Study in Acculturation*. Cambridge, MA: Belknap, 1932.

Hicks, J.R. 1932. *The Theory of Wages*. London: Macmillan.

Howrwich, Isaac A. 1922. *Immigration and Labor: The Economic Aspects of European Immigration to the U.S.* C.W.Y. Huebsch and Co. 2nd edition.

Krugman, P., and J. Bhagwati. 1975. "A Decision to Migrate: A Survey." Cambridge, MA: Massachusetts Institute of Technology (Mimeo).

Lancaster, Clarise, and Frederick Scheuren. 1977. "Counting the Uncountable Illegals." Some Initial Statistical Speculations Employing Capture-Recapture Technique." Proceedings of the *American Statistical Association*, Part I.

Lewis, Oscar. 1951. *Life in a Mexican Village. Tepoztlan Restudied*. Urbana, IL: University of Illinois Press.

——————. 1966. *Tepotzotlan. Village in Mexico*. New York: Holt, Rinehart and Winston.

Peattie, Lisa. 1979. "Organizacion de los Marginales." In R. Ketzman and J.L. Reyna (eds.), *Fuerza de Trabajo y Movimientos Laborales en America Latina*. El Colegio de Mexico.

Piore, Michael. 1973. "The Role of Immigration in Industrial Growth: A Case Study of the Origins and Character of Puerto Rican Migration to Boston." Working Paper No. 122. Massachusetts Institute of Technology, Department of Economics.

——————. 1979. *Birds of Passage; Migrant Labor and Industrial Societies*. Cambridge, MA: Harvard University Press.

U.S. Department of Labor. 1979. Bureau of Labor Statistics. *Hankbook of Labor Statistics*. Washington, D.C.

——————. 1975. "Illegal Aliens Study, Statistical Highlights." Memorandum (11/18/75) from William H. Kolberg to Secretary John H. Dunlop on Study by D.S. North to Linton and Co., issued as a press release. Washington, D.C.

World Bank. 1979. Special Study on the Mexican Economy. *Major Policy Issues and Prospects*, vol. II. Washington, D.C.

Zazueta, Carlos, and Cesar Zazueta. 1977. "En las Puertas del Paraiso." CENIET. Mimeo. (Observaciones hechas en la levantamineto de la Primera Encuesta a Trabajadores Mexicanos Indocumentados Devueltos de los Estados Unidos.) 23 de octubre–13 de noviembre.

Appendix

Data Sources

Agricultural Credit 1960. Source: *Guia a los Mercados de Mexico*. la. Edicion 1960–61.

Agricultural and Livestock Credit 1976. Ssource: Banco de Mexico. Oficina de Divulgacion.

Commercial Credit 1960. Source: *Guia a los Mercados de Mexico*. la. Edicion 1960–61.

Commercial Credit 1976. Source: Banco de Mexico. Oficina de Divulgacion.

Distance by road from one state capital to another. Source: *Guia de carreteras de Mexico*. Secretaria de Turismo. 1978.

Incomes, 1970. Source: EX *Censo General de Poblacion 1970*. Mexico. Secretary de Industria y Comercio. 1975.

Index of Land Tenure 1960. Source: *VIII Censo General de Poblacion*. Mexico. Secretaria de Industria y Comercio, 1965, and Censo Agricola Ganadero y Ejidal, 1960.

Index of Land Tenure 1970. Source: *IX Censo General de Poblacion*. Mexico. Secretaria de Industria y Comercio, 1975 and Censo Agricola Ganadero y Ejidal, 1970.

Industrial Credit 1960. Source: *Guia a los Mercados de Mexico*. la. Edicion 1960–61.

Industrial Credit 1976. Source: Banco de Mexico: Oficina de Divulgacion.

Kilometers of roads by state 1970. Source: *V Censo General de Poblacion*. Mexico. Secretaria de Industria y Comercio, 1975.

Livestock Credit 1960. Source: *Guia a los Mercados de Mexico*. la. Edicion 1960–61.

Interstate Migration 1970. Source: *IX Censo General de Poblacion*. Mexico. Secretaria de Industria y Comercio, 1975.

Minimum salary in the rural areas 1970. Source: *Comision Nacional de Salarios Minimos*. Mexico 1970.

Number of Elementary School Teacher (total and rural) 1960. Source: *Guia a los Mercados de Mexico*. la. Edicion 1960–61.

III DOMESTIC AND INTERNATIONAL SHOCKS: EFFECTS ON EMPLOYMENT AND WAGES

7 WAGE AND EMPLOYMENT ADJUSTMENTS AND THE EFFICIENCY WAGE HYPOTHESIS: AN APPLICATION TO THE JAPANESE MANUFACTURING SECTOR

Isao Ōhashi

I. Introduction

In an international comparison on the behavior of wages and employment, Gordon [1982] and Grubb, Jackman, and Layard [1983] have argued that in Japan both nominal and real wages are flexible in response to business fluctuations. This response is measured in terms of the standard deviations of rates of change of manufacturing wage rates and the coefficient of wage response relative to changes in nominal GNP (Gordon), or in terms of the change in unemployment caused by wage rigidity in the wake of a real or nominal shock (Grubb and associates).[1] To explain this wage volatility, Gordon refered to the Japanese labor market institutions of lifetime employment, bonus payments, and wage negotiations that take place annually during the "spring wage offensive." In particular, he paid

I wish to acknowledge helpful comments on previous drafts from Masahiko Aoki, Nicholas M. Kiefer, Hajime Miyazaki, and other conference participants at University of Santa Clara. I have also benefited from comments by Sohichi Kinoshita and workshop participants at Nagoya University and Irako Labor Seminar. Financial support was provided by the Ishida Foundation.

attention to the combination of wage flexibility and employment stability brought by the above institutions. The focus of this chapter is to explore the problem proposed by Gordon in the framework of the neoclassical theory of employment adjustments, focusing on the relation between wage determination and employment stability.

The orthodox model of the demand for labor in the short-run developed by such individuals as Brechling [1965], Ball and St. Cyr [1966], and Nadiri and Rosen [1969], analyzes the dynamic behavior of a firm that adjusts employment toward its optimal level, assuming that the wage rate is exogenously given. But, in a labor market where the adjustment costs of employment such as training and hiring costs play an important role and information concerning wages is imperfect, the firm is in a monopsonistic position. That is, the firm that faces an imperfectly competitive labor market can control not only employment but also the wage in the dynamic process of adjustment. From this point of view Mortensen [1970], Salop [1973], and Leban [1982] analyzed the dynamic wage and employment policy of the monopsonistic firm, and drew the important conclusion that the optimizing firm never discharges excess labor. That is, when the firm wishes to reduce its labor force, it always encourages excess labor to quit by lowering the relative wage, because the lowered wage saves labor costs by reducing the labor force. But this characteristic of their models is not useful for empirical analysis on the real economy where dismissals do in fact occur.

To admit the existence of dismissals, we incorporate the elements proposed by the efficiency wage hypothesis, which focuses on the aspect that wage payments affect the productivity of workers. This allows us to analyze how quits and dismissals are combined to reduce employment. Medoff [1979] dealt with this problem empirically for U.S. manufacturing industries. Further, it is interesting to "think more in terms of the *gross* labor market flows (layoffs, quits, new hires) rather than being confined to *net* change in employment," as claimed by Hazledone [1979]. For example, it is possible that firms may hire new workers even when they wish to reduce net employment.

This study also analyzes how the speed of employment adjustment is determined and what are its determinants in the case where the firm can control the wage rate paid. The neoclassical model emphasizes the role of variables such as adjustment costs in explaining the determinants of adjustment speed. In turn, our model will show that the wage paid by the firm and the labor market condition are substantial influences as well since adjustment speed is strongly dependent on the quit behavior of workers. From another point of view, this implies that differences in the speed of adjustment among firms are due to differences in their wage payments and

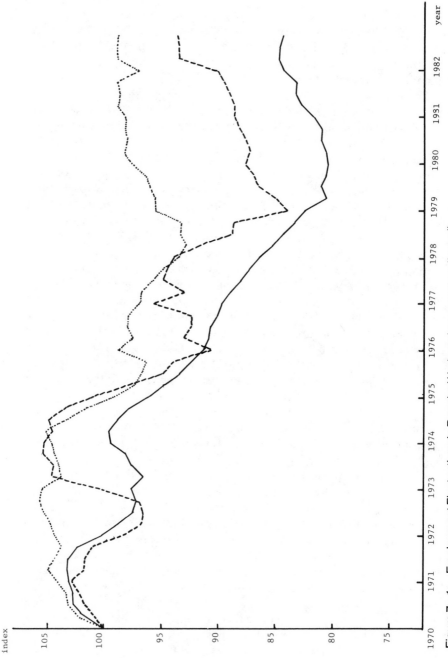

Figure 7—1. Employment Fluctuations in Regular Workers (seasonally adjusted).

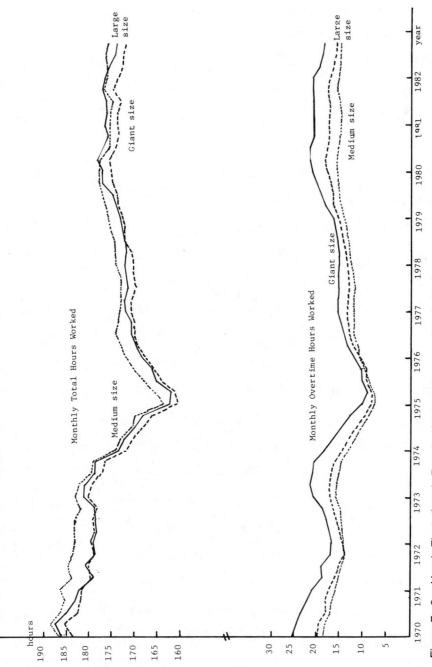

Figure 7–2. Hourly Fluctations in Regular Workers (seasonally adjusted).

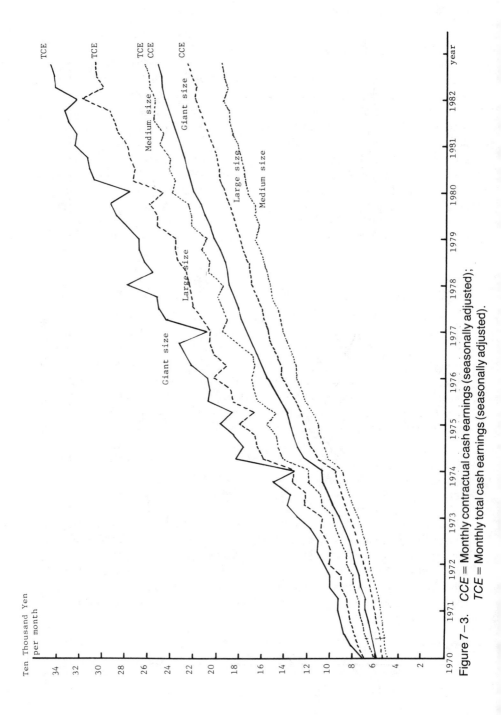

Figure 7-3.   *CCE* = Monthly contractual cash earnings (seasonally adjusted);
TCE = Monthly total cash earnings (seasonally adjusted).

the labor market condition with which they are confronted.

Finally, we test the implications of our model for the Japanese manufacturing sector with respect to firm size and discuss the problems concerning wage flexibility and employment stability, based on the empirical results obtained. We focus on differences in firm size because in Japan the earnings that individual workers receive vary widely, depending on the size of the firm in which they are employed (figures 7−1 to 7−3). For instance, according to the *Monthly Labor Survey*, the average hourly wage rates of contractual earnings differ between giant-size establishments (1,000 or more employees) and large-size (500−999) by 11%, between giant-size and medium-size (100−499 employees) by 21%, and between giant-size and small-size (30−99 employees) by 35%. If we look at their total earnings, which include bonus payments, the differences become wider, as can be seen in figure 7−3.

II. The Model

According to the efficiency wage hypothesis,[2] real wages affect the productivity of workers. This phenomenon is caused by three factors. First, so as to reduce shirking, the firm pays a higher wage and widens the gap between its own wage and the alternative wage that workers can expect when discharged. Second, it is rational for the firm to pay a higher real wage than the market-clearing rate because employees respond with added loyalty to the firm. Third, paying a higher wage makes it possible for the firm to save hiring and training costs by reducing the quits of qualified and skilled workers.

Taking account of these versions, we define an index of the workers' effort e as

$$e = w/\overline{p} - \{(1 - u)\overline{w}/\overline{p} + uz/\overline{p}\},$$

where w is the basic wage for normal hours, $\overline{p}$ is the average price level of consumption goods, u is the rate of unemployment, $\overline{w}$ is the average wage in labor market, and z is unemployment compensation. The second term is the expected gain of a separated worker. Note here that, as indicated by the efficiency wage hypothesis, increases in w and u raise the effort index, while those in $\overline{p}$ and $\overline{w}$ decrease it.[3] Using this index, we summarize the production process as follows:

$$0 = f(h, e, \beta)L, \qquad f_1 > 0, \quad f_2 > 0, \quad f_3 > 0, \quad f_{12} > 0, \quad f_{13} > 0, \qquad (7-1)$$

where 0 is output, f is the continuously twice differentiable productivity function, h is hours worked, β is the index of the amount of hiring and training costs per employee, and L is the number of workers employed. The efficiency wage hypothesis supports the assumptions concerning the positive effect of e on the marginal productivities of labor inputs, i.e., employment and hours worked, such that $f_2 > 0$ and $f_{12} > 0$. It is also reasonable to assume that $f_3 > 0$ and $f_{13} > 0$ because as the firm incurs increased costs to search for high quality workers and to train them, productivity will increase.

Denoting normal hours by h_1 and overtime or short-time hours by h_2, we have

$$h = h_1 + h_2. \tag{7-2}$$

Assuming that h_1 is historically given for the firm and noting that w is the wage payment for h_1, we define the wage function as follows,

$$v = w + g(h_2), \qquad g' > 0, \, g'' > 0, \, g(0) = 0, \tag{7-3}$$

where v is the total wage payment per worker.

In adjusting employment the firm must incur hiring and separation costs, T, such as training costs, severance pay, and employer search costs. Since these costs are assumed to be a quadratic function of net new hires, N (i.e., new hires or dismissals), the adjustment cost function is given by,

$$T = \beta N^2/2. \tag{7-4}$$

Note that the adjustment costs crucially depend on β, which is assumed to affect labor productivity.

Defining Q as quits, we have the quit function,

$$q = q(w - \bar{w}, u)L, \qquad q_1 < 0, \, q_{11} > 0, \, q_2 < 0. \tag{7-5}$$

Since the quit function of this type is standard, we do not discuss its justification here (see Salop [1973], for example). Quits and net new hires give us a dynamic identity equation,

$$\dot{L} = N - q(w - \bar{w}, u)L, \tag{7-6}$$

where $\dot{L}$ is the rate of change of employment with respect to time.

The firm is assumed to maximize the present value of its flow of profits over an infinite planning horizon, X,

$$X = \int_0^\infty (p0 - vL - T)e^{-rt}dt, \tag{7-7}$$

subject to the dynamic identity equation (7-6) with respect to h_2, w, and N, where P is defined as the price of the firm's product. To solve this problem we define the Hamiltonian as

$$H = pf(h_1 + h_2, \ w/\overline{p} - (1 - u)\overline{w}/\overline{p} - uz/\overline{p}, \ \beta)L - (w + g(h_2))L$$
$$- \beta N^2/2 + \lambda(N - q(w - \overline{w}, u)L), \tag{7-8}$$

where λ is the current-value shadow price associated with employment. The first-order and canonical conditions are

$$pf_1 - g' = 0, \tag{7-9}$$

$$pf_2/\overline{p} - 1 - \lambda q_1 = 0, \tag{7-10}$$

$$-\beta N + \lambda = 0, \tag{7-11}$$

$$\dot{\lambda} = (r + q)\lambda - (pf - w - g), \tag{7-12}$$

$$\dot{L} = N - qL, \tag{7-13}$$

where $L \neq 0$ is assumed.

A. The Short-run Equilibrium

We first deal with the short-run equilibrium of the system consisting of equations (7–9), (7–10), and (7–11) by assuming that λ and L are given. To explore the properties of the short-run solutions, we depict equations (7–9) and (7–10) graphically. Differentiating (7–9) with respect to w, we have

$$\frac{dh_2}{dw} = \frac{-pf_{12}/\overline{p}}{pf_{11} - g''} > 0,$$

where the inequality is obtained from the Legendre-Clebsch conditions (i.e., second-order conditions), which require that the Hessian matrix from (7–9), (7–10), and (7–11) must be negative definite (see appendix 7–A). Therefore, equation (7–9) can be represented by the positively sloped curve (7–9) in figure 7–4, where w^* is defined as satisfying,

$$pf_1(h_1, \ w^*/\overline{p} - (1-u)\overline{w}/\overline{p} - uz/\overline{p}, \ \beta) - g'(0) = 0. \tag{7-9}'$$

It is easily shown that increases in p, β, and u shift the curve upwards and hence decrease w^*. On the other hand, increases in h_1 and $\overline{w}$ shift it downwards and hence increase w^*.

Differentiating (7–10) with respect to w, we have

$$\frac{dh_2}{dw} = \frac{\lambda q_{11}\overline{p} - pf_{22}/\overline{p}}{pf_{21}} > 0,$$

where the inequality is again obtained from the Legendre-Clebsch conditions. Furthermore, using these conditions, we can also show that the slope

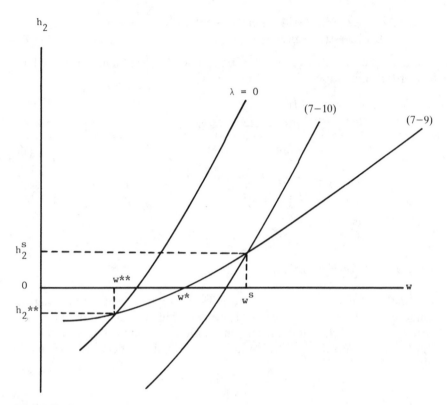

Figure 7–4.

of the curve $(7-10)$ is steeper than the curve $(7-9)$, as depicted in figure
$7-4$. Thus, the short-run equilibrium solutions (w^s, h_2^s) can be obtained as
an intersection of the two curves.

In order to analyze how the firm adjusts hours worked and employment in
response to a business slump, we first differentiate equation $(7-10)$ with
respect of λ, holding h_2 constant, to yield

$$\frac{dw}{d\lambda} = \frac{q_1^{\bar{p}}}{pf_{22}/\bar{p} - \bar{p}q_{11}} > 0,$$

This implies that the curve $(7-10)$ moves downwards as λ increases. We
here define the curve satisfying $\lambda = 0$ in equation $(7-10)$, that is,

$$pf_2(h_1 + h_2, w/\bar{p} - (1 - u)\bar{w}/\bar{p} - uz/\bar{p}, \beta) - \bar{p} = 0. \qquad (7-10)'$$

We also define the point (w^{**}, h_2^{**}) as the intersection of the curve $(7-9)$

and the curve $\lambda = 0$. Note here that since the curve $(7-10)$ moves upwards as λ decreases, if $\lambda < 0$ $(\lambda > 0)$, then the curve $(7-10)$ is higher (lower) than the curve $\lambda = 0$ and hence $w^s < w^{**}$ $(w^s > w^{**})$. In turn, equation $(7-11)$ shows that if $\lambda < 0 (\lambda > 0)$, then $N < 0$ $(N > 0)$. Therefore, the relative position of w^s to w^{**} is associated with the occurrence of dismissals such that if $w^s < w^{**}$, then $N < 0$, and vice versa.

The problem of whether dismissals are more unlikely to occur than short-time operation during periods of business slump depends on w^{**} and w^*. If $w^{**} < w^*$, then short-time operation is more likely because $w^s < w^{**}$ (i.e., dismissals) always implies $w^s < w^*$ (i.e., short-time operation) and the reverse does not hold. Unfortunately, we cannot answer decisively the question of which case is more likely to hold in our economy, but can analyze, if we wish, how changes in β, h_1, u, and $\bar{w}$ affect w^* and w^{**} and hence the likelihood of occurrence of each case by conducting comparative statics on the system of $(7-9)$ and $(7-10)'$.

B. The Stationary State

Define the stationary state solutions as $h_2{}^c$, w^c, λ^c, N^c, and L^c, which are assumed to be positive in the economy. Then they satisfy $\lambda = 0$ and $L = 0$, so that the following relations hold,

$$pf_1(h_1 + h_2^c, e^c, \beta) - g'(h_2^c) = 0, \tag{7-9a}$$

$$pf_2(h_1 + h_2^c, e^c, \beta) - \bar{p} - \lambda^c \bar{p} q_1(w^c - \bar{w}, u) = 0, \tag{7-10a}$$

$$\lambda^c = \beta N^c \tag{7-11a}$$

$$(r + q(w^c - \bar{w}, u))\lambda^c = pf(h_1 + h_2^c, e^c, \beta) - w^c - g(h_2^c), \tag{7-12a}$$

$$N^c = q(w^c - \bar{w}, y)L^c. \tag{7-13a}$$

where $e^c \equiv w^c/\bar{p} - (1 - u)\bar{w}/\bar{p} - uz/\bar{p}$. We obtain h_2^c, w^c, and λ^c by solving equations $(7-9a)$, $(7-10a)$, and $(7-12a)$, and we obtain N^c and L^c from solving equations $(7-11a)$ and $(7-13a)$.

After this exercise in comparative statics, we have the results concerning the effects of β, p, $\bar{p}$, h_1, u, and $\bar{w}$, which are shown in table $7-1$. The following points are worth mentioning. First, an increase of β raises h_2^c and w^c, reducing q^c. This is consistent with the fact that in large-size firms wages and overtime hours worked are relatively high and the quit rate is low (see table $7-2$ and figures $7-2$ and $7-3$). In turn, the effects of β on N^c and L^c are ambiguous. Our calculation leads to $dN^c/d\beta = pf_3^c/(r + q) - N^c$, where the first term in the right-hand side is the present value of an additional

Table 7−1. Pattern of Structural Effects

Changes in	Effects on							
	h_2^e	w^e	$w^e/\bar{p}$	$w^e-\bar{w}$	q^e	λ^e	N^e	L^e
β	+	+	+	+	−	+	?	?
P	+	+	+	+	−	+	+	+
$\bar{p}$	?	+	−	+	−	−	−	?
h_1	?	+	+	+	−	+	+	+
u	+	?	?	?	?	+	+	?
u with fixed q	+	−	−	−	fixed	+	+	+
$\bar{w}$	?	?	?	−	+	−	−	−
$\bar{w}$ with fixed q	constant	+	+	−	fixed	−	−	−

Note: In order to obtain the effect of $\bar{p}$ on w^e, we assume that the wage elasticity of quit behavior is less than one.

Table 7−2. Voluntary Quit Rate and Separation Rate in Relation to Establishment Size

Year	Establishment Size (number of employees)			
	30−99	*100−299*	*300−999*	*1,000 and over*
1975	0.14 (0.18)	0.14 (0.19)	0.12 (0.16)	0.07 (0.09)
1976	0.15 (0.17)	0.15 (0.18)	0.11 (0.14)	0.08 (0.10)
1977	0.14 (0.18)	0.14 (0.18)	0.11 (0.14)	0.08 (0.09)
1978	0.13 (0.16)	0.13 (0.18)	0.10 (0.13)	0.07 (0.09)
1979	0.14 (0.16)	0.13 (0.16)	0.10 (0.12)	0.07 (0.09)
1980	0.14 (0.16)	0.13 (0.15)	0.10 (0.12)	0.07 (0.10)
1981	0.13 (0.14)	0.12 (0.15)	0.10 (0.12)	0.07 (0.09)
1982	0.13 (0.15)	0.13 (0.15)	0.10 (0.12)	0.07 (0.08)

Source: The Employment Trend Survey (Ministry of Labor).
Notes: Voluntary quits means separations caused by personal reasons, mandatory retirement, death, illness, and discharge, but not by employment contract expired and managerial problems.

The separation rate is in parentheses.

increase in β, discounted by the rate of interest and the possibility of quit, and the second term is the costs. If the former is larger than the latter, then the effects of β on N^e and L^e are positive. If not, the effect on N^e is negative and the effect on L^e is ambiguous.

Second, under the assumption that the wage elasticity of quit behavior is less than one, the consumer price index has a positive effect on the nominal wage. This is because the firm attempts to avoid a decrease in the effort index by raising the wage as far as circumstances permit. On the other hand, if the wage elasticity of quit behavior is sufficiently large, then the firm responds by decreasing the wage and inducing quits, which leads to a decrease in its employment. It can be also shown that the effect of $\bar{p}$ on the real wage is negative, independent of the wage elasticity of quit behavior. That is, when the nominal wage is increased, its degree is less than that of $\bar{p}$. Thus our model predicts that in the Philips relation the coefficient of the rate of change of the consumer price index is less than one.

Third, as derived in appendix $7-B$, the effect of u on N^e is positive. This is because an increase in u raises the present value of an additional new hire by enhancing workers' efforts and reducing the quit rate. But its effect on w^e and L^e are ambiguous since unemployment has an effect not only on the efficiency behavior of workers but also on the quit behavior. If we focus only on the former's effect by assuming in appendix $7-B$ that the quit rate is not sensitive to changes in the wage and unemployment, then we know that an increase in unemployment decreases the wage. This is because in higher unemployment the firm can maintain workers' effort by the lower wage. On the other hand, if we assume that its effect on efficiency behavior is negligible an increase in unemployment raises the wage through reducing quits and making it easy for the firm to amortize its training and hiring costs. The issue of which effect dominates in the Japanese economy is empirical. In Japan it appears that the efficiency behavior of workers is more important since the quit rate is low and stable over time, as shown in table $7-2$.

Similarly, we can know the effects of the average wage level in the labor market although they are opposite to those of unemployment. For example, when efficiency behavior is dominant, an increase in the average wage level has a spillover to the firm's wage, decreasing employment. One important difference in the effect between $\bar{w}$ and u is that even in the general case an increase in $\bar{w}$ decisively reduces the gap between the firm's own wage and the average wage and hence suppresses the quit rate, while the effect of u on the firm's own wage is ambiguous.

C. Adjustment Path

We now consider the dynamic behavior of the firm along its adjustment path. To begin with, since equation $(7-12)$ is nonlinear in h_2, w, and λ, we approximate the dynamic behavior of the firm, for simplicity, by linear expansions about the stationary state solution as follows:

$$\dot{\lambda} - \{r + q^e + q_1^e(w - w^e)\}\lambda + pf^e - w^e - g(h_2^c)$$
$$+ (pf_2^e/\bar{p} - 1)(w - w^e) + (pf_1^e - g'(h_2^c))(h_2 - h_2^c) = 0.$$

Using equations (7−9) and (7−10), we have in the simplest form,

$$\dot{\lambda} - (r + q^e)\lambda + pf^e - w^e - g^e = 0. \qquad (7-14)$$

Solving this first-order differential equation gives us

$$\lambda = \lambda^e + Ae^{(r+q^e)t}, \qquad (7-14)$$

where A is the integrating constant. The transversality condition, $\lim\limits_{t\to\infty}$ $\lambda e^{-rt} = 0$, requires that A be zero. Hence we have

$$\lambda = \lambda^e = \frac{pf^e - w^e - q^e}{r + q^e}, \qquad (7-15)$$

where the second equality is obtained by equation (7−12a). Substituting this into equation (7−11) and using (7−11a), we obtain

$$N = \lambda^e/\beta = N^e. \qquad (7-16)$$

Equation (7−15) also implies that

$$w = w^e. \qquad (7-17)$$

Thus to achieve that optimum of the dynamic process, the firm sets its new hires and wage rate at the stationary state solution. Technically this conclusion is associated with our assumption that the production function has a fixed coefficient with employment. If we assume a production function of more general form, then the wage rate will change in response to employment.[4] But it makes our discussion more complex without enriching it. The production function assumed here presents our basic idea more neatly and conveniently.

Substituting equations (7−16) and (7−17) into (7−13), we obtain

$$\dot{L} = N^e - q(w^e - \bar{w}, u)L. \qquad (7-18)$$

Thus, we discover that the speed of employment adjustment is coincident with the quit rate, which is a function of the firm's own wage, the average wage in the labor market, and unemployment. It is interesting to note here that the adjustment speed depends on both the adjustment costs and labor market conditions. That is, as was shown in table 7−1, an increase in β lowers the quit rate through raising the wage, which leads to a decrease in the adjustment speed. In turn, an increase in unemployment reduces the adjustment speed through directly affecting the quit rate and indirectly the wage. Up to now, many of the studies of short-run employment have

stressed the role of technologically determined adjustment costs as important determinants of the adjustment speed, while placing much less emphasis on labor market conditions. In the present model this implicitly
assumes that the quit rate is stable relative to changes in labor market
conditions over time, or at least in the short run. For, if this is not so, they
cannot estimate the stable coefficient of adjustment speed by regressing
employment on its lagged value. As for Japanese manufacturing industries,
this assumption is possibly justified by table 7−2, which shows that
voluntary quit rates are stable over time in each of the different-sized
establishment groups. Voluntary quit rates change at most by 0.03 from 1975
to 1982 in establishments having 100−299 workers and less in firms of other
sizes.

Interestingly, the present analysis also shows that differences in the speed
of employment adjustment among the firms of different size are mainly due
to differences in their wages. That is, the speed of employment adjustment is
slow in high-wage sectors and high in low-wage sectors because the quit rate
is a decreasing function of the wage. This leads us to expect that the
adjustment speed is slow in large-size firms and high in small-size firms.[5]

III. Empirical Analysis

We now test the implications of the preceding analysis for Japanese
manufacturing industries by estimating the employment and the wage
function. To begin with, noting that the level of new hires L^e and the wage
rate w^e in the stationary state are functions of product price, the consumption index, the unemployment rate, normal hours, and the average wage in
the labor market overall, we specify equations $(7−18)$ and $(7−17)$ in a
linear stochastic form for estimation as follows,

$$L_t = a_0 + a_1 p + a_2 \bar{p} + a_3 u + a_4 h_1 + a_5 \bar{w} + a_6 L_{t-1} + \varepsilon$$
$$a_1 > 0, a_2 < 0, a_3 > 0, a_4 > 0, a_5 < 0, a_6 > 0, \qquad (7−19)$$

$$w_t = b_0 + b_1 p + b_2 \bar{p} + b_3 u + b_4 h_1 + b_5 \bar{w} + \delta$$
$$b_1 > 0, b_2 > 0, b_3 < 0, b_4 > 0, b_5 = ? \qquad (7−20)$$

where ε and δ are random terms and each of the signs of the coefficients is
indicated by table 7−1. In estimating equation $(7−19)$, we assume that the
quit rate is not sensitive to the wage rate over time because, if not, we cannot
obtain stable estimates on the coefficients of L_{t-1} and hence on the
adjustment speed of employment $(1 - a_6)$. This assumption can be justified
by table 7−2, which shows that voluntary quit rates are stable over time. It

should be stressed here that while quit rates are stable over time, they widely differ among firms of different size. This fact is not inconsistent with analysis, which attempts to explain differences in the adjustment speed among firms based on those in the quit rate. For it is assumed in our model that the quit rate is a function of the gap between the present-firm wage and the alternative. This gap is stable over time since both wages behave similarly over time, as was implied by the preceding analysis. On the other hand, when we look at the cross-sectional aspect, the above gap differs among firms. This is because the present-firm wage differs among firms, but the alternative, which is assumed to be the average wage in the labor market, is common to them.

The employment and the wage equations were estimated with quarterly time series data from 1970I to 1982IV for each of the establishment groups of different size for the Japanese manufacturing industries.[6] The results are shown in tables 7−3 and 7−4, and the definitions and the data sources are given in appendix 7−C.

The estimated results indicate the following. First, the speed of employment adjustment is lower in larger firms (see table 7−3). For example, compare the coefficients of L_{t-1} in equations (E1), (E5), and (E9). The adjustment speed is 0.105 in giant firms, 0.123 in large firms, and 0.287 in medium firms. This result supports our hypothesis that the adjustment speed is low in the high-wage sector where the quit rate is low. Concerning the stability of employment in Japan,[7] Gordon [1982] argued that the larger share of nonlabor income in Japan helps to explain how large Japanese firms can afford to offer their employees lifetime employment. In turn, the present model does not depend on wage flexibility to explain employment stability. It is determined by the level of wage which affects the quit rate and hence the adjustment of employment. In this sense our model provides an alternative explanation for this employment stability.

To explain this employment stability, Gordon also referred to the Japanese bonus system, which is regarded as a form of profit-sharing and functions as a buffer to insulate the remainder of the wage bill. This idea originating from Hashimoto [1979], is consistent with the fact that employment is more stable in larger firms in which the share of the bonus in the wage bill is relatively high. But there are two contrary facts for which to account. First, although total cash earnings (TCE), which includes bonuses, is more volatile than contractual cash earnings (CCE), unemployment is not statistically significant in the estimated wage equations where TCE is used as the dependent variable (see equations (W4), (W10), and (W16) in table 7−4). This implies that bonus payments are not necessarily responsive to labor market conditions at least on the basis of the more disaggregated data.

Table 7-3. Estimates of the Employment Equations, 1970 to 1982

Establishment size	Giant-Size Establishment L_t (Mean = 1887.28 thousands)				Large-Size Establishment L_t (Mean = 969.80 thousands)				Medium-Size Establishment L_t (Mean = 2616.43 thousands)			
Dependent Variable												
Equation	(E1)	(E2)	(E3)	(E4)	(E5)	(E6)	(E7)	(E8)	(E9)	(E10)	(E11)	(E12)
Procedure	SUR	OLS	OLS	OLS	SUR	OLS	OLS	OLS	SUR	OLS	OLS	OLS
P	3.260 (2.18)	3.294 (2.03)	4.753 (4.29)	4.147 (3.89)	1.493 (1.36)	1.485 (1.257)	2.002 (2.54)	0.796 (2.34)	4.039 (2.73)	4.034 (2.52)	5.142 (3.75)	1.700 (1.53)
$\bar{P}$	2.423 (0.78)	2.423 (0.71)	-3.378 (3.76)	---	-1.936 (0.84)	-1.968 (0.79)	-1.345 (1.96)	---	-6.453 (2.12)	-6.467 (1.97)	-8.277 (2.763)	---
h_1	4.561 (1.65)	5.564 (1.85)	8.007 (2.97)	6.545 (2.50)	3.017 (1.82)	3.127 (1.75)	3.669 (2.67)	2.406 (1.62)	9.652 (5.43)	9.647 (5.04)	10.571 (5.87)	7.673 (4.56)
u	-8.196 (0.28)	-13.719 (0.44)	---	-2.521 (0.09)	-23.051 (1.02)	-22.277 (0.92)	---	-33.052 (2.27)	-40.763 (1.44)	-40.696 (1.33)	---	-65.971 (2.36)
$\bar{w}$	-4.477 (2.19)	-4.053 (1.83)	---	-2.681 (2.50)	1.070 (0.73)	1.123 (0.71)	---	---	3.530 (1.87)	3.528 (1.74)	3.913 (1.93)	-0.098 (0.11)
L_{t-1}	0.895 (16.21)	0.937 (15.5)	0.963 (17.07)	0.937 (15.58)	0.877 (12.08)	0.889 (11.30)	0.892 (11.82)	0.884 (12.17)	0.713 (12.23)	0.713 (11.36)	0.736 (12.07)	0.743 (11.82)
Constant	-626.3 (1.16)	-887.7 (1.52)	-1369.7 (2.42)	-1043.9 (1.96)	-364.7 (1.11)	-395.5 (1.11)	-530.9 (1.94)	-272.6 (0.88)	-824.7 (2.59)	-825.4 (2.41)	-1082.6 (3.79)	-583.9 (1.77)
SEE	21.09	22.43	22.92	22.45	15.23	16.39	16.35	15.82	20.02	21.55	21.74	22.23
$\bar{R}^2$	0.989	0.989	0.987	0.988	0.934	0.934	0.934	0.936	0.956	0.956	0.955	0.953

Notes: SUR—seemingly unrelated regression; OLS—ordinary least squares.
Equations (E1), (E5), and (E9) are jointly estimated with the wage equation including all the exogenous variables.
The absolute value of the *t*-statistics are in parentheses.

Table 7-4. Estimates of the Wage Equations, 1970 to 1982

Establishment Size	Giant-Size Establishment						Large-Size Establishment						Medium-Size Establishment					
Dependent Variable	CCE Mean = 159.0 (thousand yen)			Logarithm of TCE Mean = 12.30	CCE/TCE/W Mean = 913 (yen)	Logarithm of CCE/TCE/W Mean = 6.72	CCE Mean = 149.3 (thousand yen)			Logarithm of TCE Mean = 12.18 (yen)	CCE/TCE/W Mean = 819 (yen)	Logarithm of CCE/TCE/W Mean = 6.62	CCE Mean = 127.1 (thousand yen)			Logarithm of TCE Mean = 12.06	CCE/TCE/W Mean = 725 (yen)	Logarithm of CCE/TCE/W Mean = 6.49
Equation	(W1)	(W2)	(W3)	(W4)	(W5)	(W6)	(W7)	(W8)	(W9)	(W10)	(W11)	(W12)	(W13)	(W14)	(W15)	(W16)	(W17)	(W18)
Procedure	SUR	OLS	OLS	SUR	OLS	OLS	SUR	OLS	OLS	SUR	OLS	OLS	SUR	OLS	OLS	SUR	OLS	OLS
P	-0.081 (0.86)	0.250 (3.11)	…	0.001 (0.38)	-0.995 (2.01)	-0.002 (0.64)	0.025 (0.33)	0.196 (3.34)	…	0.003 (1.26)	0.012 (0.02)	-0.001 (0.33)	-0.321 (3.64)	-0.031 (0.40)	-0.547 (4.29)	-0.0001 (0.03)	-1.919 (3.83)	-0.002 (0.66)
$\bar{P}$	0.939 (4.79)	…	0.813 (5.76)	-0.022 (3.35)	4.769 (4.57)	-0.014 (2.43)	0.481 (3.03)	…	1.299 (11.59)	-0.019 (3.48)	3.086 (2.42)	-0.015 (2.95)	0.861 (4.53)	…	1.933 (10.15)	-0.015 (2.95)	5.927 (5.50)	-0.013 (2.42)
h_1	0.804 (5.01)	1.172 (6.44)	0.901 (6.95)	0.020 (3.76)	-4.395 (5.14)	-0.035 (7.45)	0.391 (3.36)	0.561 (4.74)	0.083 (0.594)	-0.022 (5.47)	-4.964 (5.29)	-0.024 (7.08)	-0.160 (1.30)	0.078 (0.56)	-0.599 (3.61)	-0.024 (7.08)	-6.245 (8.96)	-0.033 (8.97)
u	-6.757 (3.66)	-2.293 (1.12)	-5.734 (3.26)	0.014 (0.22)	16.832 (1.71)	0.034 (0.81)	2.187 (1.41)	4.721 (3.12)	4.910 (2.74)	0.039 (0.73)	43.894 (3.51)	-0.041 (0.81)	-1.986 (1.08)	2.175 (1.08)	-1.972 (0.70)	-0.041 (0.81)	6.779 (0.65)	0.039 (0.72)
$\bar{w}$	1.084 (7.78)	1.599 (13.69)	1.130 (8.00)	0.036 (7.70)	7.528 (10.12)	0.031 (7.62)	1.013 (8.67)	1.290 (14.9)	…	0.027 (6.58)	5.396 (5.74)	0.029 (7.41)	1.061 (7.44)	1.55 (13.24)	…	0.029 (7.41)	5.218 (6.45)	0.028 (6.64)
Time	1.156 (10.19)	1.182 (8.00)	1.152 (9.33)	-0.006 (1.65)	3.373 (5.49)	-0.008 (2.41)	1.078 (10.93)	1.069 (9.35)	1.587 (11.30)	0.001 (0.33)	4.977 (6.27)	-0.004 (1.18)	0.392 (3.23)	0.440 (2.61)	0.876 (5.55)	-0.004 (1.81)	1.112 (1.61)	-0.005 (1.48)
Constant	-130.2 (4.74)	-187.9 (5.91)	-147.2 (6.78)	14.477 (15.91)	-652.0 (4.46)	11.27 (14.12)	-65.073 (3.17)	-93.48 (4.32)	-22.86 (0.91)	14.789 (20.54)	762.9 (4.57)	15.117 (24.30)	28.77 (1.27)	-10.142 (0.39)	99.480 (3.16)	15.117 (24.30)	1019 (7.95)	10.98 (16.60)
SEE	1.30	1.66	1.39	0.04	6.90	0.04	1.05	1.21	1.80	0.04	8.43	0.04	1.30	1.62	1.98	0.04	7.31	0.04
$\bar{R}^2$		0.999	0.999		0.999	0.993		0.999	0.999		0.999			0.999	0.998		0.999	0.993
$D-W$	1.47	1.53	1.48	1.76	1.49	0.87	1.45	1.54	1.32	1.56	1.18	1.20	1.47	1.41	1.22	1.20	1.80	1.15

Notes: SUR—seemingly unrelated regression; OLS—ordinary least squares.
Equations (W1), (W4), (W7), (W10), (W13), and (W17) are jointly estimated with the employment equation including all the exogenous variables by the seemingly unrelated regression method.
The absolute value of the t-statistics are in parentheses.

Second, as is presented by Sano [1981] based on data from individual large firms, the wage gain is minimally correlated with profit, but highly correlated with the average wage gain in the industry specific to the firm.

Next, according to table 7−4, wages are not responsive to unemployment in general. More specifically, the negative effect of unemployment on wages is statistically insignificant at the 10% level of confidence except in giant-size firms. Further, if we use the logarithm of TCE or hourly wage rate (CCE/THW) as the dependent variable, unemployment is insignificant even in giant firms. In addition, as shown in table 7−3, unemployment is also statistically insignificant in the employment equations as far as the consumer price index is included. These results make us speculate that the effect of unemployment on the efficiency behavior of workers is not important in Japan. That is, the preceding comparative statics analysis has predicted that a rise in unemployment decreases the wage rate and increases employment through the efficiency behavior, under the assumption that the quit rate is inelastic to the wage and unemployment (see table 7−1). But our evidence rejects this prediction. The reason why the effect of unemployment on the efficiency behavior is not significant is probably that, since the level of unemployment is very low in Japan, that is, around 2%, workers are not much concerned with the possibility of being unemployed, but rather with the wage reduction brought about by a dismissal under the seniority wage system.

Finally, as is indicated in table 7−4, the null hypothesis that the average wage in the labor market is not relevant to the wage determination of the firm is rejected at the 5% level of confidence in all the establishment groups.[8] In other words, $\bar{w}$ has a statistically significant positive effect on the wage. According to our comparative statics results in table 7−1, the effect of $\bar{w}$ on w^e is positive when the quit rate is fixed and otherwise ambiguous. This implies that the average wage in the labor market plays an important role in wage determination through affecting the efficiency behavior of workers in Japan. On the other hand, the effect of the average wage on employment is not decisive. Only in giant firms it is statistically significant at the 5% level of confidence, and its expected sign is negative. But, contrary to our expectation, the effect of $\bar{w}$ on L_t in large and medium firms is positive and insignificant. As for this, we may infer that other factors such as the product price, which are highly correlated with $\bar{w}$, are dominant in the determination of employment.

Appendix 7A

The Legendre-Clebsch conditions are the following:

$$|A| \equiv \begin{vmatrix} pf_{11} - g'' & pf_{12}/\bar{p} & 0 \\ pf_{21} & pf_{22}/\bar{p} - \lambda q_{11}\bar{p} & 0 \\ 0 & 0 & -\beta \end{vmatrix} \quad < 0$$

$$|B| \equiv \begin{vmatrix} pf_{11} - g'' & pf_{12}/\bar{p} \\ pf_{21} & pf_{22}/\bar{p} - \lambda q_{11}\bar{p} \end{vmatrix} \quad > 0$$

$$pf_{11} - g'' < 0 \; (pf_{22}/\bar{p} - \lambda q_{11}\bar{p} < 0)$$

Appendix 7B

Differentiating equations (7−9a), (7−10a), and (7−12a) with respect to u, we have

$$\begin{bmatrix} pf_{11}-g'' & pf_{12}/\bar{p} & 0 \\ pf_{21} & pf_{22}/\bar{p}-\lambda q_{11}\bar{p} & -q_1\bar{p} \\ 0 & 0 & r+q \end{bmatrix} \begin{bmatrix} \dfrac{dh_2}{du} \\ \dfrac{dw}{du} \\ \dfrac{d\lambda}{du} \end{bmatrix} = \begin{bmatrix} -pf_{12}(\bar{w}-z)/\bar{p} \\ -pf_{22}(\bar{w}-z)/\bar{p}+\lambda q_{12}\bar{p} \\ pf_2(\bar{w}-z)/\bar{p}-\lambda q_2 \end{bmatrix}$$

where the superscript e showing the stationary state solution is deleted for simplicity of notation. Solving this system gives us

$$\frac{dh_2}{du} = \frac{\lambda pf_{12}(r+q)\{q_{11}(\bar{w}-z)-q_{12}\}}{(r+q)\,|B|} > 0,$$

$$\frac{dw}{du} = ?$$

$$\frac{d\lambda}{du} = \frac{\{pf_2(\bar{w}-z)/\bar{p}-q_2\lambda\}|B|}{(r+q)|B|} > 0,$$

where it is assumed that $q_{12} \leq 0$, impling that the function of the wage suppressing the quit rate becomes more effective as unemployment increases.

Using the above results, we have

$$\frac{dN}{du} = \frac{1}{\beta}\frac{d\lambda}{du} > 0,$$

$$\frac{dL}{du} = \frac{1}{q}\frac{dN}{du} - \frac{q_2}{q}L - \frac{q_1}{q}\frac{dw}{du}$$

Appendix 7C: Definitions and Data Sources*

CCE = Monthly contractual cash earnings including payments to overtime (Monthly Labor Survey, Ministry of Labor).

TCE = Monthly total cash earnings including special payments such as bonus (Monthly Labor Survey, Ministry of Labor).

THW = Monthly total hours worked (Monthly Labor Survey, Ministry of Labor).

L   = Regular workers (Monthly Labor Survey, Ministry of Labor).

P   = Wholesale price indexes of manufacturing products (Wholesale Price Index, Bank of Japan).

h_1 = Monthly scheduled hours worked (Monthly Labor Survey, Ministry of Labor).

u   = Ratio of total unemployed to the labor force (Labor Force Survey, Prime Minister's Office).

w   = Nominal wage indexes of the whole industry (Monthly Labor Survey, Ministry of Labor).

*All data are seasonally adjusted.

Notes

1. Put differently, real wage rigidity is measured by the inverse of the long-run coefficient on unemployment in the wage equation, and nominal wage rigidity by real wage rigidity multiplied by the sum of the average lags in the wage and price equations. Ono [1985] also used the coefficients on unemployment in the regressions of the Phillips relation as a measure of wage responsiveness to labor market conditions.

2. See Stiglitz [1984] for a survey.

3. Strictly speaking, a linear function of the worker's effort with respect to the real wage is not appropriate as a formulation of the efficiency wage hypothesis because it is not assured of being consistent with the utility-maximizing behavior of the worker. But, even if we assume a nonlinear function of the worker's effort, the derived implications will be essentially the same as ours. See Shapiro and Stiglitz [1984] for a more sophisticated formulation of the efficiency behavior of workers.

4. For example, see Takayama [1974].

5. Note in the present model that β affects not only adjustment costs but also labor productivity. Importantly β is assumed to be an exogenous variable which differs among firms. That is, differences in the wage payment and the quit rate among firms are caused by β in our model. In turn, it is generally agreed that workers in large firms are more productive and paid more than those in small firms because large firms invest more in improving labor quality, training and hiring. Therefore, β can be assumed to represent firm size.

6. Although the data on small-size firms (30−99 employees) are available, we discarded them by the following two reasons: one is that the firm analyzed in the preceding section is assumed to be monopsonistic in the labor market. But small-size firms may not satisfy this assumption since their wage payments are overwhelmingly affected by the market wage. The other is that the employment data on small-size firms are not reliable because of the data discontinuities caused by sample changes. That is, Monthly Labor Survey changes its sample every three years. We can check how much each sample change brings about the gap between old and new data on employment. In the case of small-size firms its gap is more than 9% upward at each of the sample changes in the recession period we deal with, while in the case of others they are negligible but about 6.8% downward in giant-size firms in April, 1979.

7. For a comparison on the employment adjustments between the United States and Japan, see Shimada and associates [1982] and Muramatsu [1983]. In so doing, they estimated short-run employment functions for the manufacturing industries by two-digid. Akiyama, Okuno and Matsuyama [1984] compared the United States and Japan, focusing on the differences in the function of inventory fluctuations. Shinozuka [1980] estimated for the Japanese manufacturing industries by relation to firm scale. See Ueda and Yoshikawa [1984] for a survey on this issue.

8. According to Monthly Labor Survey, the percentage of regular workers employed by the establishments larger than medium-size in the manufacturing industries within the establishments having more than 30 employees in all the industries is 37.5% in 1970 and 26.3% in 1982.

References

Akiyama, T., M. Okuno, and K. Matsuyama. 1984. "Zaiko Hendō to Koyō Chōsei." (Inventory Fluctuations and Employment Adjustments) *Kinyū Kenkyū* 3 (July): 1−24.

Alchian, A.A., and H. Demsetz. 1972. "Production, Information Costs, and Economic Organization." *The American Economic Review* 62 (December): 777−795.

Ball, R.J., and E.B.A. St. Cyr. 1966. "Short Term Employment Functions in British Manufacturing Industry." *Review of Economic Studies* 33(July): 179−208.

Brechling, F. 1965. "The Relationship Between Output and Employment in British Manufacturing Industries." *Review of Economic Studies* 32(July): 187−216.

Gordon, J.J. 1982. "Why U.S. Wage and Employment Behavior Differs from that in Britain and Japan." *Economic Journal* 92(March): 13−14.

Grubb, D., R. Jackman, and R. Layard. 1983. "Wage Rigidity and Unemployment in OECD Countries." *European Economic Review* 21: 11−39.

Hashimoto, M. 1979. "Bonus Payments, On-the-job Training and Lifetime Employment in Japan." *Journal of Political Economy* 87(October): 1086−1104.

Hazledine, T. 1979. "'Employment Functions' and the Demand for Labor in the Short Run." In Hornstein, Z., J. Grice, and A. Webb (eds.), *The Economics of the Labor Market*. London: HMSO.

Leban, R. 1982. "Employment and Wage Strategies of the Firm over a Business Cycle." *Journal of Economics and Control* 4:371–394.

Medoff, J.L. 1979. "Layoffs and Alternatives Under Trade Unions in U.S. Manufacturing." *The American Economic Review* 69(June): 380–395.

Mortensen, D.T. 1970. "A Theory of Wage and Employment Dynamics." In E.S. Phelps et al. (eds.), *Microeconomic Foundations of Employment and Inflation Theory*. New York: Norton.

Muramatsu, K. 1983. Nihon no Rōdō Shijō Bunseki (An Analysis of the Japanese Labor Market). Hakutō Shobo.

Nadiri, M., and S. Rosen. 1969. "Interrelated Factor Demand Functions." *The American Economic Review* 57(September): 457–571.

Ono, A. 1985. "Saikin no Tei Keizai Seichō to Kongo no Rōdō Shijyō" (Depressed Economic Growth Today and the Labor Market in Future). In Minami, R., and A. Mizuno (eds.), *Senshin Kōgyō Koku no Koyō to Shitsugyo*. Chikura Shobō.

Salop, S.C. 1973. "Wage Differentials in a Dynamic Theory of the Firm." *Journal of Economic Theory* 6: 321–344.

Sano, Y. 1981. *Chingin to Koyō no Keizaigaku* (Economics of Wage and Employment). Chuo Keizai Sha.

Shapiro, S., and J.E. Stiglitz. 1984. "Equilibrium Unemployment as a Worker Discipline Device." *The American Economic Review* 74(June): 433–444.

Shimada, H., et al. 1982. "Chingin oyobi Koyō Chōsei Katei no Bunseki" (An Analysis of Wage and Employment Adjustment). *Keizai Bunseki* 84 (March): Economic Planning Agency.

Shinozuka, E. 1980. "Kigyō Kibobetsu ni mita Saikin no Koyō Chōsei" (A Recent Development of Employment Adjustment by Relation to Firm Size). In Nakamura, R., and S. Nishikawa (eds.), *Gendai Rodo Shijo Benseki*. Sōgō Rōdō Kenkyūsho.

Stiglitz, J.E. 1984. "Theories of Wage Ridigity." NBER Working Paper Series 1442.

Takayama, A. 1974. *Mathematical Economics*. Chicago: The Dryden Press.

Ueda, K., and Yoshikawa, H. 1984. "Rōdō Shijō no Macro Keizai Bunseki" (An Macro-economic Analysis of the Labor Market). *Kikan Gendai Keizai* (Spring): 62–77.

8 THE COLLECTIVE IMPACT OF SECTORAL SHOCKS ON AGGREGATE EMPLOYMENT FLUCTUATIONS

Joseph G. Altonji and John C. Ham

I. Introduction

This chapter examines the role of sectoral shocks in employment fluctuations. We discuss theory and evidence regarding two mechanisms through which sectoral shifts may influence growth. The first mechanism is based upon the role in the natural rate of unemployment of reallocation of labor across markets. A number of economists, including Alchian [1970], Archibald [1970], and Lucas and Prescott [1974], argued in the late 1960s and '70s that the position of the short-run Phillips curve is affected by the rate at which shocks arrive in specific sectors of the economy. The basic idea is that idiosyncratic shocks to specific firms and to specific sectors influence the

We would like to thank David Card, George Jakubson, Angelo Melino, Whitney Newey, Richard Rogerson, Aloysius Siow, and especially Ernst Stromsdorfer for very helpful comments and discussions. We are also indebted to participants at a Conference on Adjustments in Labor Markets at the University of Santa Clara and to members of the aggregate labor market group of the NBER's summer workshop on economic fluctuations. Dwayne Benjamin provided exceptional research assistance. SSHRC, Canada, provided generous financial support. We emphasize that we alone are responsible for any shortcomings of the chapter.

natural rate of unemployment because it is costly and time-consuming to reallocate resources across sectors in response to shifts in labor demand. Consequently, the natural rate of unemployment depends in part upon the variance of these sectoral shocks. In an important set of papers David Lilien [1982a, 1982b] has presented empirical evidence on the extent to which changes over time in unemployment have been due to changes in the natural rate resulting from changes in the variance of sectoral shocks. This "Reallocation Hypothesis" has attracted growing attention, as demonstrated by the recent work of Lilien, Abraham, and Katz [1985], Medoff [1983], and Neelin [1985].

Second, disaggregate shocks to particular sectors of the economy may collectively induce fluctuations in aggregate employment even in the absence of reallocation. Since aggregate employment is the sum of employment in the individual sectors, sectoral shocks may account for some of the variance in aggregate employment growth if the shocks to specific sectors have sufficiently high variance. This mechanism, which we refer to as the "Collective Impact" hypothesis, is the main focus of the chapter. Most macro-economic analyses (including the discussions of the effects of the variance of sectoral shifts on the natural rate of unemployment) have assumed that such sectoral shocks are small enough to cancel out at the aggregate level, but there is little evidence on the validity of this assumption.

In an earlier study, we began an investigation of the collective impact hypothesis by estimating an empirical model which allowed us to measure the influence of sectoral shocks on the variation in aggregate employment growth. In this chapter we have three objectives. The first is to provide a theoretical foundation for our empirical work and to consider alternate theoretical models which lead to different specifications. We hope that this theoretical model will not only clarify the benefits and limitations of our earlier work but will also prove helpful in developing more structural approaches to the problem.

Our second objective is to provide an accessible summary of the methodology and empirical results in our previous work. This work involves some difficult econometric issues as well as estimation of dynamic models involving almost 100 parameters for several specifications. This, in turn, may impose a large cost on those readers who have little interest in technical issues and are concerned primarily with the main results of the study. Here we also take the opportunity to contrast the reallocation mechanism with the collective impact mechanism, since these mechanisms are in no way mutually exclusive. Our final objective is to extend our earlier work to analyze the role played by sectoral, national, and external shocks in the greater economic instability of the 1970s and '80s.

The chapter is organized as follows. Section II provides an overview of the reallocation hypothesis and the collective impact hypothesis and our motivation for examining ther.i. Section III presents a disaggregate theoretical model of employment growth. The model serves as the basis for a more formal discussion of the collective impact hypothesis and provides a foundation for the econometric model used to examine the role of sectoral shocks in employment fluctuations. In section IV we summarize an econometric model developed and implemented in Altonji and Ham [1985] to investigate the collective impact hypothesis and discuss our main findings. In section V we extend this methodology to provide a preliminary investigation of changes over time in the importance of aggregate and sectoral shocks in aggregate employment growth. In section VI we review the results of recent studies investigating the reallocation mechanism. We then conclude the chapter.

II. The Potential Role of Sectoral Shocks in Aggregate Fluctuations

Our main interest in this study is in assessing the role of sectoral specific disturbances in *aggregate* fluctuations of employment growth. In this section, we discuss two reasons for examining the role of sectoral shocks in aggregate fluctuations. The first is that aggregate models of economic fluctuations have not been entirely successful. The second is that there are several plausible mechanisms through which sectoral shocks may be expected to influence aggregate employment. It would, of course, make a great deal of difference to policy whether national business cycles result from aggregate sources (such as changes in monetary policy, changes in investor confidence, or other aggregate sources), result from a combination of unrelated shocks to particular sectors, or result from a combination of aggregate and sectoral factors.

Over the past few decades most business cycle analyses have emphasized factors that shift aggregate demand and supply. As James Tobin [1971] has noted, a basic assumption underlying this work is that "this [macroeconomics] can be done without much attention to the constituents of the aggregate, that is to the behavior and fortunes of particular households, business firms, industries or regions."[1]

A number of aggregate economic variables have been suggested as the main cause of business cycles. The most prominent of these include unstable fiscal policy, swings in expectations about the profitability of capital (e.g., animal spirits), changes in consumer confidence, and shocks to the availability of raw materials. There would be less cause for studying disaggregate shocks if the models examining the above aggregate factors produced consistent evidence on the sources of economic fluctuations. Many economists have used structural and reduced form econometric models (e.g. Barro [1977, 1979], Mishkin [1984], and Sargent [1976]) to assess the importance of monetary policy, fiscal policy, "productivity" shocks, real interest rate shocks, changes in consumption, and other factors in explanations for aggregate fluctuations. Others have investigated these issues using descriptive time series methods (e.g., Sims [1973, 1980], Litterman and Weiss [1984], and Lawrence and Siow [1985]). Unfortunately, these studies produce conflicting results, and no clear answer has emerged on the primary causes of business cycles. In part the inconsistency in the evidence may reflect the limitations of current econometric tools, data problems, and the inadequacy of current aggregate theoretical models of economic activity. More satisfactory results may emerge as the search continues for a tight, unified explanation of business cycles. However, it is also possible that aggregate fluctuations arise from a variety of sources and simply do not have a tight, unified aggregate explanation.[2] Consequently, there may be a payoff to research on the role of disaggregate shocks in economic fluctuations.

In the remainder of this section, we discuss mechanisms through which disaggregate shocks may influence aggregate fluctuations.

A. Sectoral Shocks, Aggregate Employment, and the Reallocation Hypothesis

Lilien [1982a, 1982b] has explored one mechanism through which disaggregate shocks may influence aggregate employment and unemployment. (See also the discussion in Lilien and Hall [1984].) Lilien hypothesized and provided some empirical support for the view that the level of unemployment at any point in time is related to the variance of shocks affecting specific industries because of the time that is required for resources to be reallocated among industries. This view is related to a number of earlier discussions of the natural rate of unemployment, including Alchian [1971], Archibald [1971], Lucas and Prescott [1974], and others. (See the studies cited in Lilien [1982a].)

The formal model in Lilien [1982b] has the following features. First, the labor market is segmented into different sectors because of costs of information about opportunities in other sectors, transportation costs, and human capital that is specific to firms in a particular sector. Consequently, the supply of labor to a particular sector adjusts only slowly to shifts in the demand for labor. Second, there are important sector-specific shocks. Third, these shocks have a multiplicative rather than additive effect on the revenue generated by a given quantity of labor in the sector. Consequently, sectoral specific shocks alter the efficient allocation of labor among sectors. Until the supply of labor adjusts to the changes in the marginal revenue product of labor in the various sectors, the overall productivity of labor is reduced. This occurs because of a worsening in the match between where labor is located and where labor is most productive. Consequently, employment and output fall and, with a fixed labor force, unemployment rises following a shift in the composition of demand.

In a world in which sectoral shifts occur continuously, the rate at which the shifts occur will affect the overall demand for labor and thus the unemployment rate. Lilien hypothesized that the volatility (variance) of sectoral shifts varies considerably over time and is responsible for a substantial part of the movement in both the natural rate of unemployment and the total amount of employment.

Sectoral Shocks with Segmented Labor Markets and Downward Wage Rigidity. It is interesting to explore the relationship between Lilien's model and discussions of unemployment in the Phillips Curve literature, such as Lipsey (1960), Archibald (1970) and Tobin (1972), since this earlier literature emphasizes that the position of the Phillips curve is affected by mismatches between employment demand in various sectors and the supply of labor to these sectors.

Lilien's (1982b) model assumes that the short run supply of labor and the demand for labor in each sector are continuously in equilibrium. Wage stickiness does not play a role in his analysis. Unemployment arises because the lower productivity of labor (resulting from mismatching across markets) lowers the sum (across sectors) of the employment levels which clear the sectoral labor markets. While the earlier Phillips curve literature also is based upon the view that labor markets are highly segmented, it assumes (in contrast to Lilien) an asymmetric wage adjustment process in which downward adjustments in wages take longer than upward adjustments. The unemployment rate within a given sector rises if demand falls to the point that the constraint on downward wage adjustment becomes binding. The overall unemployment rate is related to the fraction of labor markets in which the downward wage adjustment is slow or in which wage floors are binding.

How would an increase in the dispersion of sector specific shocks to labor demand or supply affect the unemployment rate in an economy with segmented labor markets and an asymmetric wage adjustment mechanism? An increase in the variance in these shocks will increase the variance of the market clearing wage level for any given sector. This, in turn, will increase the probability that the wage floor will be binding for a given market. Thus, the fraction of labor markets with binding constraints on wage adjustments will increase and the unemployment rate will rise with an increase in the variance in shocks affecting specific sectors. This will be true even if there is no reallocation of labor.

B. Sectoral Shocks and Aggregate Employment: The Collective Impact Hypothesis

In models such as those of Lilien and Lucas and Prescott, sectoral shocks may have a positive effect on unemployment as a result of the reallocation process even if they sum to zero in every period. This is also true in the segmented labor market models with asymmetric wage adjustment discussed by Lipsey, Tobin, and others. In this chapter and in Altonji and Ham [1985] we investigate a somewhat different question, namely, the extent to which independent sectoral specific shocks affect the overall level of business activity simply because the weighted average of a set of independent shocks need not equal zero in every period.

Suppose that sectoral specific shocks have a large variance relative to aggregate shocks. In this case sectoral shocks will obviously be important for employment variation in a particular sector. However, since the national employment change is a weighted sum of industry and regional components, it is possible that the variance of the appropriately weighted sum of the sectoral disturbances may be large enough to explain a significant amount of the variance of the national employment change. For example, consider an economy with I sectors of equal size. Assume that the employment change Y_{it} in each sector is the sum of an aggregate shock c_t with variance σ_c^2 and a sectoral shock η_{it} with variance $\sigma_{\eta i}^2$. Thus

$$Y_{it} = c_t + \eta_{it}, \ i = 1, \ \ldots, \ I.$$

For simplicity, assume that the aggregate and sectoral shocks are serially uncorrelated, that there are no feedbacks from past employment changes to current employment changes, that all shocks are independent, and that $\sigma_{\eta i}^2 = \sigma_\eta^2$ for all sectors. Then the variance in employment in sector i is

$$\text{Var}(Y_{it}) = \sigma_c^2 + \sigma_\eta^2,$$

and the variance in the change in aggregate employment $Y_{ct} = \Sigma_i Y_{it}$ is

$$\text{Var}(Y_{ct}) = I^2 \sigma_c^2 + I \sigma_\eta^2.$$

The correlation of employment changes across sectors is

$$\text{Corr}\ (Y_{it}, Y_{i't}) = \frac{\sigma_c^2}{\sigma_c^2 + \sigma_\eta^2}, \qquad (i \neq i'),$$

Table 8–1.   Correlation Across Sectors and Fraction of Aggregate Employment
Variation Due to Sectoral Shocks

	σ_η^2/σ_c^2			
	.5	1	2	3
A. Correlation across sectors[a]	.667	.500	.333	.250
B. Share of aggregate employment variation due to sectoral shocks[b]				
I = 3	.182	.250	.400	.500
I = 5	.118	.167	.286	.375
I = 10	.063	.091	.167	.231
I = 20	.032	.050	.091	.130

[a]Correlation across sectors $= 1/(1 + \sigma_\eta^2/\sigma_c^2)$.
[b]Share due to sectoral shocks $= (\sigma_\eta^2/\sigma_c^2)/(1 + \sigma_\eta^2/\sigma_c^2)$.

and the fraction of the variance in the aggregate employment change
accounted for by the sectoral shocks is

$$\frac{\sigma_\eta^2/\sigma_c^2}{[I + \sigma_\eta^2/\sigma_c^2]}$$

In table 8–1 we have computed the correlation in employment across
sectors and the fraction of the variance in aggregate employment which is
due to sectoral shocks for various values of I and the relative variance of η_t
and c_t.

A role for disaggregate shocks in aggregate fluctuations through the
collective impact mechanism is clearly a theoretical possibility. However,
the empirical importance of such shocks is unclear. The early studies of
Burns and Mitchell [1946] and Mitchell [1951], and the more recent work of
Lehmann [1982] suggest that economic activity in different industries and
regions of the economy moves together, which is an important reason for
believing that the construction of simple aggregative models of economic
activity will ultimately be successful. (See for example, the discussion in
Lucas [1977].) On the other hand, the extent and stability of the co-
movements may be exaggerated. As many have noted, over the last 20 years
there has been great diversity in the behavior of employment across regions
and industries in both the United States and Canada. This diversity is only
partially accounted for by differences in trend growth rates, with service
industries growing faster than manufacturing, the sunbelt states growing
more rapidly than the Northcentral states in the United States, and the
Western provinces growing more rapidly than the Central and Maritime
provinces in Canada.

To shed some light on this issue, we present the correlation of annual
changes in the log of Canadian employment by one-digit SIC industry in

Table 8–2. Correlation Matrix for Industrial Employment[a]

	Forestry	Mining	Manufacturing	Construction	Transportation	Trade	Finance	Service	Government
Forestry	1.	.497	.689	.478	.590	.396	.468	.296	-.097
Mining		1.	.451	.462	.533	.373	.077	.307	-.194
Manufacturing			1.	.793	.621	.821	.472	.589	-.150
Construction				1.	.567	.692	.369	.523	-.057
Transportation					1.	.614	.410	.276	.142
Trade						1.	.563	.570	.105
Finance							1.	.403	.325
Service								1.	-.050
Government									1.

[a]Measured in log first differences.

Table 8–3. Correlation Matrix for Industrial Employment[a] After Accounting for United States Effects

	Forestry	Mining	Manufacturing	Construction	Transportation	Trade	Finance	Service	Government
Forestry	1.	.596	.397	.365	.523	.115	.180	-.071	-.104
Mining		1.	.572	.486	.548	.365	.028	.296	-.190
Manufacturing			1.	.788	.692	.812	.198	.444	-.174
Construction				1.	.649	.642	.265	.494	-.027
Transportation					1.	.582	.286	.123	.157
Trade						1.	.437	.457	.145
Finance							1.	.204	.397
Service								1.	-.042
Government									1.

[a]Measured in log first differences.

Table 8–4. Correlation Matrix for Provincial Employment[a]

	Newfoundland	Nova Scotia/ New Brunswick	Quebec	Ontario	Saskatchewan/ Manitoba	Alberta	British Columbia
Newfoundland	1.	.853	.830	.818	.610	.263	.764
Nova Scotia/ New Brunswick		1.	.896	.768	.639	.558	.868
Quebec			1.	.884	.707	.579	.877
Ontario				1.	.644	.493	.853
Saskatchewan/ Manitoba					1.	.519	.673
Alberta						1.	.662
British Columbia							1.

[a]Measured in log first differences.

Table 8–5. Correlation Matrix for Provincial Employment[a] After Accounting for United States Effects

	Newfoundland	Nova Scotia/ New Brunswick	Quebec	Ontario	Saskatchewan/ Manitoba	Alberta	British Columbia
Newfoundland	1.	.799	.731	.695	.582	.069	.617
Nova Scotia/ New Brunswick		1.	.868	.697	.601	.497	.831
Quebec			1.	.815	.705	.491	.802
Ontario				1.	.672	.351	.742
Saskatchewan/ Manitoba					1.	.482	.669
Alberta						1.	.605
British Columbia							1.

[a]Measured in log first differences.

table 8−2. While the results show substantial positive correlations between many of the industry pairs, the correlations are less than .5 in 23 out of 36 cases. In table 8−3 we present the partial correlations between industry pairs after controlling for the influence of an aggregate external disturbance proxied by the current value and first lag of the change in the log of United States GNP. Again, while significant correlations arising from a common domestic disturbance remain, there is much movement that is uncorrelated across industries.

On the other hand, the correlations for the provinces are considerably stronger than those for the industries (see tables 8−4 and 8−5). While one can debate whether these correlations are large or small, these results indicate that sectoral shocks potentially play a large enough role in employment behavior at the industry and province level to warrant a careful evaluation as a possible source of aggregate fluctuations. This is especially true given that these correlations could arise, in part, from feedback effects across provinces or industries of shocks that are initially province or industry specific. This chapter and Altonji and Ham [1985] are the first systematic attempts to measure the overall contribution of industry-specific, region-specific, and combined industry- and region-specific shocks to aggregate fluctuations.

III. A Disaggregate Model of Employment Growth

In this section we present a simple structural model of the labor market. The model serves as a basis for discussion of how aggregate shocks and disaggregate shocks affect the economy over time. The formal model is basically consistent with the econometric framework developed in Altonji and Ham [1985] that is discussed below. Thus, it serves as a concrete example of a model that is consistent with the empirical work on the collective impact hypothesis below, and makes it easier to assess the pluses and minuses of this framework.

A. Basic Equations

We assume that each province p and industry i of the labor market constitutes a specific sector denoted by pi. The model consists of equations for the position of the output demand function of sector pi, the demand for labor in sector pi, the supply of labor in sector pi, the wage in sector pi, and employment in sector pi. In the initial discussion we assume that the labor market in sector pi clears each period. We then consider the nonmarket clearing case.

The Demand for Output. Let D_{pit} denote an index of the change in the position of the output demand function of sector pi. D_{pit} is determined by

$$D_{pit} = a_{opi} + a_{1pi}Y_{ct-1} + a_{2pi}Y_{p \cdot t-1} + \varepsilon_{pit}^D, \qquad (8-1a)$$

where

$$\varepsilon_{pit}^D = a_{4pi}c_t^D + a_{5pi}\eta_{it}^D + a_{6pi}v_{pt}^D + u_{pit}^D, \qquad (8-1b)$$

where Y_{ct-1} is the change in the growth of aggregate employment in $t-1$, and $Y_{p \cdot t-1}$ is the change in employment growth in province p in period $t-1$. In equation (8–1b), ε_{pit}^D is a composite demand shock that depends upon a national component c_t^D, an industry component η_{it}^D, a province component v_{pt}^D, and a combined province-industry component u_{pit}^D. The shock c_t^D is an index of determinants of aggregate demand, including monetary and fiscal policy, the expectations of consumers and investors, and foreign demand.[3]

We specify that Y_{ct-1} affects D_{pit}, with a combined province-industry specific coefficient, since Y_{ct-1} is related to current and future labor and nonlabor income in the economy and thus to consumer demand.[4] Since some industries, such as retail trade, services, and finance, have local markets, we also permit lagged employment in province p, $Y_{p \cdot t}$, to affect D_{pit} with a combined province-industry-specific coefficient. Demand is affected also by the industry-specific shock η_{it}^D. This variable captures changes in the composition of demand for goods resulting from changing technology of production and consumption, changes in preferences, and changes in export demand or import competition that are specific to particular sectors. A change in tariffs or quotas affecting a particular industry, such as textiles, would be one example. Demand is also affected, with a coefficient that is larger for goods with local markets, by the province-specific shocks v_{pt}^D. The province shocks are most likely to reflect changes in government policy. Alternate spending and taxation policies, including regional development programs of the Federal government, shift the demand for an industry's output in a given region.

The Demand for Labor. The growth of demand for labor in sector pi is denoted by Y_{pit}^d and is determined by

$$Y_{pit}^d = b_{opi} + b_{1pi}D_{pit} + b_{2pi}Y_{pit-1} + b_{3pi}\omega_{pit} + \varepsilon_{pit}^d, \qquad (8-2a)$$

where

$$\varepsilon_{pit}^d = b_{4pi}c_t^d + b_{5pi}\eta_{it}^d + b_{6pi}v_{pt}^d + u_{pit}^d. \qquad (8-2b)$$

Labor demand depends upon the output demand index D_{pit} for obvious reasons. The slope coefficient b_{1pi} depends on the parameters of the production function and the product demand curve. Lagged employment growth enters the equations since there are likely to be adjustment costs associated with hiring and training, severance pay, and unemployment insurance payments. We expect this variable to enter with a positive sign, with $b_{2pi} > 0$.

Employment demand depends negatively upon the wage ω_{pit}, with $b_{3pi} < 0$. Finally, national, industry, and province-specific shocks to productivity, costs of other inputs of production, and nonwage labor costs, such as unemployment insurance payments, affect employment demand. Note that one might expect some correlation between these shocks and the factors in equation (8–1) that influence labor demand through the product demand function. After substituting for D_{pit} from equation (8–1a) one may write Y_{pit}^d as

$$Y_{pit}^d = (b_{opi} + b_{1pi}a_{opi}) + b_{1pi}a_{1pi}Y_{ct-1} \qquad (8-3)$$
$$+ b_{1pi}a_{2pi}Y_{p \cdot t-1} + b_{2pi}Y_{pit-1}$$
$$+ b_{3pi}\omega_{pit} + b_{1pi}\varepsilon_{pit}^D + \varepsilon_{pit}^d.$$

The Supply of Labor. The supply of labor Y_{pit}^s is determined by

$$Y_{pit}^{s \cdot} = q_{opi} + q_{1pi}Y_{ct-1} + q_{2pi}Y_{p \cdot t-1} + q_{3pi}Y_{\cdot it-1} \qquad (8-4a)$$
$$+ q_{4pi}Y_{pit-1} + q_{5pi}\omega_{pit} + \varepsilon_{pit}^s,$$

where

$$\varepsilon_{pit}^s = q_{6pi}c_t^s + q_{7pi}v_{pt}^s. \qquad (8-4b)$$

In equation (8–4a), $Y_{\cdot it-1}$ is the lagged growth rate of employment in industry i. Labor supply is a function of an aggregate labor supply shift index c_t^s that summarizes the effects of demographic shifts, such as the baby boom and changes in the labor supply behavior of young workers, married women, and older men and women, as well as the effects of taxes and subsidies and the unemployment insurance system. To some extent, these shifts may be region specific as in the Canadian worker disability programs and entitlement provisions in the unemployment insurance legislation, and thus the variable v_{pt}^s is included. Due to moving costs and costs of changing firms (seniority-based fringe benefits, wages, job security provisions, and vacation pay), Y_{pit}^s is a positive function of Y_{pit-1}. The variable Y_{pit}^s can also be positively related to $Y_{\cdot it-1}$ and $Y_{p \cdot t-1}$ due to industry-specific human capital and the costs of geographic mobility.

Labor supply will also depend positively upon perceived current and future employment opportunities in pi, and negatively upon perceived employment opportunities in other provinces and other industries. If lagged employment is positively related to employment opportunities in pi after controlling for the wage, this is a second reason to expect Y_{pit}^s to depend (in a positive fashion) on Y_{pit-1}. By the same reasoning, higher levels of employment in other provinces and industries in the previous period will have a negative effect on Y^s_{pit}. Consequently, the variable Y_{ct-1} appears in equation (8−4a) with a negative coefficient. (The coefficients on $Y_{\cdot it-1}$, $Y_{p\cdot t-1}$, and Y_{pit-1} are net of the effects that these variables have through Y_{ct-1}.)

B. Market Equilibrium: The Market Clearing Case

Initially, we assume the wage ω_{pit} in each sector adjusts to equate labor supply and demand, with $Y_{pit} = Y^s_{pit} = Y^d_{pit}$. The implied equation for the growth in the wage is

$$\omega_{pit} = \alpha_{pi}[b_{opi} + b_{1pi}a_{opi} - q_{opi}] + \alpha_{pi}[b_{1pi}a_{1pi}$$
$$- q_{1pi}]Y_{ct-1} + \alpha_{pi}[b_{1pi}a_{2pi} - q_{2pi}]Y_{p\cdot t-1} - \alpha_{pi}q_{3pi}Y_{\cdot it-1}$$
$$+ \alpha_{pi}[b_{2pi} - q_{4pi}]Y_{pit-1} + \alpha_{pi}b_{1pi}\varepsilon^D_{pit} + \alpha_{pi}\varepsilon^d_{pit}$$
$$- \alpha_{pi}\varepsilon^s_{pit}, \tag{8-5}$$

where $\alpha_{pi} = 1/(q_{5pi} - b_{3pi})$.
Substituting (8−5) into equation (8−3) or (8−4) leads to the employment equation

$$Y_{pit} = [\alpha^d_{pi}(b_{opi} + b_{1pi}a_{opi}) + \alpha^s_{pi}q_{opi}] + [\alpha^d_{pi}b_{1pi}a_{1pi}$$
$$+ \alpha^s_{pi}q_{1pi}]Y_{ct-1} + [\alpha^s_{pi}q_{2pi} + \alpha^d_{pi}b_{1pi}a_{2pi}]Y_{p\cdot t-1}$$
$$+ \alpha^s_{pi}q_{3pi}Y_{\cdot it-1} + [\alpha^s_{pi}q_{4pi} + \alpha^d_{pi}b_{2pi}]Y_{pit-1}$$
$$+ \alpha^s_{pi}\varepsilon^s_{pit} + \alpha^d_{pi}b_{1pi}\varepsilon^D_{pit} + \alpha^d_{pi}\varepsilon^d_{pit}, \tag{8-6}$$

where

$$\alpha^s_{pi} = -b_{3pi}\alpha_{pi} \text{ and } \alpha^d_{pi} = 1 - \alpha^s_{pi}.$$

A few observations can be made about equation (8−6). First, note that the relationship between Y_{pit} and the lagged employment terms could arise through the effects of these variables on product demand, labor demand, and labor supply. Second, the greater the wage responsiveness of labor supply, the larger the effect of product demand shocks and labor demand shocks on Y_{pit}. If the labor supply response to the wage is large, then the amount of labor supplied accommodates the shift in labor demand without a large wage increase.

Third, although industry shocks and province shocks have only a local effect in the initial period, they affect employment in other industries and provinces in subsequent periods through the lagged employment terms. In part, the lagged employment terms enter because adjustment costs affect the response of the supply of and the demand for labor to ε^s_{pit} and ε^d_{pit}. This mechanism, particularly in the labor supply equation, is closely related to the discussion of reallocation costs in Lilien and others. In part, the lagged employment terms enter because past employment affects the demand for output. This might occur through the mechanism discussed by Long and Plosser [1983]. In their work, interrelationships among industries in the production process imply a link between past employment levels in a given industry and product demand in other industries. These lagged terms could also enter through the effect of lagged employment on consumer income and consumer demand, as discussed above. Finally, the lagged employment terms could enter because they are correlated with current and future employment prospects, and thus influence the supply of labor to various industries.

The fourth point, which is closely related to the third, is that the behavior of employment in a given market cannot be analyzed independently of the other markets. Let $\underline{Y}_t$ denote the $PI \times I$ vector of the Y_{pit} for the P provinces and I industries. Since Y_{ct}, $Y_{p \cdot t}$, and $Y_{\cdot it}$ are weighted sums of the Y_{pit}, one may express Y_{ct}, $Y_{p \cdot t}$, and $Y_{\cdot it}$ in terms of $\underline{Y}_t$. The expression for national employment growth is given by

$$Y_{ct} = \Sigma_{pi} w_{pi} Y_{pit}, \qquad (8-7a)$$

where w_{pi} is the share of Canadian employment accounted for by province p-industry i. Employment growth in industry i equals

$$Y_{\cdot it} = \Sigma_p w_p^i \cdot Y_{pit}, \qquad (8-7b)$$

where w_p^i. is the share of industry i employment accounted for by employment in province p-industry i. Provincial employment growth equals the weighted sum of growth rates over the industries in province p,

$$Y_{p \cdot t} = \Sigma_i w_{\cdot i}^p Y_{pit} \qquad (8-7c)$$

where $w_{\cdot i}^p$ is the fraction of employment in province p due to employment in province p-industry i.

Consequently, one may combine equation $(8-6)$ for each pi into a system of equations given by equation $(8-8)$

$$\underline{Y}_t = \underline{\lambda} + \pi \underline{Y}_{t-1} + \underline{\tilde{\varepsilon}}_t^s + \underline{\tilde{\varepsilon}}_t^D + \underline{\tilde{\varepsilon}}_t^d \qquad (8-8)$$

where the pi^{th} elements of $\underline{\tilde{\varepsilon}}_t^s$, $\underline{\tilde{\varepsilon}}_t^D$ and $\underline{\tilde{\varepsilon}}_t^d$ are

$$\tilde{\varepsilon}_{pit}^s = \alpha_{pi}^s \varepsilon_{pit}^s, \quad \tilde{\varepsilon}_{pit}^D = \alpha_{pi}^d b_{1pi} \varepsilon_{pit}^D$$

and

$$\tilde{\varepsilon}_{pit}^d = \alpha_{pi}^d \varepsilon_{pit}^d.$$

The elements of the vector of constants $\underline{\lambda}$ and the matrix π are functions of the parameters in the equations for each of the Y_{pit} and the weights defined above. If the economy is subject to no shocks, the equilibrium values of the employment change variables are determined by equation $(8-8)$. The solution for the steady state value of $\underline{Y}$ is

$$\underline{Y} = [I - \pi]^{-1}\underline{\lambda}. \qquad (8-9)$$

Equation $(8-8)$ and the variances and serial correlation properties of the various shocks determine the steady state variance of employment growth in the various sectors. The variance of the aggregate employment change Y_{ct} is a weighted sum of the variances and covariances of employment changes in the individual sectors. Consequently fluctuations in sector-specific shocks contribute to fluctuations in aggregate employment growth. This is the collective impact hypothesis.

Fifth, the parameters of the product demand, labor demand, and labor supply equations must be consistent with the long-run equilibrium of wages across sectors, taking account of compensating wage differentials. If the compensating wage differentials are stable as a percentage of the wage, then equilibrium wage growth in all of the sectors should be the same. We omit a discussion of the nature of these restrictions since we do not examine them in the empirical work below.

Employment Determination: The Nonmarket Clearing Case. It is useful to explore the implications of the behavior of the labor market in the case in which wages do not instantaneously adjust to equate the short-run supply of and demand for labor in each sector. We work with a variant of the contract wage models of Fischer [1977] and Phelps and Taylor [1977] that have formed the basis for a number of theoretical and empirical studies of wage behavior. The basic idea of these models is that the wage is set in period $t-1$ to the value that would clear the market in period t in the absence of unanticipated shocks to the economy or the sector. Ex post, the wage does not clear the market if unanticipated shocks shift the labor demand and supply schedules. We assume that in the event of a discrepancy between supply and demand at the preset wage, the actual employment level is a weighted average of the two.

The implied equation for the growth in the wage is

$$\begin{aligned}
\omega_{pit} = {} & \alpha_{pi}[b_{opi} + b_{1pi}a_{opi} - q_{opi}] + \alpha_{pi}[b_{1pi}a_{1pi} \\
& - q_{1pi}]Y_{ct-1} + \alpha_{pi}[b_{1pi}a_{2pi} - q_{2pi}]Y_{p \cdot t-1} \\
& - \alpha_{pi}q_{3pi}Y_{\cdot it-1} + \alpha_{pi}[b_{2pi} - q_{4pi}]Y_{pit-1} \\
& + \alpha_{pi}b_{1pi}\varepsilon_{pit-1}^{D} + \alpha_{pi}\varepsilon_{pit-1}^{d} - \alpha_{pi}\varepsilon_{pit-1}^{s}. \qquad (8-10)
\end{aligned}$$

In equation $(8-10)$ we have temporarily assumed that the various shocks in the model follow random walks in levels to avoid having to introduce additional notation, so that c_t^D, etc., are the innovations in the shocks. Let μ_{pi}^s denote the weight of labor supply and μ_{pi}^d denote the weight of labor demand in employment $(\mu_{pi}^d + \mu_{pi}^s = 1)$ so that the employment growth equation may be written as[5]

$$Y_{pit} = \mu_{pi}^s Y_{pit}^s + \mu_{pi}^d Y_{pit}^d. \qquad (8-11)$$

Using equation $(8-10)$ to eliminate ω_{pit} from equations $(8-3)$ and $(8-4)$ for Y_{pit}^d and Y_{pit}^s and substituting into equation $(8-11)$ leads to the nonmarket clearing employment equation

$$
\begin{aligned}
Y_{pit} = {} & \alpha_{pi}^s q_{opi} + \alpha_{pi}^d b_{1pi} a_{opi} + [\alpha_{pi}^s q_{1pi} + \alpha_{pi}^d b_{1pi} a_{1pi}] Y_{ct-1} \\
& + [\alpha_{pi}^s q_{2pi} + \alpha_{pi}^d b_{1pi} a_{2pi}] Y_{p \cdot t-1} + \alpha_{pi}^s q_{3pi} Y_{\cdot it-1} \\
& + [\alpha_{pi}^s q_{4pi} + \alpha_{pi}^d b_{2pi}] Y_{pit-1} + \mu_{pi}^d b_{1pi} \varepsilon_{pit}^D + \mu_{pi}^d \varepsilon_{pit}^d \\
& + \mu_{pi}^s \varepsilon_{pit}^s + \alpha_{pi} b_{1pi} (\mu_{pi}^d b_{3pi} + \mu_{pi}^s q_{5pi}) \varepsilon_{pit-1}^D \\
& + \alpha_{pi} (\mu_{pi}^d b_{3pi} + \mu_{pi}^s q_{5pi}) \varepsilon_{pit-1}^d - \alpha_{pi} (\mu_{pi}^d b_{3pi} \\
& + \mu_{pi}^s q_{5pi}) \varepsilon_{pit-1}^s + \alpha_{pi}^d b_{opi} \qquad (8-12)
\end{aligned}
$$

The coefficients on the lagged employment terms in equation $(8-12)$ are identical to the market clearing employment equation $(8-6)$. However, the coefficients on the shocks ε_{pit}^D, ε_{pit}^d, and ε_{pit}^s are different unless the weights (μ_{pi}^s, μ_{pi}^d) happen to equal $(\alpha_{pi}^s, \alpha_{pi}^d)$. Furthermore, in the nonmarket clearing case the first lag of each shock affects employment. This occurs since one period is required for wages to adjust to the shocks. Consequently, the econometric specification discussed below, in which we assume that the lagged shocks have a coefficient of zero in the model, is inconsistent, in general, with the nonmarket clearing model. However, in the special case where (μ_{pi}^s, μ_{pi}^d) equal $(\alpha_{pi}^s, \alpha_{pi}^d)$, the lagged shocks do not affect employment in the nonmarket clearing case, and equations $(8-6)$ and $(8-12)$ are equivalent.

Extensions. In this section, we discuss extensions of the basic model. First, we discuss the role of unemployment. Second, we consider the possibility that labor supply responds (with a lag) to permanent changes in the demand for labor in a given sector.

A straightforward means of incorporating unemployment into the model is to assume that the change in unemployment in a given sector is a negative function of the change in employment in that sector. Such a relationship is implied by the nonmarket clearing model discussed above, especially if labor demand receives a larger weight in employment determination than labor supply. A negative relationship is also consistent with a market clearing model where some workers respond to a reduction in current wages by increasing consumption of leisure or by searching more intensely for alternate employment opportunities. Specifically, we assume that U_{pit}, the change in the unemployment rate in pi, is determined by

$$U_{pit} = \theta Y_{pit}, \qquad (8-13)$$

where θ is negative. The specific value of θ depends upon the extent to which reductions in the number and quality of job opportunities in equations $(8-6)$ or $(8-12)$ translate into changes in unemployment or changes in labor force participation. Let U_{ct} denote the change in the aggregate unemployment rate, where U_{ct} is a weighted average of the U_{pit}. If the weights are similar to the weights of Y_{pit} in Y_{ct}, then one may use equation $(8-13)$ to approximate U_{ct} as

$$U_{ct} = \theta Y_{ct}. \qquad (8-14)$$

We assume that, with a one period lag, an increase in the unemployment rate increases the supply of workers to all sectors of the economy with a positive coefficient q_{8pi}. In this case the supply equation $(8-4a)$ becomes

$$
\begin{aligned}
Y_{pit}^{s} = q_{opi} &+ (q_{1pi} + q_{8pi}\theta)Y_{ct-1} + q_{2pi}Y_{p\cdot t-1} \\
&+ q_{3pi}Y_{\cdot it-1} + q_{4pi}Y_{pit-1} + q_{5pi}\omega_{pit} + \varepsilon_{pit}^{s}. \qquad (8-15)
\end{aligned}
$$

In the market clearing case the employment equation becomes

$$
\begin{aligned}
Y_{pit} = [\alpha_{pi}^{d}(b_{opi} &+ b_{1pi}a_{opi}) + \alpha_{pi}^{s}q_{opi}] + [\alpha_{pi}^{d}b_{1pi}a_{1pi} \\
&+ \alpha_{pi}^{s}q_{1pi} + \alpha_{pi}^{s}q_{8pi}\theta]Y_{ct-1} \\
&+ [\alpha_{pi}^{s}q_{2pi} + \alpha_{pi}^{d}b_{1pi}a_{2pi}]Y_{p\cdot t-1} + \alpha_{pi}^{s}q_{3pi}Y_{\cdot it-1} \\
&+ [\alpha_{pi}^{s}q_{4pi} + \alpha_{pi}^{d}b_{2pi}]Y_{pit-1} + \alpha_{pi}^{s}\varepsilon_{pit}^{s} + \alpha_{pi}^{d}b_{1pi}\varepsilon_{pit}^{D} \\
&+ \alpha_{pi}^{d}\varepsilon_{pit}^{d}. \qquad (8-16)
\end{aligned}
$$

One obtains an equation for Y_{pit} that, after rearrangement of coefficients, is identical to equation $(8-6)$ in a reduced-form sense. A similar result holds for equation $(8-12)$. Thus, both the employment equations $(8-6)$ and $(8-12)$ are consistent with the above model of unemployment. It is easy to extend the model to allow for the possibility that unemployment in region p has a larger effect on the supply of labor to region p than to other regions (because of moving costs), and to allow for the possibility that unemployment in industry i has a larger effect on the supply of labor to industry i than to other industries. These modifications would result in further changes in the interpretation of the coefficients of the lagged employment terms in equations $(8-6)$ and $(8-12)$.

Nevertheless, the above view of unemployment is highly restrictive. It requires the assumption that the effect of shocks to labor supply and demand on unemployment are proportional to their effects on the level of employment. One might expect demographic shifts or changes in unemployment insurance provisions to have different impacts upon the effective supply of labor (Y_{pit}^{s}) and upon the decision to participate in the labor force. In this case, it would be necessary to add an error term to equations (8−14) and (8−15). The reader may verify that in this case an additional source of shocks (dated $t-1$) are added to the employment equations (8−6) and (8−12).

Differential Responses to Temporary and Permanent Shocks.   Discussions of structural unemployment and reallocation across sectors of the labor market frequently make a distinction between the effects of transitory demand shocks and permanent demand shocks. A transitory demand reduction (resulting from either a product demand shift or a technology shock) is likely to have a smaller effect on the supply of labor to a particular sector than a demand change which is perceived to be permanent. Workers are less likely to incur the fixed costs of moving between industries or between regions in response to a transitory sectoral shock than to a permanent one. (See, for example, the discussion in Topel [1986].) Lilien [1982b] assumes explicitly that the supply of workers to a given sector responds only to permanent shifts in the sectoral composition of demand. The extent to which structural unemployment is a problem depends in part on the amount of time required for workers to recognize that the shifts in demand are permanent, the size of the supply response to these shocks, and the speed with which decreases in employment in a given sector induce individuals to increase their supply of labor to other sectors.

Let ξ_{pit} denote a *permanent* sector-specific shift in labor demand, which may arise either from a shift in product demand or a shock to technology or the prices of nonlabor inputs. To avoid having to define a completely new set of notation, we assume momentarily that all other demand disturbances defined previously are transitory and simply add ξ_{pit} to the labor demand equation (8−3). This leads to

$$Y_{pit}^d = (b_{opi} + b_{1pi}a_{opi}) + b_{1pi}a_{1pi}Y_{ct-1}$$
$$+ b_{1pi}a_{2pi}Y_{p \cdot t-1} + b_{2pi}Y_{pit-1}$$
$$+ b_{3pi}\omega_{pit} + b_{1pi}\varepsilon_{pit}^D + \varepsilon_{pit}^d + \xi_{pit}. \qquad (8-17)$$

Further, we assume that workers learn with a one period lag that the shock is permanent, and that Y_{pit}^s is a positive function of ξ_{pit-1}. This leads to the supply equation

$$Y_{pit}^s = q_{opi} + q_{1pi}Y_{ct-1} + q_{2pi}Y_{p \cdot t-1} + q_{3pi}Y_{\cdot it-1}$$
$$+ q_{4pi}Y_{pit-1} + q_{5qi}\omega_{pit} + \varepsilon_{pit}^s + q_{9pi}\xi_{pit-1}. \qquad (8-18)$$

Following through on the earlier substitutions leads to the employment equation for the market clearing case

$$Y_{pit} = [\alpha_{pi}^d(b_{opi} + b_{1pi}a_{opi}) + \alpha_{pi}^s q_{opi}] + [\alpha_{pi}^d b_{1pi}a_{1pi}$$

$$+ \ \alpha^s_{pi}q_{1pi}]Y_{ct-1} + [\alpha^s_{pi}q_{2pi} + \alpha^d_{pi}b_{1pi}a_{2pi}]Y_{p \cdot t-1}$$
$$+ \ \alpha^s_{pi}q_{3pi}Y_{\cdot it-1} + [\alpha^s_{pi}q_{4pi} + \alpha^d_{pi}b_{2pi}]Y_{pit-1}$$
$$+ \ \alpha^s_{qi}\varepsilon^s_{pit} + \alpha^d_{pi}b_{1pi}\varepsilon^D_{pit} + \alpha^d_{pi}\xi_{pit} + \alpha^d_{pi}\varepsilon^d_{pit}$$
$$+ \ \alpha^s_{pi}q_{9pi}\xi_{pit-1}. \tag{8-19}$$

This modification to the model also introduces lagged values of shocks into the employment growth equation.

Note that policies intended to retrain or assist in the relocation of workers (e.g., the Manpower Development and Training Act of 1962 or the current Job Training Partnership Act of 1982 in the United States) should increase the response of labor supply to a permanent shock and also presumably increase the responsiveness of supply for a given sector to unemployment in other sectors. An increase in the level and duration of unemployment benefits could reduce these responses.

In this section we have considered several theoretical models of employment determination in a given sector. We now turn to the issue of moving from a theoretical model to an equation which can be estimated from available data. We focus on reduced-form models which are compatible with the market clearing model $(8-6)$, although the same approach could be used to consider other models.

IV   An Econometric Model of the Analysis of Employment Variation

B. Estimating Equations

In the market-clearing model outlined above, and in particular equation $(8-6)$, the basic unit of an analysis is employment growth in a specific province-industry pair. In this model, employment growth depends on a set of observable variables and a set of unobservable shocks. The observable variables consist of: (1) the growth in Canadian employment in the previous year; (2) the growth in employment in the own industry in the previous year; (3) the growth in employment in the own province in the previous year; and (4), the growth in employment in industry i-province p. The unobservable shocks to province p-industry i consist of: (1) a national (Canadian) shock; (2) a shock to industry i; (3) a shock to province p; and (4), an idiosyncratic shock to province p-industry i.

As it stands, equation $(8-6)$ is too general to be used for empirical estimation. Thus we consider a model that implicitly imposes a number of restrictions on the theoretical equation $(8-6)$. First, we assume that all coefficients (including those on the shocks) have only an i subscript, and do not differ across provinces for the same industry. Imposing this restriction results in an equation of the form

$$Y_{pit} = \lambda_i + \gamma_i Y_{ct-1} + \delta_i Y_{p.}t_{-1} + \theta_i Y_{\cdot it-1}$$
$$+ \phi_i Y_{pit-1} + \alpha_i^d \varepsilon_{pit}^d + \alpha_i^d b_{li} \varepsilon_{pit}^D + \alpha_i^s \varepsilon_{pit}^s, \qquad (8-20)$$

where

$$\gamma_i = \alpha_i^s q_{1i} + \alpha_i^d b_{1i} a_{1i} \qquad (8-21a)$$

$$\delta_i = \alpha_i^s q_{2i} + \alpha_i^d b_{1i} a_{2i} \qquad (8-21b)$$

$$\theta_i = \alpha_i^s q_{3i} \qquad (8-21c)$$

$$\phi_i = \alpha_i^s q_{4i} + \alpha_i^d b_{2i}. \qquad (8-21d)$$

It should be emphasized that γ_i, δ_i, θ_i, and ϕ_i are reduced form parameters that combine a number of structural effects as given in equations (8-21a) through (8-21d). Next, we further restrict the theoretical model by simplifying the error structure in equation (8-20). To clarify this simplification, we first write each of the errors in equation (8-20) in terms of reduced-form coefficients on the respective national, industrial, provincial, and idiosyncratic shocks

$$\alpha_i^s \varepsilon_{pit}^s = \alpha_i^s g_{6i} c_t^s + \alpha_i^s g_{7i} v_{pt}^s$$
$$= f_i^s c_t^s + g_i^s v_{pt}^s, \qquad (8-22a)$$

$$\alpha_i^d \varepsilon_{pit}^d = \alpha_i^d b_{4i} c_t^d + \alpha_i^d b_{5i} \eta_{it}^d + \alpha_i^d b_{6i} v_{pt}^d + \alpha_i^d u_{pit}^d$$
$$= f_i^d c_t^d + h_i^d \eta_{it}^d + g_i^d v_{pt}^d + k_i^d u_{pit}^d, \qquad (8-22b)$$

and

$$\alpha_i^d b_{1i} \varepsilon_{pit}^D = \alpha_i^d b_{1i} a_{4i} c_t^D + \alpha_i^d b_{1i} a_{5i} \eta_{it}^D$$
$$+ \alpha_i^d b_{1i} a_{6i} v_{pt}^D + \alpha_i^d b_{1i} u_{pit}^D$$
$$= f_i^D c_t^D + h_i^D \eta_{it}^D + g_i^D v_{pt}^D + k_i^D u_{pit}^D \qquad (8-22c)$$

The coefficients h_i^d, h_i^D, k_i^d, and k_i^D are not identified, and we normalize them to 1.0.[6] To simplify the model for empirical implementation, we make the following approximation[7]:

$$f_i c_t \approx f_i^s c_t^s + f_i^d c_t^d + f_i^D c_t^D \qquad (8-23a)$$

and

$$g_i v_{pt} \approx g_i^s v_{pt}^s + g_i^d v_{pt}^d + g_i^D v_{pt}^D. \qquad (8-23b)$$

We also use the following definitions:

$$\eta_{it} = \eta_{it}^d + \eta_{it}^D \qquad (8-23c)$$

and

$$u_{pit} = u_{pit}^d + u_{pit}^D. \qquad (8-23d)$$

Given these simplifications, our equation for employment growth in pi becomes

$$Y_{pit} = \lambda_i + \gamma_i Y_{ct-1} + \delta_i Y_{p \cdot t-1} + \theta_i Y_{\cdot it-1} + \phi_i Y_{pit-1} + \varepsilon_{pit}, \quad (8-24a)$$

where

$$\varepsilon_{pit} = f_i c_t + g_i v_{pt} + \eta_{it} + u_{pit}. \quad (8-24b)$$

These approximations represent strong restrictions on the error structure that are unlikely to hold in practice. For example, in terms of the national shock, equation (8-23a) will only be strictly valid if $f_i^s = f_i^d = f_i^D$ or $c_t^s = m_1 c_t^d = m_2 c_t^D$ in each period. Indeed, one may argue that using only one index of national shocks is too restrictive, given the many plausible sources of shocks at this level. Our response to this objection is threefold. First, in the empirical work below we use the growth in U.S. GNP as a second index of aggregate shocks. Second, even the restricted model is quite complex, so it seems sensible to begin by determining whether the data are rich enough to support the restricted model before proceeding to more general specifications. Third, the restricted model gives the sectoral shocks their best chance to play a role in the variation of aggregate employment growth. If sectoral shocks do not appear to play a major role using the restricted model, for our purposes there is little point in moving to more complex models.

Two further modifications to equation (8-24a) are useful. For simplicity, the theoretical models discussed above ignored any impact of external shocks. However, it is important in the empirical work to allow external shocks (particularly those arising from the United States) to influence employment growth in the Canadian sectors. To do so, we assume that the current and lagged growth rate in real U.S. GNP, US_t and US_{t-1}, affect employment growth in pi with an industry-specific coefficient. Second, we found that including the own lag Y_{pit-1} had no effect on the empirical results, and thus for clarity we set $\phi_i = 0$ for all i in the discussion that follows. Thus our empirical equation takes the form[8]

$$Y_{pit} = \lambda_i + \gamma_i Y_{ct-1} + \delta_i Y_{p \cdot t-1} + \theta_i Y_{\cdot it-1}$$
$$+ B_{1i} US_t + B_{2i} US_{t-1} + \varepsilon_{pit}, \quad (8-25)$$

where ε_{pit} is given by (8-24b).

Since Y_{ct-1}, $Y_{p \cdot t-1}$, and $Y_{\cdot it-1}$ (taken together) depend on the $PI \times 1$ vector $\underline{Y}_{t-1}$ (through the weights defined in (8-7a), (8-7b), and (8-7c)), we can write this modified system as

$$\underline{Y}_t = \underline{\lambda} + \pi \underline{Y}_{t-1} + \underline{B}_1^* US_t + \underline{B}_2^* US_{t-1} + \underline{\varepsilon}_t,$$

where

$$\underline{B}_1 = [B_{11}, \ldots, B_{1I}]', \quad \underline{B}_2 = [B_{21}, \ldots, B_{2I}]'$$

$$\underline{B}_1^{*\prime} = [\underline{B}_1', \underline{B}_1', \ldots, \underline{B}_1'] \text{ and } \underline{B}_2^{*\prime} = [\underline{B}_2', \ldots, \underline{B}_2']. \tag{8-26}$$

Thus, equation (8–26) can be viewed as a restricted autoregressive model, where the matrix π depends on the national, industry, and province weights and the regression parameters[9]

$$\underline{\gamma}' = [\gamma_1, \ldots, \gamma_I], \ \underline{\delta}' = [\delta_1, \ldots \delta_I] \text{ and}$$
$$\underline{\theta}' = [\theta_1, \ldots, \theta_I].$$

As noted above, ε_{pit} is assumed to follow a factor structure of the form

$$\varepsilon_{pit} = f_i c_t + \eta_{it} + g_i v_{pt} + u_{ipt}, \tag{8-24b}$$

where c_t = Canadian shock affecting all province-industry pairs with industry-specific coefficient f_i; $\mathrm{Var}(c_t) = \sigma_c^2$.

η_{it} = industry-specific shock affecting industry i; $\mathrm{Var}(\eta_{it}) = \sigma_{\eta i}^2$.

v_{pt} = province-specific shock affecting all industries in province p with industry specific weight g_i; $\mathrm{Var}(v_{pt}) = \sigma_{vp}^2$.

u_{pit} = idiosyncratic disturbance relecting special conditions affecting only pi; $\mathrm{Var}(u_{pit}) = \sigma_{upi}^2$.

We assume that the national shock c_t, the vector $\underline{\eta}_t = (\eta_{1t}, \ldots, \eta_{It})'$ of industry disturbances, the vector $\underline{v}_t = (v_{1t}, \ldots v_{pt})'$ of province disturbances, and the vector $\underline{u}_t = (u_{11t}, \ldots, u_{PIt})'$ of province-industry shocks, are mutually uncorrelated at all leads and lags. For example, c_t is assumed uncorrelated with the shock that is specific to manufacturing. It is natural to decompose the variance of the employment disturbances in this way. However, in our empirical work we also make the much stronger assumption that the industry shocks η_{it} are uncorrelated across industries, that the province shocks v_{pt} are uncorrelated across provinces, and that the combined province-industry shocks u_{pit} are uncorrelated across provinces and industry pairs. In any error components model of this type, restrictions are necessary for identification, and the interpretation of results are conditional on these identifying restrictions. In our model the independence assumptions *within* the vector of industry errors $\underline{\eta}_t$, provincial errors $\underline{v}_t$ and idiosyncratic errors $\underline{u}_t$ represent identifying restrictions. Intuitively our procedure can be viewed as asking whether we gain anything by starting from a baseline model with a national shock and then adding sets of independent industry shocks and independent provincial shocks. The justification for this approach is that empirically it will be extremely difficult to distinguish between models with only national shocks and models with correlated provincial and industry shocks. Moreover, even if this empirical distinction could be made, it would not be an interesting distinction for interpreting theoretical models.

From the error structure shown in equation (8−24b) and the identifying independence assumptions, we can calculate the model's prediction for the correlation between ε_{pit} and $\varepsilon_{p'i't}$. For the case of different industries ($i \neq i'$) in different provinces ($p \neq p'$), only the national shock c_t makes a contribution and

$$\text{cov}(\varepsilon_{pit}, \ \varepsilon_{p'i't}) = f_i f_{i'} \sigma_c^2. \qquad (8-27a)$$

If the industries differ, but are located in the same province, v_{pt} also makes a contribution and

$$\text{cov}(\varepsilon_{pit}, \ \varepsilon_{pi't}) = f_i f_{i'} \sigma_c^2 + g_i g_{i'} \sigma_{vp}^2. \qquad (8-27b)$$

On the other hand, if the provinces differ ($p \neq p'$) but the industries are the same, η_{it} makes a contribution and

$$\text{cov}(\varepsilon_{pit}, \ \varepsilon_{p'it}) = f_i^2 \sigma_c^2 + \sigma_{\eta i}^2 \qquad (8-27c)$$

Finally, if both the provinces and the industries are the same, then η_{it}, v_{pt}, and u_{it} all make a contribution and

$$\text{Var} \ (\varepsilon_{pit}) = f_i^2 \sigma_c^2 + \sigma_{\eta i}^2 + g_i^2 \sigma_{vp}^2 + \sigma_{upi}^2. \qquad (8-27d)$$

Equation (8−25) summarizes the effect of current Canadian shocks, lagged and current growth in U.S. GNP, and the lagged employment growth across Canadian sectors, on the current employment growth across Canadian sectors. Equations (8−27a) through (8−27d) present the covariance structure between errors. Before we can obtain an expression for the impact of U.S. and Canadian shocks on fluctuations in steady state growth in Canadian employment, it is necessary to specify the form of the processes determining US_t and the Canadian shocks c_t, $\underline{v}_t$, η_t, and $\underline{u}_t$. We assume that US_t follows a second order autoregressive process

$$US_t = \rho_1 US_{t-1} + \rho_2 US_{t-2} + \varepsilon_{ust}, \qquad (8-28)$$

where ε_{ust} is a white noise error (i.e., uncorrelated over time) with variance σ_{US}^2. In terms of the Canadian shocks, a priori we rule out autocorrelation in $\underline{u}_t$. Empirically, we found no evidence of autocorrelation in c_t and η_t, and evidence of only a small degree of autocorrelation in $\underline{v}_t$. Moreover, allowing for this autocorrelation had no impact on the empirical results. Thus in the interests of clarity, we proceed as if c_t, η_t, and $\underline{v}_t$ can all be treated as white noise.

Recalling that national employment growth takes the form

$$Y_{ct} = \underline{w}' \underline{Y}_t, \tag{8-7a}$$

where $\underline{w}$ is the vector of national weights (for ease of notation we have dropped the c subscript), it is straightforward to show that the steady state variance in national employment growth $V(Y_{ct})$ takes the form

$$V(Y_{ct}) = \underline{w}' H_{US} \underline{w} + \underline{w}' H_c \underline{w} + \underline{w}' H_\eta \underline{w} + \underline{w}' H_v \underline{w} + \underline{w}' H_u \underline{w}. \tag{8-29}$$

The first term in equation (8-29) is the contribution of the US shock to $V(Y_{ct})$ where H_{US} is a $PI \times PI$ matrix depending on π, $\underline{B}_1$, $\underline{B}_2$. σ_{us}^2, ρ_1 and ρ_2.[10] (Recall that π, in turn, is a function of $\underline{\theta}$, $\underline{\delta}$, $\underline{\gamma}$, and the national, provincial, and industrial weights.) The contribution of the Canadian shock c_t to the steady state variance in national employment growth is given by the second term in this equation, where H_c depends on π, $\underline{f}$ and σ_c^2. The contributin of the $I \times 1$ vector of industrial shocks η_t is represented by the third term in (8-29), where H_η is a function of π and the vector of industry variances. The fourth term in equation (8-29) indicates the contribution of the $P \times 1$ vector of provincial shocks $\underline{v}_t$, where H_v depends on π, $\underline{g}$, and the vector of provincial variances. Finally the contribution of the PI vector of idiosyncratic shocks $\underline{u}_t$ is given by the fifth term, where H_u depends on π and the vector of idiosyncratic variances. The fraction of the variance in national employment growth due to any one of these shocks (or set of shocks) is given by the ratio of the respective term in equation (8-29) to the sum of all of the terms.

B. Estimation Methods

The above model provides a straightforward method of comparing the role of sectoral shocks relative to the role of national and external shocks in fluctuations of national employment growth. Of course, before the model can be implemented, one must estimate the parameters in equations (8-25) and (8-27a-d).[11] Estimation of the regression parameters $\underline{\theta}$, $\underline{\delta}$, $\underline{\gamma}$, $\underline{B}_1$, and $\underline{B}_2$ is straightforward. The appropriate estimation method is either OLS or TSLS, depending on the degree of autocorrelation in c_t, η_t, $\underline{v}_t$, and $\underline{u}_t$ and how one wants to interprete equation (8-25). In practice the variance decomposition of equation (8-29) is insensitive to the method used to estimate equation (8-25).

The method used to estimate the parameters defined in equations (8-27a-d) will be less familiar to some readers and thus deserves a more detailed discussion. To carry out this estimation, one first takes the $PI \times 1$ vectors of residuals from equation (8-25) for each time period and forms the empirical covariance matrix of the residuals

$$S = \Sigma_t \hat{\underline{\varepsilon}}_t \hat{\underline{\varepsilon}}_t' / T. \qquad (8-30a)$$

A typical element of S takes the form

$$S_{pip'i'} = \Sigma_t \hat{\varepsilon}_{pit} \hat{\varepsilon}_{p'i't} / T. \qquad (8-30b)$$

If $p \neq p'$ and $i \neq i'$, the error structure shown in equation $(8-24b)$ predicts that this empirical covariance in equation $(8-30)$ should take the form given by equation $(8-27a)$. Alternatively, if $p = p'$ but $i \neq i'$ the model predicts this empirical covariance will be given by equation $(8-27b)$, and a similar argument can be made concerning equations $(8-27c)$ and $(8-27d)$. Of course, even a correct model will not predict perfectly, but on average it should predict correctly. Analogous to least squares estimation, one can obtain "minimum distance" estimates of the $\underline{f}$ and $\underline{g}$ terms, as well as the variances of the national, provincial, industrial, and idiosyncratic shocks, by choosing the values of these parameters which minimize the sum of squared differences between the sample covariances given in equation $(8-30)$ and the predicted covariances chosen from the appropriate expression in equations $(8-27a-d)$.

C. An Overview of the Empirical Results

In estimating the model described in section IV, we faced a number of difficult technical econometric problems that we could not fully resolve. We also considered several further modifications of the model. In general our results were not sensitive to these modifications, but some specific para-meter estimates were affected. A full discussion of these technical problems and our sensitivity analysis is inappropriate in the present context; however, it is important to emphasize that we view our empirical work as a significant first step but not, in any way, as the final word on these issues. Moreover, even ignoring these technical issues, the basic model contains almost 100 parameters, and their interpretation is complicated by the dynamic nature of the model. Here we provide a basic summary of the results in the hope that this will enable readers to gain the flavor of the results without incurring the cost of carefully reviewing each set of parameter estimates and simulation results.

The basic data for the study are annual observations on employment growth for the period 1961−82 disaggregated by one digit industry and province.[12] In our analysis we (separately) aggregate the Nova Scotia and New Brunswick data and the Manitoba and Saskatchewan data. Observa-

Table 8–6. Average Percentage Share in Canadian Employment[a] by Province and Industry: 1961 – 1982

	Newfoundland	Nova Scotia/ New Brunswick	Quebec	Ontario	Saskatchewan/ Manitoba	Alberta	British Columbia	Row Totals
Forestry	.042	.132	.281	.170	.027	.034	.306	.992
Mining	.078	.129	.369	.509	.175	.427	.172	1.859
Manufacturing	.200	.934	7.499	12.078	.984	.844	1.956	24.495
Construction	.123	.339	1.445	2.125	.432	.689	.606	5.759
Transportation	.229	.680	2.715	3.402	1.095	.883	1.272	10.276
Trade	.281	.969	4.168	6.620	1.488	1.464	1.803	16.793
Finance	.040	.203	1.320	2.163	.366	.369	.527	4.988
Services	.461	1.616	7.282	10.746	2.360	2.486	2.942	27.893
Government	.143	.521	1.607	2.761	.623	.587	.703	6.945
Column totals[b]	1.597	5.523	26.686	40.574	7.550	7.783	10.287	

[a]Defined as sum over industries and provinces listed.
[b]May not sum to 100% because of rounding.

Table 8–7. Means and Standard Deviations of the Log First Differences in Industry and Provincial Employment

A. Industry

	Forestry	Mining	Manu-facturing	Con-struction	Trans-portation	Trade	Finance	Services	Government
Mean	−.0113	.0171	.0128	.0179	.0168	.0349	.0476	.0482	.0317
Standard Deviation	(.0760)	(.0514)	(.0364)	(.0560)	(.0179)	(.0218)	(.0231)	(.0165)	(.0223)

B. Province/Region

	Newfoundland	Nova Scotia/New Brunswick	Quebec	Ontario	Saskatchewan/Manitoba	Alberta	British Columbia
Mean	.0293	.0214	.0241	.0295	.0244	.0525	.0395
Standard Deviation	(.0287)	(.0206)	(.0241)	(.0182)	(.0175)	(.0213)	(.0290)

tions for Prince Edward Island, the Yukon, and the North West Territories are not used in the analysis. Summary statistics for the data are given in tables 8−6 and 8−7.

In addition to the variance decomposition given in equation (8−29), the results of our estimation can be summarized in terms of: (1) the feedback effects of Y_{ct}, $Y_{p \cdot t}$, and $Y_{\cdot it}$ on current employment growth in pi; (2) the effects of the current shocks ε_{ust}, c_t, η_t, and $\underline{v}_t$ on current employment growth; and (3) impact of the shocks on the time pattern of employment growth. ·

In terms of the feedback effects our results can be summarized as follows:

1. Lagged Canadian employment growth has a negative impact on all industries except construction, government, and services. The largest feedback effects occur in forestry, mining, manufacturing, and construction.

2. The lagged change in own provincial employment growth has a substantial positive impact on current employment growth in most industries. The largest effects of this variable are found in mining, manufacturing, construction, transport, and finance.

3. The effects of lagged own industry employment are mixed in sign and relatively small.

The effects of the current shocks on current employment growth may be summarized as follows:

1. U.S. GNP has a positive impact effect on all industries except government. It has a strong effect on forestry, manufacturing, and construction, a moderate effect on trade and finance, and a relatively weak effect on mining.

2. The current Canadian shock has its largest impact on forestry, mining, and construction. It has an intermediate effect in manufacturing and transportation. Government employment growth reacts negatively to the national shock.

3. The own industry shock is more important than the national shock in finance, service, and trade. The national shock is more important than the own industry shock in mining, manufacturing, forestry, and construction.

The province shocks, somewhat surprisingly, have their largest impact on forestry and mining and somewhat smaller effects on transportation and manufacturing. An anomolous result is that the construction response to the province shock is often estimated to be negative. The provincial variances, except for Newfoundland, are relatively small. It should be noted that the estimates of industry and province variances are imprecise, and some point estimates are less than zero.[13]

The impact of provincial and industry shocks on the time pattern of employment growth is quite complex. Thus we limit ourselves to summarizing the dynamic response to one-time U.S. and national shocks. The industries' response to the national shock is similar to their response to the U.S. shock. In response to a U.S. shock, the growth rate of national employment rises above its initial level for three periods and then returns to zero. In most industries the impact of the shock is always positive. However, in forestry, manufacturing, and finance the growth rate first rises in response to a U.S. shock and then falls before returning to its initial value. In government, the U.S. shock first lowers and then raises employment growth.

The most interesting result of our empirical work concerns the decomposition of the steady state variance in the national employment growth. We find that the changes in U.S. GNP dominate the variance of Canadian national employment growth, accounting for 62% to 67% of this variation. The next most important source of variation is the Canadian national shock, which accounts for 24% to 28% of the variance in national employment growth. The contribution of the industry shock ranges from approximately 5% to 9%. The contribution of the province shocks range from less than 1% to 2.5%. The idiosyncratic shocks account for 1.5% to 2% of the variance. The combination of industry-specific, province-specific, and the combined province-industry-specific shocks account for 7% to 12% of the steady-state variance in Canadian employment growth. Thus while the sectoral shocks account for only a small portion of the variation in national employment growth, they account for a significantly higher fraction of the variation due to Canadian sources.

V. Structural Shift in the Variance of Aggregate Employment Growth

Most economists would agree that the aggregate economy demonstrated greater instability in the 1970s and the early 1980s than in the 1960s. An important issue is the source of this greater instability. In this section we present the results of a preliminary investigation of the causes of structural shift in the variance of aggregate economic activity.

We focus on the variance of aggregate Canadian employment growth over this period. We examine the contribution of the U.S. shocks, the national shock, industrial shocks, provincial shocks, and the combined province-industry specific (idiosyncratic) shocks to the steady-state variance of employment growth in the subperiods 1963−70 and 1972−82. We assume that the regression coefficients in equation (8−25), the U.S. autoregressive parameters in equation (8−28), and the response coefficients f and g in equations (8−27a−d) are constant across the subperiods, but allow the

Table 8–8. Investigating Structural Shift in the Steady-State Variance of Aggregate Employment Growth (Full Model Estimates)

Sample Period	$V(Y_{ct})$	Percentage Contribution of					
		U.S. Shocks	National Shocks	Industry Shocks	Province Shocks	Idiosyncratic Shocks	All Sectoral Shocks[e]
1.[a]							
1963–1970	0.557×10^{-3}	68.2	22.6	1.2	3.0	4.9	9.1
1972–1982	1.2023×10^{-3}	61.2	26.7	8.5	2.2	1.1	11.8
2.[b]							
1963–1970	0.568×10^{-3}	68.8	23.3	1.3	1.8	4.7	7.8
1972–1982	1.224×10^{-3}	60.1	30.0	7.2	1.4	1.2	9.8
3.[c]							
1963–1970	0.529×10^{-3}	74.0	24.5	-2.1	-1.6	5.2	1.5
1972–1982	1.158×10^{-3}	63.5	27.8	8.6	-0.9	0.9	8.6
4.[d]							
1963–1970	0.532×10^{-3}	73.6	24.8	-2.1	-1.4	5.0	1.5
1972–1980	1.193×10^{-3}	61.7	80.8	7.4	-0.5	0.7	7.2

[a]Full sample estimates of $\underline{f}$ and $\underline{g}$ used. Negative variance estimates set to 0.
[b]Parameters $\underline{f}$ and $\underline{g}$ reestimated. Negative variance estimates set to 0.
[c]Full sample estimates of $\underline{f}$ and $\underline{g}$ used. Negative variance estimates *not* set to 0.
[d]Parameters $\underline{f}$ and $\underline{g}$ reestimated. Negative variance estimates *not* set to 0.
[e]Sum of the contribution of industry, province, and idiosyncratic shocks.

variance terms σ^2_{US}, σ^2_c, as well as the industry, province, and idiosyncratic variances, to differ across the periods. We use two approaches in re-estimating the model. In each approach we use the full sample regression coefficients and the full sample estimates of the U.S. autoregressive parameters, and estimate σ^2_{US} for the two sample periods. In the first approach we fix $\underline{f}$ and $\underline{g}$ at the full sample parameter estimates and then calculate separate estimates of the (non-U.S.) variance parameters for the subperiods. In the second approach, we re-estimate $\underline{f}$ and $\underline{g}$ and the period-specific variance parameters jointly. Here we allow the variances to differ in the subperiods but constrain the response coefficients $\underline{f}$ and $\underline{g}$ to be constant over the subperiods. Given parameter estimates from each of these approaches, we calculate an estimate of the steady-state variance in national employment growth for the two subperiods, and the percentage contribution to this variance of U.S. shocks, a national Canadian shock, provincial shocks, industrial shocks, and idiosyncratic province-industry specific shocks.

It is important to note that each of these approaches places stringent demands on the available data. For example, in the 1963–70 period we estimate a fairly rich factor model from covariances based on eight annual observations. As we note below, there is evidence that this model is, in fact, too rich for the available data. Thus we also consider a simpler model.

In panel 1 of table 8–8 we report the results of the variance decomposition when the loading factors $\underline{f}$ and $\underline{g}$ take on their full sample point estimates.[14] As in our earlier work, in calculating the variance decompositions we have set negative point estimates of the variances to zero. In panel 2 of the table we present the variance decomposition results when $\underline{f}$ and $\underline{g}$ are re-estimated under the assumption that each vector is constant over the two periods. There is remarkably little difference in the results produced by the two procedures, and thus we focus on the results in panel 1.

These results indicate that the variance in national employment growth doubled in the second period. Further, the relative contribution of the U.S. shock, the idiosyncratic shocks, and perhaps the provincial shock appear to have diminished in the 1970s while the relative contribution of the national and industrial shocks appear to have increased during this period. However, it is important to note that the absolute level of the contribution to steady-state variance increased substantially for all of the sources of variance except the idiosyncratic shocks.

There are two reasons for exercising considerable caution when examining the results in panels 1 and 2 of the table. First, standard errors are not available for the contributions to the steady-state variance, and the changes in the respective contributions in the two periods may not be large relative to

Table 8–9. Investigating Structural Shift in the Steady-State Variance of Aggregate Employment Growth (No Provincial Shocks)

Sample Period	$V(Y_{ct})$	Percentage Contribution of					
		U.S. Shocks	National Shocks	Industry Shocks	Province Shocks	Idiosyncratic Shocks	All Sectoral Shocks[e]
1.[a]							
1963–1970	0.545×10^{-3}	71.7	22.3	1.4	---	4.5	5.9
1972–1982	1.197×10^{-3}	61.5	28.5	8.4	---	1.5	9.9
2.[b]							
1963–1970	$.544 \times 10^{-3}$	71.8	22.2	1.5	---	4.5	6.0
1972–1982	1.213×10^{-3}	60.7	32.2	6.7	---	0.4	7.1
3.[c]							
1963–1970	0.531×10^{-3}	73.7	23.0	-1.2	---	4.6	3.4
1972–1982	1.182×10^{-3}	62.3	28.9	8.3	---	0.4	8.7
4.[d]							
1963–1970	0.529×10^{-3}	73.9	22.8	-1.3	---	4.6	3.3
1972–1982	1.213×10^{-3}	60.7	32.2	6.7	---	0.4	7.1

[a]Full sample estimates of $\underline{f}$ used. Negative variance estimates set to 0.
[b]Parameters $\underline{f}$ reestimated. Negative variance estimates set to 0.
[c]Full sample estimates of $\underline{f}$ used. Negative variance estimates *not* set to 0.
[d]Parameters $\underline{f}$ reestimated. Negative variance estimates *not* set to 0.
[e]Sum of the contribution of industry and idiosyncratic shocks.

sampling error. Second, in each approach approximately 30% of the point estimates of the (non-idiosyncratic) variance parameters are negative. Moreover, in contrast to the variance decompositions over the full sample, we find that *not* setting these variables to zero in the variance decompositions can affect somewhat the interpretation of the contributions, particularly the total contribution of sectoral shocks reported in the last column of the table (see panels 3 and 4).

Since these problems may indicate that a model with national, industry, and provincial shocks is too complex for estimation on the subperiods, we repeated our calculations for a model that excludes provincial shocks. Thus, the provincial variances equal zero and g drops out of the model. These results are reported in table 8−9, where each panel corresponds to the respective panel in table 8−8.[15] The results in table 8−9 are very similar to those in table 8−8 discussed above. However, we must note that again approximately 30% of our point estimates of the variance parameters were negative.

Thus the results in tables 8−8 and 8−9 must be considered preliminary.[16] However, these results indicate that increases in the variances of all shocks except the idiosyncratic ones lead to the greater instability of aggregate Canadian employment growth in the 1970s and 1980s.

VI. A Review of Evidence on Sectoral Shifts and the Reallocation Hypothesis

The above analysis indicates that sectoral shocks play only a modest role in fluctuations in employment growth in Canada via what we have called the collective impact mechanism. However, we wish to emphasize that our results do not rule out the possibility that sectoral shocks play a substantial role in employment fluctuations through the reallocation mechanism. Our findings, while preliminary, indicate that the direct effect of the average value of the sectoral shocks (weighted by the size of the specific sectors) has only a modest variance relative to the variance in aggregate employment growth. However, in the reallocation hypothesis, Lilien is concerned with the effect of fluctuations in the *variance* of sectoral shocks rather than fluctuations in the *average* of the sectoral shocks that occur in a particular time period. In fact, Lilien assumes explicitly that the average of the sectoral shocks is zero in every period. In our analysis the variance of the average of the sectoral shocks is not zero and is an increasing function of the variances of the individual shocks.

Several recent studies have examined the reallocation hypothesis, with mixed results. We briefly summarize the main methods and results rather than attempt a comprehensive survey, since research on the reallocation hypothesis is very active and appears to be in a state of flux. Readers are also referred to the survey in Lilien and Hall [1984, pp. 61–71].

Lilien [1982a] proxies the variance in sectoral shifts by constructing the employment growth dispersion measure σ_t. This dispersion index is defined as the square root of the weighted sum of squared deviations of industry growth in employment from aggregate employment growth. The reallocation hypothesis suggests that an increase in the dispersion in employment demand should increase layoffs, holding total accessions constant. Lilien finds that a measure of σ_t constructed from data for 21 manufacturing industries has a strong positive effect on the layoff rate in manufacturing even after one controls for the quit rate and the aggregate change in manufacturing employment.

Lilien [1982a] also finds that current and lagged values of a measure of σ_t, constructed from employment growth in 11 one-digit industries, has a positive relationship to the unemployment rate even after one controls for aggregate demand fluctuations as proxied by a distributed lag on Barro's unanticipated money growth variable. Taken at face value, Lilien's results are impressive in that they indicate that shifts in the natural rate associated with σ_t account for 36% of the variance in the detrended unemployment rate. The relationship is much stronger during the 1970s than during the '60s. This is consistent with casual evidence that structural shifts were more important during the 1970s, although our findings for Canada indicate that the variability in sectoral shocks rose by only a modest amount *relative* to the variance in aggregate and external shocks.

However, Lilien [1982b] noted that the dispersion measure σ_t will be correlated with *aggregate* shocks affecting all industries if the responses to such shocks are industry specific, as in the model we present above. Although Lilien [1982b, p. 22] does not take a stand on the impact that this would have on his earlier findings, Abraham and Katz [1985] show that under plausible assumptions aggregate shocks (not controlled for by un-anticipated money growth) will induce a positive correlation between σ_t and the unemployment rate. This calls Lilien's initial findings into question.

The subsequent evidence in Lilien [1982b] and Abraham and Katz [1985] is mixed on whether Lilien's initial results are due to a spurious correlation between σ_t and some aggregate shock. Lilien approaches the issue directly by repeating his earlier analysis but with an alternative dispersion level, SIG_t. This variable is based upon the residuals of a model for industry employment growth that controls for the effects of aggregate shocks with time effects for each year and a distributed lag of unanticipated money growth. (Lilien disaggregates by industry, and the time effects are equivalent to the national shock c_t with coefficient vector f in (8−24b).) He finds that a distributed lag of SIG_t has a strong positive effect on the unemployment rate in a regression that also includes a trend and a distributed lag of unanticipated money shocks. These results basically confirm the findings of his first study. It is worth noting, however, that Lilien's model (see his equation 24) implies that he should have also included the estimates (that depend on his estimated time effects as well as unanticipated money) of the aggregate shock (D_t in his notation) and its square as additional regressors in the unemployment equation. It is possible that (1) unanticipated money growth, and the other controls that Lilien reported trying, do not adequately control for D_t, and that (2) the level and/or square of D_t happens to be correlated with the estimates of SIG_t. In this case, some bias might remain, although we do not have any evidence that this problem is important. Note, however, that our results in section V suggest that in Canada, *both* aggregate shocks and sectoral shocks had higher variance during the 1970s and early 1980s than during the 1960s.

Abraham and Katz argue that an increase in sectoral shifts should be accompanied by higher vacancy levels (an outward shift in the Beverage curve), while aggregate demand shocks would have a negative effect on vacancy rates. They find that Lilien's σ_t is negatively related to the Help Wanted index for the United States (controlling for unanticipated money growth). They also obtain a negative relationship between a measure of σ_t for the British economy and a British series on job vacancies that is less subject to criticism than the Help Wanted index. Finally, they find that the sectoral dispersion measure SIG_t constructed by Lilien [1982b] is also negatively related to the Help Wanted index. Abraham and Katz provide some speculation on why SIG_t might be correlated with aggregate demand, and conclude that neither Lilien's analysis using σ_t nor the analysis using SIG_t provide "... a firm basis for establishing that sectoral shifts have been an important source of cyclical fluctuations in unemployment" (p. 19). Lilien and Hall [1984] are more positive in their assessment of the evidence.

Two additional studies deserve mention. Medoff [1983] identifies sectoral shifts with geographical changes in labor demand. He presents evidence that is loosely consistent with Lilien's [1982a] analysis of industry shifts. He also presents evidence suggesting that the Beverage curve has shifted out over time. This finding would be consistent with the reallocation hypothesis, but may also be related to other factors which have caused the short-run Phillips curve to shift. Medoff also finds that a weighted sum of squared *state* employment growth rates (not the squared deviations from the national employment growth rate) has a positive association with the Help Wanted index. He also finds that the weighted sum of squared *industry* employment growth rates has a positive association with the Help Wanted index. However, these results are not necessarily inconsistent with Abraham and Katz's finding of a negative association between the Help Wanted index and both σ_t and SIG_t, since Medoff's dispersion measure is different from the ones used by Lilien and Abraham and Katz. Moreover, Medoff controls for the prime age male unemployment rate while these other studies do not. Medoff also finds a negative link between dispersion in growth rates and labor productivity. This result is consistent with the reallocation hypothesis. Overall, his research supports a role for reallocation in an outward shift of the short run Phillips curve during the 1970s.

Finally, Neelin [1985] has recently analyzed the reallocation hypothesis for Canada. First, she finds an insignificant relationship between the Help Wanted index and measures of σ_t for Canada calculated on an industry, region, and combined industry-region basis. Thus, she obtains ambiguous results when using Abraham and Katz' check on Lilien's [1982a] procedure. Second, Neelin decomposes the variance in sectoral shifts into a component induced by past deviations of GNP from trend and a component induced by shocks to employment in each sector that are orthogonal to the lagged GNP variable. She finds that after controlling for eight lags of the unemployment rate and the current and lagged values of various proxies for aggregate demand shifts, all of the link between σ_t and unemployment is due to the component of σ_t induced by GNP rather than the dispersion component induced by sectoral shocks, when σ_t is computed on an industry or combined industry-region basis. When σ_t is computed by regions, the component of σ which is exogenous with respect to GNP has a small effect. Overall Neelin's results for Canada point to a much smaller role for the reallocation hypothesis in unemployment fluctuations than that suggested by Lilien's results for the United States.

Clearly, the current evidence on the reallocation mechanism is mixed. As is the case with the collective impact hypothesis, further research is required before any firm conclusions may be drawn.

VII. Concluding Remarks

In this chapter we analyze two mechanisms through which disaggregate shocks affecting specific sectors of the economy may induce aggregate fluctuations. The first, which we call the collective impact hypothesis, simply acknowledges that aggregate employment may reflect fluctuations in an appropriately weighted average of the disaggregate shocks. We develop a disaggregate model of employment in which sectoral shocks enter through product demand, labor demand, and labor supply. The theoretical model provides a foundation for the econometric time series model that we have used in our research on the contribution of disaggregate shocks to aggregate fluctuations. However, it is oversimplified in a number of respects and hopefully can be improved upon in future research. An interesting avenue for future research would be to introduce nonlinearities into the model that would permit shifts in the variance parameters of the sectoral shocks to affect the expected value of the growth in the log of aggregate employment, as suggested by the reallocation hypothesis. In our model the variances in the sectoral shocks affect only the variance of aggregate employment. Unfortunately, this represents a difficult task, and such a nonlinear model will raise further econometric problems.

The empirical analysis of the collective impact hypothesis indicates that industry-specific and province-industry specific shocks account for 7% to 12% of the variation in Canadian employment growth over the period 1961-82. U.S. shocks and aggregate Canadian shocks account for 62% to 67% and 24% to 28% of the variance, respectively. Thus, our results suggest that sectoral shocks play only a modest role in aggregate fluctuations in employment, although they play a more important role in terms of variation due to Canadian sources.

We also find a large increase between the 1960s and the 1970s in the contribution of sectoral shocks to aggregate employment fluctuations, although in absolute terms the contributions of the United States and the national Canadian shock also more than double. While the relative importance of sectoral shocks appears to have increased, the greater variability of output during the 1970s and early 1980s appears to be due primarily to aggregate sources. However, these estimates should be treated very cautiously, since the model estimates used to compute the variance decompositions for the subperiods are far from satisfactory.

Although the collective impact hypothesis has received little attention in the literature, a number of recent studies have examined the importance of the hypothesis that changes in the variance of sectoral shocks induce changes in employment because of the time and resources lost as labor adjusts in response to the changing composition of demand. This "reallocation" mechanism and the collective impact mechanism are not mutually exclusive, although no existing study (including our own) allows for both in a single model. The results of existing studies of the reallocation mechanism are mixed, and it is too early for strong conclusions to be drawn about it.

Notes

1. We learned of Tobin's paper from Lilien [1982b], who also uses this quote. Note that Tobin, in his American Economic Association presidential address, states, "The myth of macroeconomics is that relations among aggregates are enlarged analogues of relations among corresponding variables for individuals, households, firms, industries, markets. The myth is a harmless and useful simplification in many contexts, but sometimes it misses the essence of the phenomenon." [Tobin, 1972, p. 9]. Tobin presents a view of the natural rate of unemployment that is similar to Lilien's, aside from an assumption that sectoral wages adjust more slowly to excess supply than to excess demand. However, Tobin does not emphasize fluctuations in the natural rate that might result from changes in the variance of sectoral shocks.

2. The recent study by Blanchard and Watson [1984] is one of a number of studies that suggests that *aggregate* shocks arise from a number of sources.

3. In aggregating various determinants of aggregate demand into one index that enters the equation for D_{pit} with a sector-specific coefficient, we are implicitly assuming that differences across sectors in the response of D_{pit} to the components of aggregate demand are the same for all components. For example, the assumption implies that the ratio of the response of the demand for manufacturing products from a given region to a change in the money supply and to a change in military expenditure changes is the same for all regions. This is a strong assumption.

4. The product price does not appear in equation (8−1a) because D_{pit} indexes changes in the position of the product demand curve rather than product demand itself. We substitute D_{pit} directly into the condition which determines labor demand, so that the product price does not appear there either.

5. Fischer assumes that employment is demand determined, in which case the parameters $\mu_{pi}^s = 0$ for all p, i.

6. We allow the variance of industry shocks η_{it} to differ by industry and the variance of idiosyncratic shocks μ_{pit} to differ by industry-province pair.

7. It is also necessary to normalize the $\underline{f}$ and $\underline{g}$ vectors. One possible normalization is $f_1 = 1$ and $g_1 = 1$.

8. We also experimented with a province specific constant in equation (8−25), but this did not change the results.

9. Given that $PI = 63$ in our work and $T = 20$, it is not possible to leave π as an unrestricted matrix to be determined by the data.

10. The explicit expressions are quite lengthy and are omitted to save space. These expressions are given in Altonji and Ham [1985].

11. The model that we estimate falls into the general class of index models discussed in Engle and Watson [1981]. Models in this class incorporate direct feedback from past values of the observed variables to the current values as well as serial correlation in the unobserved variables that drive the system. See Altonji and Ham [1985] for a discussion of other possible approaches to assessing the importance of sectoral shocks, including the use of multiregional structural econometric models of the type surveyed in Bolton [1980], and vector autoregressive models.

12. It is not possible to obtain a finer industrial classification when also disaggregating by region.

13. For the sample used in section V, 3 of the 17 point estimates of the variances were negative, although none of these was significantly different from zero.

14. All of the estimates in tables 8−8 and 8−9 are based on the residuals when OLS is used to estimate equation (8−25) and data on Newfoundland are excluded. We carried out some

limited experiments with other sets of residuals, and our results did not change.

15. The model excluding provincial shocks was estimated on the full sample period 1963–82. The resulting parameter estimates for f were used to calculate the results in panels 1 and 3 of table 8–9.

16. In future work it would be interesting to investigate the structural shift issue using parameter estimates based on quarterly or monthly data. Using a finer degree of time aggregation would allow the data to be more informative in each of the subperiods, although it would also complicate the estimation considerably.

References

Abraham, Katherine, and Lawrence Katz. 1985. "Cyclical Unemployment: Sectoral Shifts or Aggregate Disturbances?" Cambridge, MA: The Sloan School, Massachusetts Institute of Technology (revised June).

Alchian, Armen. 1970. "Information Costs, Pricing, and Resource Unemployment." In E.S. Phelps (ed.), *Microeconomic Foundations of Employment and Inflation Theory*. New York: Norton.

Altonji, Joseph, and John Ham. 1985. "Variation in Employment Growth in Canada: The Role of External, National, Regional and Industrial Factors." Princeton NJ: Industrial Relations Section, Princeton University, Working Paper No 201 (November).

Archibald, G.C. 1970. "The Structure of Excess Demand for Labor." In E.S. Phelps (ed.), *Microeconomic Foundations of Employment and Inflation Theory*, New York; Norton.

Barro, Robert. 1977. "Unanticipated Money Growth and Unemployment in the United States." *American Economic Review* 67 (March): 101–115.

———. 1977. "Unanticipated Money, Output, and the Price Level in the United States." *Journal of Political Economy* 86 (August): 549–580.

Blanchard, Olivier, and Mark Watson. 1984. "Are Business Cycles All Alike?" Cambridge, MA: National Bureau of Economic Research, Working Paper No. 1392 (June).

Bolton, Roger. 1980. "Multiregional Models: Introduction to a Symposium." *Journal of Regional Science* 20 (May): 131–142.

Burns, Arthur, and Wesley Mitchell. 1946. *Measuring Business Cycles*. New York: National Bureau of Economic Research.

Fischer, Stanley. 1977. "Long-Term Contracts, Rational Expectations, and the Optimal Money Supply Literature." *Journal of Political Economy* 85 (February): 191–205.

Lawrence, Colin, and Aloysius Siow. 1985. "Interest Rates and Investment Spending: Some Empirical Evidence for Post-War Producer Equipment." *Journal of Business* (forthcoming).

Lilien, David. 1982a. "Sectoral Shifts and Cyclical Unemployment." *Journal of Political Economy* 90 (August): 777–793.

———. 1982b. "A Sectoral Model of the Business Cycle." MRG Working

Paper No. 8231, Los Angeles, CA: Department of Economics, University of
Southern California. (December).

——————— and Robert Hall. 1984. "Cyclical Fluctuations in the Labor Market." In
O. Ashenfelter and R. Layard (eds.), *The Handbook of Labor Economics.*
Amsterdam: North Holland (forthcoming).

Lipsey, Richard, 1960. "The Relation between Unemployment and the Rate of
Change of Money Wages in the United Kingdom, 1862–1957: A Further
Analysis." *Economica* 27 (February): 1–41.

Litterman, Robert, and Lawrence Weiss. 1985. "Money, Real Interest Rates and
Output: A Reinterpretation of Postwar U.S. Data." *Econometrica* 53 (January):
129–156.

Lehmann, Bruce. "What Happens during Business Cycles?" New York: Graduate
School of Business, Columbia University (October). Mimeo.

Long, John, and Charles Plosser. 1983. "Real Business Cycles." *Journal of Political
Economy* 91 (February): 39–69.

Lucas, Robert E., Jr. 1972. "Expectations and the Neutrality of Money." *Journal of
Economic Theory* 4 (April): 103–124.

——————— . 1977. "Understanding Business Cycles." In K. Brunner and A. Meltzer
(eds.), *Stabilization of the Domestic and International Economy.* Carnegie-
Rochester Conference on Public Policy, vol. 5. Amsterdam: North Holland.

——————— and Edward Prescott. 1974. "Equilibrium Search and Unemployment."
Journal of Economic Theory 7 (February): 188–204.

Medoff, James. 1983. "U.S. Labor Markets: Imbalance, Wage Growth, and
Productivity in the 1970s." *Brookings Papers on Economic Activity* 1: 87–128.

Mitchell, Wesley Claire. 1951. *What Happens During Business Cycles: A Progress
Report.* New York; National Bureau of Economic Research.

Miskin, Fredrick, 1983. *A Rational Expectations Approach to Macroeconomics:
Testing Policy Ineffectiveness and Efficient Market Models.* Chicago, IL: University of Chicago Press.

Neelin, Janet. 1985. "Canadian Unemployment and Sectoral Shifts." Princeton, NJ:
Industrial Relations Section. Princeton University (September). Mimeo.

Phelps, Edmund S. 1970. "Introduction: The New Microeconomics in Employment
and Inflation Theory." In E.S. Phelps (ed.), *Microeconomic Foundations of
Employment and Inflation Theory.* New York: Norton.

——————— and John Taylor. 1977. "Stabilizing Powers of Monetary Policy under
Rational Expectations." *Journal of Political Economy* 85 (February): 163–190.

Sargent, Thomas J. 1976. "A Classical Macroeconomic Model for the United
States." *Journal of Political Economy* 84 (April): 207–237.

Sims, Christopher A. 1972. "Money, Income and Causality." *American Economic
Review* 62 (September): 540–552.

— ——————. 1980. "Macroeconomics and Reality." *Econometrica* 48 (January):
1–48.

Tobin, James. 1971. "Introduction" in *Essays in Economics, Vol. 1, Macroeconomics*,
Chicago: Morkam.

Tobin, James. 1972. "Inflation and Unemployment." *American Economic Review* 62 (March): 1–18.
Topel, Robert. 1986. "Local Labor Markets." *Journal of Political Economy* 94 (June): S111–S143.
Watson, Mark, and Robert Engle. 1982. "The EM Algorithm for Dynamic Factor and MIMIC Models." Economics Department Working Paper 82–6. San Diego, CA: Department of Economics, University of California.

IV COMPENSATION OF DISPLACED WORKERS

9   JOB SECURITY VERSUS INCOME SECURITY

G. C. Archibald and Peter T. Chinloy

I. Introduction

. . . the effects of unemployment insurance are typically measured by regressing the unemployment rate on some measure of unemployment benefits, together with whatever set of control variables yields a believable coefficient on the variable measuring unemployment benefits. Review of the results of various studies reveals that different sets of control variables yield sometimes markedly disparate estimates of the effect of unemployment insurance. Hence, the results obtained are suspect.

This highlights the need for a theory of the effect of unemployment insurance which is built up on microfoundations, since the rigorous use of consumer theory in constructing the model to be estimated imposes discipline on the choice of variables to be included as controls.—W.E. Diewert, in H.G. Grubel and M.A. Walker (eds.), Unemployment Insurance: Global Effects of its Effects on Unemployment, Vancouver, B.C.: Fraser Institute, 1976, p. 89.

The theme of this series of chapters is how labor markets adjust to shifts in competitiveness and external shocks. This chapter examines some stylized

Research assistance from Dexter Chu and Susan Ghan is acknowledged. We are grateful to the Social Sciences and Humanities Research Council of Canada for research funding under grant 464−84−0033. We are particularly grateful to Ben Craig, Kazuo Koike, Daniel Hamermesh, Masanori Hashimoto, Diana Hancock, and Carl Mosk for their comments.

facts on the behavior of employment, labor force participation, and the cost of hiring and retaining workers during 1964–82 for the United States, Canada, Japan, Germany, and the United Kingdom.

Two general conclusions arise from these cross-country data. First, the United States and Canada have been relatively successful in absorbing into employment the large postwar baby boom cohort. The labor force participation rate of young men and women increases, as does the employment rate. The reverse appears to be the case in Germany and the United Kingdom.[1] In Japan, while the unemployment rate for young workers remains stable, their participation rate decreases. Second, the United States and Canada have experienced growth in total employment during the period, while in Germany, the United Kingdom, and Japan, total employment has remained stagnant or declined.

It is our contention that these observations are associated with the degree of flexibility in labor market institutions. This is not to suggest a monocausal explanation, as employment and participation are affected by aggregate economic policy, international shocks, and other institutional factors. Yet, the institutions of labor markets can affect the level of employment. The working hypothesis is "easy to fire, easy to hire." The higher the costs of creating a job, arising through longer job tenure or severance payments, the less willing is the employer to hire workers. Where there are barriers to increasing or decreasing the size of the work force, new hires cannot easily be absorbed. This flexibility is not entirely exogenous, but is a part of the response to workers' preferences. Workers derive utility not just from income but also from the security of income. If this security is not universally provided, demands are placed on the firm for job protection and employment guarantees.

Markets for labor, as for other services, operate more efficiently if the transactions costs of altering the level of employment are reduced. Where the firm is required to provide all security, barriers to hiring and firing arise. Barriers include layoff restrictions, seniority rules on promotion, and recall rights. Transaction costs for the firm associated with hiring and firing can be reduced by income-support programs, suggesting that their socially optimal level is nonzero.[2]

Differentiable labor demand functions may not be obtainable because of discontinuities in the demand function for labor for the firm. Aggregation over firms, where the relevant conditions are satisfied, can produce continuously differentiable demand functions.[3] Data at the level of the industry, region or economy, are likely to produce estimates that differ from those we should obtain at the firm level. Estimates derived under conventional maximization conditions must be interpreted cautiously.[4] For this reason, the empirical focus of this chapter is on qualitative properties of the data rather than on estimation of demand functions.

In section II, a theory of the labor market is developed. On the supply side, the worker maximizes utility, dependent on the level of income and the security of its gain. Security is provided by income from either more stable employment or income support. As income support increases, workers are more willing to accept lower job security from the employer.

Two cases on the demand side for labor are distinguished. In the completely flexible case, the firm determines the current employment level from the current wage, prices per unit of other inputs and outputs, levels of fixed goods, and technology. In the completely rigid case, the firm is unresponsive to the current wage, viewing labor as a fixed or quasi-fixed factor. These polar cases are easily defined, but less so are intermediate situations in which a firm varies employment less than it would in the completely flexible case, but obviously more than it would in the rigid case.

In section III, we examine the qualitative implications of the model. On quantities, an international comparison of the behavior of employment, labor force participation, and unemployment is carried out for men and women aged 16−24 and 25−64.

On prices, when workers constitute a fixed or quasi-fixed factor of production, the current wage is not the appropriate price per hour hired. What is required is the price of the services delivered per hour by a potential long-term employee. This requires the construction of a user cost of labor. We define the user cost of labor as the price of renting the services of one hour of a worker's time. The user cost depends on the length of tenure, the opportunity cost of the capital investment made by the firm in the employee, and the asset price of labor.

The asset price of labor is defined as the price that purchases the career services of one worker per hour. It is the present value of the sequence of wage payments per hour over the career. It depends on length of tenure, the wage sequence, and the discount rate used to capitalize the stream of future costs. The user cost and asset price differ in that the former is the price of the services per hour of a worker, and the latter is the price of adding one worker. The user cost and asset price include both wage and benefit payments while on the job, and any requirement to make payments on separation or termination. Their construction requires details on the institutions covering hiring and firing.

An explicit part of the argument for removal of institutions such as unemployment insurance, job training, and welfare is that their absence would encourage greater flexibility of work arrangements and increase employment. Given that security provides utility to workers, if it is not provided through income support while unemployed, then the demand for it will be expressed in arrangements between employees and employers.

Removing unemployment insurance coverage or increasing experience rating is likely to reduce hiring and mobility, making markets less, rather than more, flexible. Reduction in public pensions, such as Social Security in the United States, increases the pressure on the individual employer to provide security. The consequence is more rigidity of employment.

With security provided by general institutions, the user cost of adding one hour to time worked for an existing employee is equal to that for the first hour of a new employee. The elasticity of output with respect to hours worked and employment are equal. Firms are more willing to hire secondary or high risk workers if it is easier to discharge them, and the workers themselves have more opportunity to search for a career on the job.

With security provided by the firm, the user cost of adding one hour to time worked for an existing employee is lower than that for the first hour of a new employee. If a production function can be estimated, the elasticity of output with respect to hours exceeds that with respect to employment.[5] The response to a shift in demand is not necessarily to absorb secondary workers, given the possibility of a long-term tenured obligation. Employers must resort to increased screening for the rationed job slots, involving extensive and possibly wasteful investment in education and training.

The above does not pretend to cover the issues raised by the public provision of income security. There are costs associated with such programs. These include the subsidization of time spent outside of employment, incentives to remain in or move to regions of high unemployment if benefits vary regionally, and the tendency for seasonal industries to lay workers off during a predictable slowdown. These would be included in a complete cost-benefit analysis of unemployment insurance.

Where unemployment insurance is paid on predictable phenomena, such as seasonal shutdowns, cross-subsidization from other industries is not easily defensible. What our arguments suggest is that a general trend to experience rating can ossify the labor market.

There are benefits from rigid markets. These include an incentive for workers to accept specific training, and potentially less unproductive rivalry if promotion is based on seniority. Yet quality of life surveys show that countries with relatively flexible labor markets, such as Canada, have the most satisfied workers, and countries with rigid markets such as Japan the least.[6] Our results may provide an explanation for this observation.

II. Labor Markets and Security

A. Labor Supply, Income, and Job Security

Let the degree of security, or probability of continued employment, be q. If $q = 1$, the employer provides employment regardless of the state of demand, reflected by the price of output. If $q < 1$, there is no security of employment. Depending on the price of output, the worker can be laid off, whereupon unemployment compensation at level X is paid. If employed, the wage is W. The security level q can also be a function of the price of output. A value of q less than unity is the probability of employment given a realization of the state of demand.

Each worker has a state-independent von Neumann-Morgenstern utility function, and seeks to maximize expected utility where:

$$E(U) = qU(W) + (1-q)U(X). \qquad (9-1)$$

This depends on the degree of security provided by the firm q, the form of the utility function, the wage W, and the level of jobless payments X. The utility function is monotone increasing, strictly quasi-concave, and twice differentiable. Jobs are offered in a package of wage and hours, with hours worked fixed, so there is no wage-hour substitution by workers. If a worker is guaranteed employment, q is unity regardless of the outcome of demand for output[7]. While the model is based on a one-period case, the same qualitative implications apply to a multi-period case. In a multiperiod context, for period t, the contribution to the maximand is $z(t) = q(t)U(W(t)) + (1-q(t))U(X(t))$. The individual maximizes $\int_{t=h}^{T+h} a(t)z(t)dt$, where $a(t)$ is a discount factor, h is hiring date, and T is length of tenure.

Total differentiation of $(q - 1)$ yields, at $U = \bar{U}$, with U' being the first derivative of U in its argument,

$$qU'(W)dW + U(W)dq + U'(X)dX - qU'(X)dX - U(X)dq = 0 \qquad (9-2)$$

whereupon the slope of the level surface in $W-q$ space is

$$dW/dq_{(U=\bar{U})} = -[U(W) - U(X)]/qU'(W) \equiv r(W, X, q) < 0. \qquad (9-3)$$

This is the worker's marginal rate of substitution between wages and security. Further, by rearranging (9-2),

$$dq/dX_{(U=\bar{U}, W=\bar{W})} = -(1-q)U'(X)/(U(U(W) - U(X)) < 0. \qquad (9-4)$$

The worker is willing to accept, given the level of utility $U = \bar{U}$, a lower level of security if jobless payments X are increased. Income security can be used to purchase less job security, wages constant. Also,

$$dW/dX_{(U=\bar{U},q=\bar{q})} = -(1-q)U'(X)/qU'(W) < 0, \qquad (9-5)$$

and the worker will accept a lower wage if income security is increased. The extent of the reduction depends on the level of security, the curvature of the utility function, and the level of wage and income support.

The first inequality (9–4) is the one we exploit. To maintain utility constant, a worker accepts a lower level of job security if unemployment compensation is exogenously increased. The worker accepts a lower wage, or together, some lower combination of q and W. To examine how the acceptable combination varies with X, we investigate the marginal rate of substitution between q and W. Workers reduce their demand for job security as income security increases. The form of the utility function determines the tradeoff between wages and security that workers accept. Attacks on general security programs appear to assume that the natural state of the labor market is spot with completely flexible demand and supply functions. This need not be the case, and the likely consequence of an increase in income security is more rather than less flexibility.

The comparative statics of the wage-security tradeoff can be examined in W, X, and q. Totally differentiating $r(W,X,q)$,

$$dr = (\partial r/\partial W)dW + (\partial r/\partial X)dX + (\partial r/\partial q)dq \qquad (9-6)$$

and

$$dr/dW = \partial r/\partial W + (\partial r/\partial X)dX/dW + (\partial r/\partial q)dq/dW.$$

Jobless payments X are exogenous, so when considering worker's preferences, $dX/dW = 0$. Also $dq/dW = 1/r$, so

$$dr/dW = \partial r/\partial W + (\partial r/\partial q)r. \qquad (9-7)$$

The response of r to a change in the wage W is:

$$\partial r/\partial W = -\{q[U'(W)]^2 - [U(W) - U(X)]qU''(W)\}/[qU'(W)]^2 \qquad (9-8)$$
$$= -1/q + rs < 0,$$

where $s(W) \equiv -U''(W)/U'(W) > 0$ is the coefficient of relative risk aversion. An increase in the wage reduces r, holding other factors constant. Since r is negative, this implies an increase in the absolute value of the slope in $W-q$ space. For a change in the security level

$$\partial r/\partial q = [U(W) - U(X)]/q^2 U'(W) \qquad (9-9)$$
$$= -r/q > 0.$$

Hence,

$$dr/dW = -2/q + rs < 0. \qquad (9-10)$$

An increase in wages causes r to steepen, for the total derivative. Higher wages cause a more inflexible tradeoff between wages and security.

For a change in security:

$$
\begin{aligned}
dr/dq &= (\partial r/\partial W)(dW/dq) + (\partial r/\partial X)(dX/dq) + \partial r/\partial q \\
&= (\partial r/\partial W)r + \partial r/\partial q \\
&= \{q[U'(W)]^2 - [U(W) - U(X)]qU''(W)\}[U(W) - U(X)]/ \\
&\quad [qU'(W)]^2 + [U(W) - U(X)]/q^2 U'(W) \\
&= r[-1/q + rs] - r/q \\
&= -2r/q + r^2 s > 0.
\end{aligned}
\qquad (9-11)
$$

The responses to changes in wages and security are related, since $dr/dq = rdr/dW$. Given that r is negative, the positive total derivative in equation $(9-11)$ implies that the slope of the marginal rate of substitution decreases in absolute value. Workers are more willing to trade between wages and security as security increases. A firm offering more secure employment is more able to obtain wage concessions.

Similar concessions can be obtained by increasing income security. Holding given the wage and job security,

$$
\partial r/\partial X = U'(X)/qU'(W) > 0. \qquad (9-12)
$$

As X increases, r decreases, and the tradeoff between wages and security becomes more flexible. An increase in jobless benefits, not experience rated, causes workers to accept a more flexible tradeoff between wages and job security. In either case, for increases in job security q and income security X, workers are more willing to substitute between wage and security. If the wage increases, but neither q nor X is changed, workers are less willing to substitute between wage and security. Job protection q and income support X are alternative methods of providing security.

Two issues regarding the provision of security are whether the worker is capable of providing self-insurance, and whether the wage includes a risk premium covering the security offered. On self-insurance, if there are complete contingent markets in the Arrow-Debreu sense, wages can be obtained for all states. Such contingent markets are non-existent, but there is a bond market where the worker can potentially lay off his or her risk, through saving.

Two problems affect the ability to use the bond market. First, there is asymmetric information between employer and employee. The employer has more knowledge on when the layoff is coming and how many are to be affected. Second, there are transaction costs, causing nonconvexities. In principle, riskier firms may pay a risk premium in the wage package. However, it cannot be assumed that the market will automatically generate the appropriate risk premiums unless there are observable characteristics of the firm used by underwriters in setting insurance premiums. Capital markets are less than uniformly successful in identifying these characteristics, and workers can hardly be expected to do better.

B. Labor demand and flexibility

The labor market is characterized by the offering of packages of wages and employment to workers. Some firms undertake to pay guaranteed wages regardless of the state of demand. These firms offer security with wage W and employment level $\bar{L}$, which we will call the fixed case. This is exemplified by working conditions in manufacturing in Western Europe, and may obtain for a sizeable minority of workers in the United States and Canada.[8] In Japan, while employment levels are fixed in large manufacturing firms, total compensation is flexible through the bonus system.

An alternative case is for the firm to offer a given wage, or to take it as given by the marketplace, but offer no security of employment. Suppose the wage is the same W as before. Intermediate arrangements between the two cases where some security of employment is given are also possible, although subject to monitoring difficulties. In intermediate cases, the employer undertakes to retain more workers than would otherwise obtain.

The firm's intertemporal maximization problem is complex. Future demand for output and prices is stochastic. Except where there is either no security or complete security, the firm can save current wages by offering more security than it would in the completely flexible case. This gives rise to a stochastic control problem that appears to be analytically intractable. For our purposes, we can adequately illustrate the properties of the variable profit function. We do this rather than adopt the devices made familiar in the implicit contract literature for several reasons. First, in that literature it is common to assume two states, Good and Bad. The firm undertakes not to lay off as many workers in the Bad state as it would in the completely flexible case. The fact that this will inhibit its hiring in the Good state is not discussed: it is implicitly assumed that it will not. This is inadmissible. Restrictions on layoffs imply restrictions on hiring. Second, the implicit contract is not incentive-compatible to the employer in the Bad state, and, given asymmetric information, unenforceable.[9] Given the problem of unenforceability and asymmetric information, the problem of the length of the fixed contract becomes crucial in the implicit contract model. The variable profit function is, however, sufficient for our purposes.

Capital is fixed in the short run at $\bar{K}$, as is the production function for output, $Y(\bar{K}, L)$. The maximum of variable profit, revenue less variable cost, given the production function, is the variable profit function π. The firm is assumed to be a price taker in the output market, with price P independent of the level of output. No qualitative results are altered by introducing an imperfectly competitive $P(Y)$ inverse demand function. The firm choosing the flexible combination of wage and security maximizes variable profit

$$\pi(W, \ P{:}\bar{K}) = \max_L \{PY(\bar{K},L) - WL\}. \qquad (9-13)$$

The variable profit function is increasing in the price of output, decreasing in the price of input, and quasi-convex in prices. It is linearly homogeneous in prices. For expository purposes, it is assumed that wages are relatively rigid and prices flexible. An initial undertaking to pay wage W is honored regardless of the price outcome P, which arises from the demand for output. The linear homogeneity in prices, with W/P entering the variable profit function, implies that which is flexible or fixed, price or wage, is relatively unimportant. Since K is fixed and W predetermined, employment responds only to the observed P, which is not necessarily known in advance. The demand for labor is

$$L = -\partial\pi(W,P{:}\bar{K})/\partial W. \qquad (9-14)$$

There are as yet no costs to altering the size of the work force.

If the firm offers a guarantee of employment, and the same wage W, variable profit is

$$\bar{\pi} = -W\bar{L} + PY(\bar{K},\bar{L}), \qquad (9-15)$$

where $\bar{L}$ is the number guaranteed employment. This relation is linear in π-P space, with slope the fixed output level $Y(\bar{K},\bar{L})$ and intercept $-W\bar{L}$. If firms offering fixed and flexible wage and security combinations paid the same wage W, prior to the realization of the price P, to which both are exposed, only at one point are profits from both strategies equal. This is where $L = \bar{L}$ and $\pi = \bar{\pi}$.

The flexible strategy dominates, and with competitive conditions, no firms would offer job guarantees. Workers are willing to trade off wages for increased security, which is provided by the firm in the fixed employment case. They would be willing to accept some wage $W_0 < W$ if employment were fixed. The wage remains fixed at W_0. The variable profit level for altering prices with guaranteed employment now shifts upward and to the left in π-P space, as is shown in figure $9-1$. The actual shift depends on the substitutability between wages and security, based on the labor supply, the degree of risk aversion of the worker, and the distribution of prices.

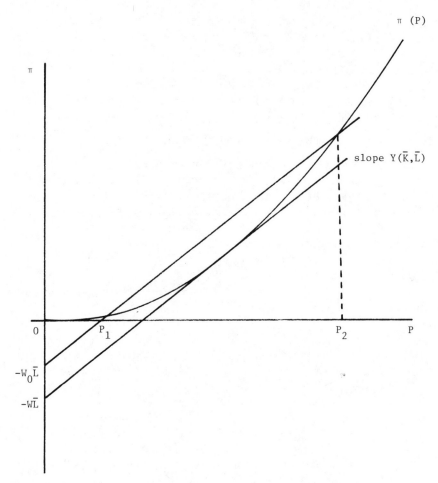

Figure 9–1.

Assume that P has support on an interval $[\underline{P}, \bar{P}]$, where $0 \le \underline{P} \le P_1 \le P_2 \le \bar{P} \le +\infty$. The three subintervals, with their implications for the level of variable profit, are as follows:

$$\begin{array}{ll} \underline{P} < P < P_1 & \bar{\pi} < \pi \\ P_1 \le P < P_2 & \bar{\pi} \ge \pi \\ P_2 \le P < \bar{P} & \bar{\pi} < \pi. \end{array} \qquad (9\text{–}16)$$

The shape of $\pi(P)$ and the tangency at $\bar{\pi}$, given the wage W, guarantees two intersections for $W_0 < W$. Since the measure of profit is variable profit, revenue less variable cost, or quasi-rents, these must be positive in the short run for the firm to operate. If total profit were being maximized, this could be negative in the short run (loss-minimization) if revenue fails to cover capital cost.

The frontier of variable profit is established by the inequalities in (9–16). For the first and third inequalities, flexible labor markets dominate, and inside the second inequality, the rigid arrangement, with employment at $\bar{L}$, dominates. An implicit contract, with a mixture of the two, presumably would produce variable profit inside the lens shape in figure 9–1. Expected variable profit depends on the density function of P. The supply model indicates that workers are willing to trade wages for security. Without this risk aversion, P_1 and P_2 cannot be obtained. One candidate for $\bar{W}$ is that needed to make $q = 0$ in the supply model. The firm extracts rent from the risk aversion of the worker.

Also from the supply analysis, as unemployment insurance benefits X are reduced, the W-q tradeoff shifts rightward and steepens. This implies increased security at the firm level, requiring the band between P_1 and P_2 to be increased. Some of this is offset by the higher wage, which reduces the gap. Nevertheless, a reduction in unemployment benefits is likely to have the effect of increasing rigidity in the labor market. If this reduction in unemployment benefits is compensated by increases in other expenditures, there is no effect on employment, but only an effect in prices until P_2 is reached. The effect of fiscal or any other policy geared at markets is blunted.

Observed labor demand is as in figure 9–2. Suppose the wage is fixed at W and prices vary. Real wages realized are measured as W/P on the vertical axis, and the variable profit-maximizing employment level L on the horizontal axis. The three regimes are as follows:

$$
\begin{aligned}
W/P > W/P_1 \qquad & L = \partial\pi/\partial P \\
W/P_1 \geq W/P \geq W/P_2 \qquad & L = \bar{L} \\
W/P_2 > W/P \qquad & L = \partial\pi/\partial P.
\end{aligned} \qquad (9\text{--}17)
$$

As P increases to P_1, the real wage W/P declines. The flexible arrangement dominates. Labor demand is $L = \partial\pi/\partial P$. As P increases, a discontinuity occurs, with the number employed jumping to $\bar{L}$ from the level $\partial\pi(P = P_1)/\partial P$. Further increases in P are accompanied by a perfectly inelastic demand for labor, until $P = P_2$, whereupon there is another jump in employment, from $\bar{L}$ to $\partial\pi(P = P_2)/\partial P$.

For given W and variable L, there will exist an interior $\bar{L}$ such that workers in $\bar{L}$ will accept $W_0 < W$ for security of employment. In figure 9–1 we have selected the $\bar{L}$ and W_0 such that $\pi = \bar{\pi}$, but there is no guarantee that actual contracts will select these levels. In any case, for any arbitrary interior

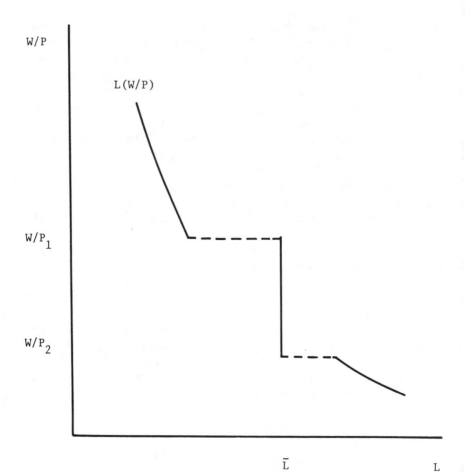

Figure 9−2.

$\bar{L}$ and $W_0 < W$, there will be a range of prices P_1, P_2 in the interval $[\underline{P}, \bar{P}]$, $\underline{P} < P_1 < P_2 < \bar{P}$, such that it will pay the firm to accept the fixity of $\bar{L}$ in exchange for the lower wage. Giving up flexibility by offering workers job security increases profits in this range. For high realizations of price $P > P_2$, profits are increased by paying the wage $W > W_0$ in return for the freedom to lay off unwanted labor. Given the utility function and density function of prices, $f(P)$, W_0, $\bar{L}$, P_1, and P_2 are jointly determined.

The labor demand is discontinuous. Layoffs and hires occur *en masse*, depending on attaining the relevant thresholds as prices respectively decrease and increase. Estimation of such demand functions requires a mixture of continuous choice and discrete choice models, with an accumulation of probability density occuring at the two jump points.

Empirically at the level of the individual firm, layoffs and hires are likely to be observed in bursts, as the relevant thresholds are attained. While the demand for labor for an individual firm is discontinuous, that for the economy can have a smooth neoclassical shape, given aggregation over firms. There is a range where the level of employment exhibits no response to real wage changes. All the above arises with no costs of severance or redundancy. These costs increase the range of the jumps, and also introduce small jump points everywhere along the underlying demand function.

It suits us to choose W_0, $\bar{L}$ from $\pi = \bar{\pi}$. However, there are many flexible pairs. If the firm attaches low probability to $P < P_1$, it may contract in such a way that it is difficult to restore variable L even at the price W. While the firm's desired behavior is discontinuous, observable behavior may not be, given transactions costs.

C. Transactions Costs and Long-Term Employment

Thus far, the firm faces no additional costs in altering the size of the work force. Despite this, the results suggest that hiring and firing are likely to occur at discrete intervals, and in jumps. This is exacerbated by the presence of transactions costs of hiring and firing.

Given our supply analysis, these are not entirely exogeneous, but arise partly from the worker's demand for security. Some hiring costs, such as interviewing and personnel costs, removal allowances, and record keeping on the number of workers employed, are exogenous to the employee-employer arrangement. Where the duration of employment is long, and firing is difficult, firms have an incentive to increase investment in pre-employment screening. Prospective employees also have an incentive to invest in activities geared at improving initial prospects at employment. In both Germany and Japan, schooling for males occurs for relatively long periods, with emphasis on passing examinations. The pressure of the labor market may extend backwards to the kindergarten.

Firing costs include severance pay, redundancy pay, experience-rated repayment of unemployment insurance, and grievance procedures to be followed before dismissal. These may be set endogenously as part of agreements between employers and employees, or be mandated by legislation. In the latter case, they may appear to be exogenous, but in the long-run sense are not. They reflect the interaction of workers' preferences and political policy, whether intermediated by unions or not.

Transactions costs require a dynamic model of the hiring decision. The present value of the costs of hiring one worker at time h are

$$D(h) = C(h) + \int_h^{h+T(h)} a(t)W(t)H(t)dt + a(h+T(h))C(h+T(h)) \quad (9-18)$$

where $T(h)$ is the expected duration of employment, $C(h)$ are net hiring costs, that can include employment subsidies, and $C(h+t(h))$ are net termination costs. The expected duration of employment $T(h)$ is not an exogenous variable. It is known ex post, and used to calculate the benefits and costs of hiring workers. Upon being hired, workers can expect employment for $T(h)$ periods. The discount factor, wage, and hours worked at experience t are, respectively, $a(t)$, $W(t)$, and $H(t)$. As experience increases

$$\partial D(h)/\partial T = a(T)W(T)H(T) + a(T)C'(T) + a'(T)C(T) \quad (9-19)$$

which is positive for typical applications. Total hiring costs $D(h)$ are increasing in $C(h)$, $C(h+T)$, wages, and hours, and decreasing in the interest rates underlying the discount factor.

The cost of adding one worker to employment depends on $D(h)$. The cost function for increasing average hours can be convex. Nevertheless, the lower the initial and terminal costs, because of general income security, the more likely it is that adjustment in labor input is made by increasing employment rather than hours.

The return received from a worker is

$$m(h) = \int_h^{h+T} a(t)M(t,v)dt, \quad (9-20)$$

where v is an index of quality. The marginal product of a worker with quality v at experience t is $M(t,v)$. The present value of the output over a career is $m(h)$ for a worker hired at h. If v indexes age, sex, education, and other characteristics, these are used in prehiring screening, since the cost of a mistake increases with T. Younger workers are less likely to be hired, and education serves as a screen to allocate workers to jobs. Higher transactions costs further widen the price range (P_1, P_2) within which perfect inelasticity in labor demand is maintained.

III. Employment and Prices of Labor

A. Introduction

The foregoing indicates that because of discontinuities, direct estimation of labor demand functions is difficult. The observed behavior of labor markets ought to comply with the basic predictions of the model. As an empirical check, we investigate labor markets for five countries: Canada, Japan, Germany, the United Kingdom, and the United States. We present data on employment, labor force participation, and unemployment.

We require a measure of the extent to which a labor market relies on job security as opposed to income security. Our procedure is to construct a user cost of labor, analogous to the user cost of capital. This user cost depends on the length of tenure, the wage sequence, the opportunity cost of capital, and discount factors. It is derived from an asset price of labor. There are two types of asset price. The first is the present value of the hourly wage to be paid, capitalized over the duration of tenure in years. The second is the asset price per worker hired, where the present value includes hours worked per year and transaction costs of hiring, redundancy, and severance. The user cost per hour depends on the asset price per hour. Higher user costs induce an incentive to economize on employment. The difference between the asset price per hour and the asset price per worker leads to jump discontinuities in the user costs.

The preference for security when it has to be achieved on the job instead of by public income support is manifested by both longer tenure and increased transaction costs of hiring and dismissal. The asset price per hour responds to the former, and hence tenure is an argument of the user cost. Higher user costs, all else equal, indicate a greater reliance on security at the firm level. The focus is on the effect of tenure, given the empirical difficulties of measuring transactions costs, though we present some evidence on these as well.

B. Employment, Unemployment, and Participation

The qualitative nature of the behavior of unemployment and labor force participation for the period 1970−82 is examined for the five countries. Four age-sex groups are distinguished: men and women aged less than 25, and aged 25−64. The latter are termed prime aged, and the former youth. Figure 9−3 shows the unemployment rates for youth. For both sexes, Canada and the United States consistently have the highest youth un-employment rates, with Germany and Japan having the lowest. The United Kingdom has low unemployment rates for young men and women until the mid 1970s, after which these rates are the highest.

The trends in labor force participation between countries are shown in figure 9−4. Canada is the only country among the five in which participation rates increase substantially during the period. In 1970, the youth unem-

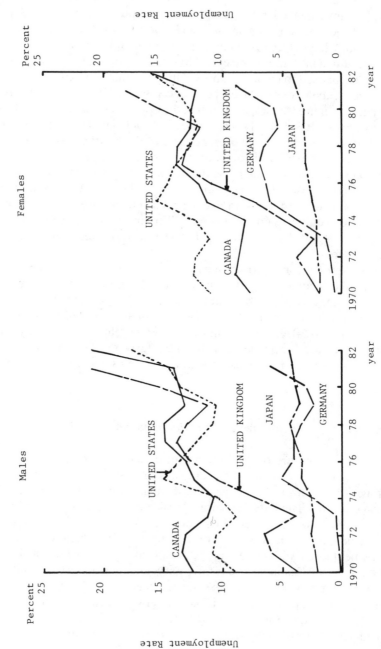

Figure 9–3. Unemployment Rates for Young Males and Females, 1970–1982.

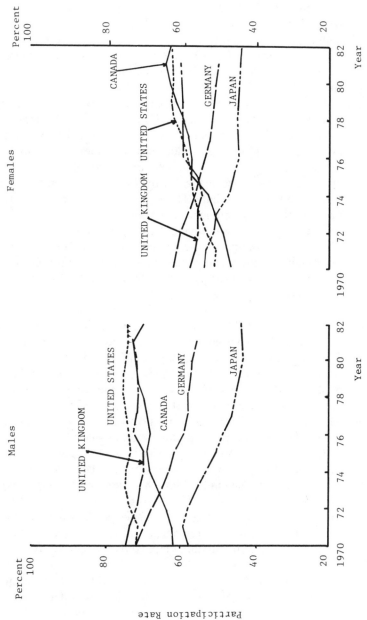

Figure 9—4. Labor Force Participation Rates in Young Males and Females, 1970—1982.

ployment rate for men is 12.6%, and the participation rate 61.8%, with 54% of the population in the age-sex category employed. In 1980, in Canada, the unemployment rate for youth is 13.7%, and the participation rate 72%, with 62% of the age group employed. During the 1970s there is an increase of eight percentage points in the proportion of the young male population in Canada employed. There is some deterioration of these markets subsequent to 1980. The unemployment rate continues to increase while the participation rate decreases.

For women, a similar comparison indicates an even greater relative increase in youth employment in Canada. The youth unemployment rate for women is 7.7% in 1970, and the participation rate 46.3%, with 42.7% of the population employed. In 1980, the youth unemployment rate is 14%, and participation rate 62%, with 53% of the population in the age-sex group employed. The performance of the labor market in the United States for young people is similar. There is a large increase in the labor force participation rate among young women.

The increase in employment for youth and women in the 1970s is a phenomenon confined to the United States and Canada among the countries examined. Youth participation rates decline in both Germany and Japan, and the United Kingdom exhibits a sharp increase in unemployment rates, with relatively stable participation rates.

In Japan, the labor force participation rate for young men declines from 57.7% in 1970 to 43.3% in 1980, and the employment rate increases from 2.1% to 4.5%. The percentage employed declines from 56.5% to 41.4%. Among young women, the participation rate in 1970 is 53.4%, with an unemployment rate of 1.9%. The percentage of the population employed is 52.4. In 1982, the participation rate declines to 43.5%, and the unemployment rate increases to 4.3%. The percentage of the population employed is 41.6. Both among young men and women, the unemployment rate has increased, and the participation rate has decreased.

Qualitatively, from figures 9-3 and 9-4, Canada has the lowest participation rate for young women among the five countries in 1970, and in 1982 it has the highest. The United States has the second lowest participation rate in this group in 1970, and in 1982 it has the second highest. By comparison, in Germany the participation rate is highest in 1970 and second lowest in 1982. Rank orders on labor force participation rates, unemployment rates, and proportion of the population employed are shown in table 9-1 for persons aged less than 25.

For persons employed as a proportion of the youth age group, Germany and the United Kingdom have a decline in rank order between 1970 and 1982 for both men and women. Japan has a decline in rank order for women, and

Table 9–1. Rank Order, Youth Labor Force Participation, and Unemployment Rates

Labor Force Participation Rates (ordered from highest to lowest)

Males		Females	
1970	1982	1970	1982
1. United Kingdom	1. United States	1. Germany	1. Canada
2. United States	2. United Kingdom	2. United Kingdom	2. United States
3. Germany	3. Canada	3. Japan	3. United Kingdom
4. Canada	4. Germany	4. United States	4. Germany
5. Japan	5. Japan	5. Canada	5. Japan

Unemployment Rates (ordered from lowest to highest)

Males		Females	
1970	1982	1970	1982
1. Germany	1. Japan	1. Germany	1. Japan
2. Japan	2. Germany	2. Japan	2. Germany
3. United Kingdom	3. United States	3. United Kingdom	3. Canada
4. United States	4. Canada	4. Canada	4. United States
5. Canada	5. United Kingdom	5. United States	5. United Kingdom

Proportion of Population Employed (ranked from highest to lowest)

Males		Females	
1970	1982	1970	1982
1. United Kingdom	1. United States	1. Germany	1. United States
2. Germany	2. Canada	2. United Kingdom	2. Canada
3. United States	3. United Kingdom	3. Japan	3. United Kingdom
4. Canada	4. Germany	4. United States	4. Germany
5. Japan	5. Japan	5. Canada	5. Japan

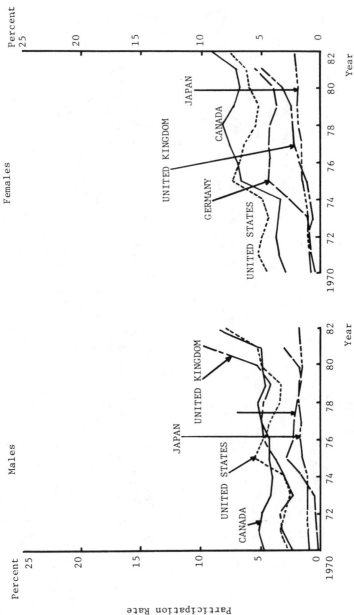

Figure 9—5.   Unemployment Rates in Prime Age Males and Females, 1970—1982.

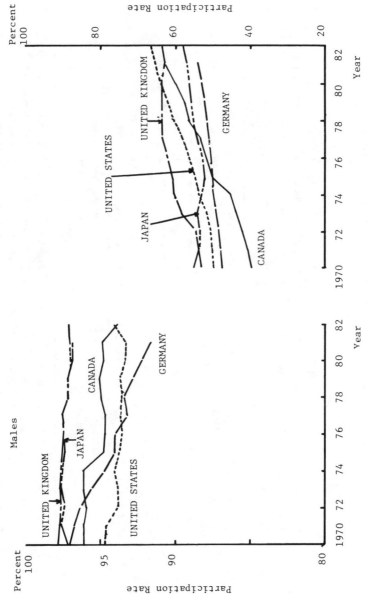

Figure 9—6.   Labor Force Participation Rates in Prime Age Males and Females, 1970—1982.

Table 9–2. Rank Order, Prime Age Labor Force Participation, and Unemployment Rates

Labor Force Participation Rates (ordered from highest to lowest)

Males		Females	
1970	1982	1970	1982
1. United Kingdom	1. United Kingdom	1. Japan	1. United States
2. Japan	2. Japan	2. United Kingdom	2. United Kingdom
3. Germany	3. United States	3. United States	3. Canada
4. Canada	4. Canada	4. Germany	4. Japan
5. United States	5. Germany	5. Canada	5. Germany

Unemployment Rates (ordered from lowest to highest)

Males		Females	
1970	1982	1970	1982
1. Germany	1. Japan	1. Japan	1. Japan
2. Japan	2. Germany	2. United Kingdom	2. United Kingdom
3. United Kingdom	3. United States	3. Germany	3. Germany
4. United States	4. Canada	4. Canada	4. United States
5. Canada	5. United Kingdom	5. United States	5. Canada

Proportion of Population Employed (ranked from highest to lowest)

Males		Females	
1970	1982	1970	1982
1. Japan	1. Japan	1. Japan	1. United States
2. Germany	2. United States	2. United Kingdom	2. United Kingdom
3. United Kingdom	3. United Kingdom	3. Germany	3. Canada
4. Canada	4. Canada	4. United States	4. Japan
5. United States	5. Germany	5. Canada	5. Germany

remains last among men, where there is also a decline in the employment rate for the population. By comparison, both Canada and the United States increase their rank order. For women, the United States and Canada had the lowest two rankings in 1970, and the highest two rankings in 1982.

Prime aged unemployment and labor force participation rates are shown in figures 9−5 and 9−6. Among men, unemployment rates are increasing over the period, and participation rates decreasing. The most pronounced decrease is in Germany, where the participation rate declines to 91.7% in 1982. Among women, there is a large increase in participation in Canada. The rank orders are indicated in table 9−2. For proportion employed, Japan remains the leader over the period among men. Among women, the ranking declines to fourth. Both Canada and the United States increase their rank order among women. There is decline in rank order in Germany in both categories. The ranking among prime aged men is relatively stable, except for a switch in positions between Germany and the United States.

In the three groups regarded as "secondary," young men, young women, and prime-aged women, the shift in ranking is most pronounced. The period is marked by a shift in the composition of total employment in Canada and the United States toward these groups, not apparent in the United Kingdom, Japan, and Germany. This shift in demographic structure has implications for family income. In Japan, the probability of observing spouses and children working is lower than in Canada or the United States. While variation in earned income can arise from the bonus in Japan, variation in family income can arise from the contribution to total income of several members. Over the life cycle, younger and older persons in the United States and Canada have a higher probability of working than in Japan.

The United States and Canada appear to have been relatively successful in absorbing the baby boom cohort born after World War II. Conversely, in Japan, Germany, and the United Kingdom, there have been increases in unemployment rates, and decreases in the proportion of the youth population employed. There is a rapid growth in participation rates in this group for the United States and Canada, not matched in the other three countries. While macro-economic, structural, trade, and other forces are also at work, the institutional features of labor markets may be partly responsible for these results.

C. User Costs of Labor Services and Asset Prices of Hiring

The asset price of labor is the present value of the hourly payments each year for hiring a worker over the average years of job tenure. Distributions of job

Table 9−3.   Distribution of Job Tenures (proportion of workers in particular tenure category)

Length of Tenure	Canada 1983	Germany 1972	Japan 1982	United Kingdom 1979	United States 1983
Under 6 months	.156	---	---	---	.215
Under 1 year	.227	---	.098	.138	.273
Under 2 years	.331	.250	.212	.244	.385
Under 5 years	.547	.490	.332	.476	.542
5 to under 10 years	.188	.219	.188	.219	.173
10 to under 20 years	.172	.219	.261	.184	.173
20 years and over	.094	.116	.219	.121	.009
Average job tenure (years)					
All workers	7.5	8.5	11.7	8.6	7.2
Males	8.6	8.9	13.5	9.6	8.4
Females	5.8	5.7	8.8	6.4	5.6

Source: OECD (1984a, chapter 5). Blank indicates not available.

tenures for the five countries are given in table 9−3.

Tenure duration data for Japan are based on an establishment survey of employers. Data for the other countries on tenure are from a household survey of the labor force. This causes two problems in the measurement of job tenure. First, a survey of persons on job tenure typically asks the duration of time spent on the current job. Since the job has not been completed, use of this estimate biases the estimate of job tenure downwards. Second, a survey of jobs rather than workers is required. Older workers are likely to have longer tenure at fewer jobs. Younger workers have shorter tenure at more jobs. The household survey excludes the adjustment for the larger number of jobs per time period of younger workers. The estimate of tenure duration is therefore biased upwards. Measured tenure has two factors contributing to bias, one in each direction. Without a job survey, the net effect of the two cannot be determined.

Tenure arises endogenously, given the response to worker preferences, but in the calculations we assume that employers view the average tenure as exogenous. In all countries, the average tenure of a worker exceeds the useful life of vehicles (three years), and equipment (five years) used in the U.S. tax code, following the 1981 Tax Equity and Fiscal Responsibility Act. Only structures have a longer useful life under the tax code. The implication is that workers must be regarded as analogous to capital. In Japan, almost half of all workers have tenure of ten years or more.

Consider a time series of hourly wages $W(t)$ for a worker hired at date h. The discount rate is $R(h)$, and $d(h)$ is the rate of depreciation and amortization. The present value of wage payments for one hour per year over the average tenure in years is

$$w(h) = \int_h^{h+T} W(t) \exp[-(R(h)+d(h))]t\,dt. \qquad (9-21)$$

If $W(t)$ is replaced by an annuity wage W, then

$$w(h) = W \int_h^{h+T} \exp[-(R(h)+d(h))]t\,dt.$$
$$= \{W/[(R(h) + d(h)]\}[1 - \exp\text{-}(R(h) + d(h))T].$$

The user cost of labor is the price of retaining the services of one worker per hour, or

$$U(h) = w(h)[R(h) + d(h)].$$
$$= W[1 - \exp\text{-}(R(h) + d(h))T]$$
$$= W[1 - \exp\text{-}(R(h)T + 2)], \qquad (9-22)$$

the last equality arising if the depreciation rate is constant and geometric, with $d(h) = 2/T$.

The user cost rank order is not generally the same as the tenure T rank order. Hence the use of the wage as opposed to the user cost can produce misleading estimates. The specification is exponential, but any monotone increasing function $F(T)$ in tenure can be applied. Then $U = WF(T)$. If $W_1 > W_2$, but $T_1 < T_2$ for two pairs, then the user cost ranking between U_1 and U_2 depends on wages and tenures. The wages entering $w(h)$ are all deductible in calculating tax liability, and $R(h)$ and $d(h)$ have no deductible portions. Here, labor is viewed as capital to the firm, but tax authorities permit only the expensing of current wages paid, and no amortization of future wage and severance costs. The economic definition of the user cost of labor to the firm is $U(h)(1-\tau)$, where τ is the marginal rate of corporate income taxes.

In calculating user costs, the hourly wage for each country is from the International Labor Office, *Handbook of Labor Statistics*, and is the series for non-agricultural employment. It is based on straight time wages, and does not include fringe benefits. The interest rate $R(h)$ used is that on long-term U.S. government bonds at each date h. The measure $w(h)$ is the asset price per hour, capitalized over a career, of hiring a worker at time h, excluding statutory fringe benefits and termination costs. The asset prices are constructed in domestic currency, and then converted to U.S. dollars using the average annual spot exchange rate as reported in the Organization for Economic Co-operation and Development, *Main Economic Indicators*.

Table 9−4. Asset (Career-Hour) Prices of Labor, 1964−1982 (in constant 1980 U. S. dollars)

Year	Canada	Japan	Germany	United Kingdom	United States
1964	15.71	7.47	8.60	9.43	17.69
1965	15.89	7.82	9.14	10.08	17.82
1966	16.79	8.80	9.78	10.62	18.51
1967	17.42	9.50	9.74	9.25	18.72
1968	17.93	10.42	10.51	9.47	19.17
1969	18.02	11.18	10.87	9.54	19.07
1970	21.37	16.26	14.45	11.48	20.83
1971	22.26	18.46	15.70	13.12	21.19
1972	21.41	19.37	17.61	12.15	20.16
1973	23.44	23.36	22.64	13.91	21.75
1974	24.92	30.13	22.95	16.83	22.92
1975	26.26	32.91	25.07	16.85	22.60
1976	24.30	39.28	23.00	14.00	21.74
1977	22.34	47.35	30.36	15.11	21.33
1978	21.26	35.38	29.48	16.13	20.46
1979	20.62	40.84	25.33	18.55	20.20
1980	20.35	35.56	20.69	20.92	19.43
1981	18.89	29.40	17.73	15.72	18.21
1982	18.74	27.68	14.79	12.93	17.62

Note: Calculated as $w(h) = W(t) \int_h^{h+T} exp(-(R+d)t)dt$, where T is the average tenure, $W(t)$ is the hourly wage in non-agricultural employment, R is the long-term U. S. bond rate, and $d = 2/T$. The source of tenure data is OECD (1984a), and wage data are from the ILO *Handbook of Labor Statistics*, various issues. Data are converted to current U. S. dollars at the annual average spot exchange rate, and deflated by the U. S. Consumer Price Index.

The prices are converted to constant 1980 U.S. dollars, using the U.S. Consumer Price Index. The asset prices $w(h)$ are reported in table 9−4 for 1964−82.

Japan has the highest asset cost of labor by the end of the sample period, being 50% greater than in the next highest country. In 1982, the asset price is 27.68 1980 U.S. dollars per hour.[10] This is the present value of hiring one worker per hour. This is the capital cost of creating another job. The comparable estimate for the United States is 17.62. In 1964, the corresponding figures, in 1980 U.S. dollars, are 17.69 for the United States and 7.47 for Japan.

In 1964, Japan has the lowest asset price of labor. By 1974, it has the highest asset price of labor, retaining this position subsequently. Canada has the second highest asset price of labor in 1964, and the second highest in

Table 9-5.   User Costs of Labor Services, per Hour (constant 1980 United States dollars)

Year	Canada	Japan	Germany	United Kingdom	United States
1964	4.55	1.45	2.22	2.41	5.32
1965	4.69	1.56	2.41	2.64	5.46
1966	4.80	1.67	2.49	2.67	5.50
1967	5.04	1.84	2.51	2.36	5.62
1968	5.16	2.00	2.69	2.40	5.72
1969	5.31	2.22	2.86	2.48	5.83
1970	5.52	2.64	3.27	2.57	5.61
1971	5.79	3.04	3.59	2.97	5.75
1972	6.46	3.99	4.76	3.25	6.31
1973	6.23	3.97	5.30	3.22	6.02
1974	5.79	4.11	4.61	3.33	5.58
1975	6.11	4.50	5.04	3.34	5.51
1976	6.15	6.18	5.10	3.07	5.74
1977	5.95	8.08	7.13	3.51	5.92
1978	6.10	6.75	7.52	4.07	6.09
1979	5.77	7.53	6.30	4.56	5.88
1980	5.61	6.41	5.06	5.06	5.58
1981	5.64	5.96	4.73	4.15	5.63
1982	5.84	5.98	4.15	3.59	5.69

Note: Calculated as $w[R + d]$, where w is the asset price of labor, R is the long-term U. S. bond rate and $d = 2/T$. Interest rates are measured in real terms by subtracting the growth rate of the U. S. Consumer Price Index.

1982, but the relative differential with other countries has narrowed. In the United Kingdom the asset price of labor is 9.43 in 1964, about half that for the United States at 17.69. In 1980, the asset price of labor in the United Kingdom exceeds that for the United States, although by 1982 the United States has a higher asset price. The relative asset price of labor between the United States and the United Kingdom in 1964 is 17.69/9.43, or 1.88, and in 1982 it is 17.62/12.93, or 1.36. The relative asset price in the United Kingdom has increased by 1.88/1.36, or 38.2% over 1964–82. The asset price of labor has increased most substantially in Japan, which has the lowest growth in employment over the period.

The real asset price of labor in the United States has remained constant during the 1970s. Real asset prices increased in Japan until the late 1970s with subsequent declines largely accounted for by exchange rate movements. Nevertheless, on this measure, the cost of creating a job, initially in Japan less than half that of the United States, had risen to more than 50%

greater than in the United States.

The presence of long-term worker attachments implies that the spot or current market wage is misleading. Long-term tenure may be required by custom or law, or from a reponse of the market to worker preferences, or because of firm-specific skills. The asset prices also depend on the wage sequences. Relative wages have increased in Japan more than in any other sample country. The wage levels themselves may be partly a consequence of requiring employers to provide security.

The user costs of labor are shown in table 9−5. The user cost of labor is the price of hiring the services of a worker for one hour. This converts the asset price, for hiring one worker per annual hour over a career, into an hourly flow cost during one year. In 1964, Japan is ranked lowest in the user cost of labor, at 1.45 1980 U.S. dollars. The United States and Canada have the highest user costs of labor, at 5.32 and 4.55, respectively, in the same units. In 1980 Japan has the highest user cost of labor, at 6.41 1980 U.S. dollars per hour, followed by Canada and the United States. The relatively high user costs of labor in the United Kingdom and Germany have been reduced subsequent to 1980 by exchange rate movements.

Relative user costs, dividing the 1982 entry by that for 1964, are:

Canada	1.28
Japan	4.12
Germany	1.87
United Kingdom	1.49
United States	1.07.

The smallest increase in relative user costs is in the United States, followed by Canada, the United Kingdom, Germany, and Japan. The greatest relative increase in user costs of labor occurs in Japan: it is more than twice the next largest relative increase, that of Germany. The ranking on relative user cost is also the exact rank order, from lowest to highest, of job tenures. Increased job tenure, or on-the-job security, is associated with an increase in the relative user cost of labor.

The data have implications for productivity measurement. Japan has the highest asset price of hiring a worker, and the highest user cost of utilizing the services of a worker. This requires that the marginal product per worker over a career with a firm, and the marginal product per hour, be higher than for the other four countries. Conversely, from table 9−6, the United Kingdom has the lowest user cost of labor per hour. In 1982, if an employer in the United Kingdom were equating marginal product with user cost in each period, the productivity per hour of a worker need be only 3.59/5.98 or 60% that for a comparable worker in Japan. Japan requires high produc-

Table 9−6. Wages per Hour (constant 1980 U. S. dollars)

Year	Canada	Japan	Germany	United Kingdom	United States
1964	5.34	1.66	2.59	2.81	6.26
1965	5.41	1.78	2.78	3.05	6.40
1966	5.64	1.92	2.90	3.13	6.50
1967	5.87	2.08	2.92	2.75	6.62
1968	6.07	2.29	2.92	2.80	6.75
1969	6.16	2.53	3.28	2.88	6.83
1970	6.32	2.81	3.55	3.12	6.84
1971	6.99	3.50	4.27	3.59	6.99
1972	7.49	4.16	4.66	3.74	7.34
1973	7.48	5.07	5.63	3.87	7.27
1974	7.50	5.37	6.36	4.23	7.05
1975	7.66	5.56	5.78	4.24	6.95
1976	8.17	6.19	6.43	3.75	7.05
1977	7.77	7.78	6.30	4.21	7.14
1978	7.07	9.56	8.38	4.76	7.19
1979	7.00	7.40	8.34	5.37	6.99
1980	6.64	8.11	6.99	5.99	6.66
1981	6.80	7.20	5.76	4.79	6.58
1982	6.80	6.57	5.41	4.09	6.57

tivity per hour from workers because it has the highest user cost of labor. There is a large increase in relative user costs during the period, increasing the incentive to raise productivity in Japan. By comparison, the United States and Canada, having the lowest relative increases in user costs, have the least incentives to raise labor productivity.

Data on wages per hour are indicated in table 9−6. In table 9−7 are rank orders on user costs and wages for all five countries. These results indicate that user costs $U(W, R, T)$ do not produce the same rankings as wages. Relative wage increases between 1964−82 are as follows:

Canada	1.27
Germany	2.09
Japan	3.96
United Kingdom	1.46
United States	1.05.

The examination of employment data on quantities and prices of labor comes to the same conclusion. The countries with the longest average job tenures have the slowest growth of employment and slowest absorption of

Table 9–7. Rank Order, User Costs of Labor and Wages, 1965–1982

| | 1965 | | 1970 | | 1975 | | 1980 | | 1982 | |
	User Costs	*Wages*	*User Costs*	*Wages*	*User Costs*	*Wages*	*User Costs*	*Wages*	*User Costs*	*Wages*
1.	United States	United States	United States	United States	Canada	Canada	Japan	Japan	Canada	Japan
2.	Canada	Canada	United States	Canada	United States	United States	Canada	Germany	Japan	Canada
3.	United Kingdom	United Kingdom	Germany	Germany	Germany	Germany	United States	Canada	United States	United States
4.	Germany	Germany	Germany	United Kingdom	Japan	Japan	Germany	United States	Germany	Germany
5.	Japan	Japan	United Kingdom	Japan	United Kingdom	United Kingdom	United Kingdom	United Kingdom	United Kingdom	United Kingdom

younger and female workers. These countries also have the highest user costs of labor.

D. Measuring the Cost to Firms of Job Severance

There are two aspects of the cost of job severance. The first is payments to workers, such as unemployment insurance. The second is the marginal cost to the firm per laid-off worker. These are measured for each of the five countries. Suppose the layoff occurs after tenure $T(h)$ for a worker hired at time h. Benefits to workers and severance costs to the firm are paid as a lump sum at the layoff point.

The hiring date present value to the worker of the unemployment insurance benefit at the end of average tenure is

$$V(h) = \exp(-RT(h))b(T(h)) \qquad (9-23)$$

where $b(T(h))$, the level of benefits paid, can depend on the tenure duration $T(h)$. At the margin, this does not impose a cost to the firm, assuming no experience rated repayments.

The severance pay requirement is

$$S(h) = \exp(-RT(h))c(T(h)) \qquad (9-24)$$

where $c(T(h))$, the severance pay requirement, can depend on the length of service. The total severance cost to the employer is $e_s S(h) + e_v V(h)$ where e_s and e_v are experience-rated repayments between zero and unity, respectively, for severance pay and unemployment insurance. These costs are added to the asset price of labor. For the worker, the total compensation obtained from the job, after taxes, is

$$A(h) = w(h)(1-\tau_w) + V(h)(1-\tau_b) + S(h)(1-\tau_s) \qquad (9-25)$$

where marginal tax rates on earnings, unemployment insurance benefits, and severance pay are, respectively, τ_w, τ_b, and τ_s.

There are other costs of severance that we cannot quantify. Thus, worker representatives must be notified prior to a layoff for economic reasons in the United Kingdom and Germany. In Japan, the high direct cost of labor reduces the number hired, and requires increases in the quality, through increases in the relative employment of prime-aged men. The high user cost of labor requires the hiring of more skilled workers, increasing the requirement for prehiring screening. In Germany, the user cost of labor is relatively low. The costs of firing delay hiring, shunting younger workers into unemployment, the school system, or otherwise outside the labor force.

Calculation of the asset price of labor after tax for each year would require an annual simulation of the entire national and local tax codes in each country. Comparisons are possible in specific years. The Organization for Economic Co-operation and Development in *Tax-Benefit Position of Production Workers* calculates the average tax rates for a married couple with two children in each country for 1981. These average tax rates are 10.61% for Canada, 2.81% for Japan, 9.74% per Germany, 19.45% for the United Kingdom, and 14.39% for the United States. State and local taxes are excluded from these calculations. Applying these to the asset prices for labor in 1981 produced for $w(h)(1-\tau_w)$, the first expression in (9–25),

Canada	20.89
Japan	30.23
Germany	19.46
United Kingdom	18.78
United States	20.83

in constant 1980 U.S. dollars. These are exclusive of employer contributions to payroll taxes, and represent the present value of career-hour returns from employment. From the supply side, or point of view of the worker, the Japanese have higher relative asset prices than on the demand side, because of the low rates of personal income taxation. In Japan provision for redundany and severance tends not to be institutionalized. (These issues are discussed in Koike [1985] in this book.) Japan has the lowest marginal tax rates but the most inflexible labor markets. Low marginal tax rates are not necessarily associated with employment growth, contrary to supply-side economics predictions.

Returning to the demand side, the total cost to the employer is the asset price of labor, grossed up by employer payroll tax contributions, and the employer cost of experience rated unemployment insurance repayments and severance, or

$$E(h) = w(h)(1+\tau) + e_v V(h) + e_s S(h). \qquad (9-26)$$

The cost to an employer of creating a permanent job is equation (9–26). Here τ is the marginal rate of employer contribution to payroll tax. The return to a worker from accepting it is equation (9–25). In the calculation of direct labor costs in $w(h)$, the United Kingdom has the lowest asset price and user cost of labor, although the relative differential has narrowed.

The low asset prices and user costs ought generally to stimulate employment in the United Kingdom relative to other countries. The reason that has not occurred may lie in the last two terms of equation (9–26), that represent the transactions costs of termination. In the United Kingdom, under the Redundancy Payments Act, a 35-year-old worker with nine years of service is entitled to nine weeks of wages as severance pay.[11] A 50-year-old with nine years of service receives 13.5 weeks of wages. Using the 1981 average wage per hour, converted as before to 1980 U.S. dollars, and projected forward over expected tenure at hire, and multiplying by 9/52 to convert the nine weeks into an annual equivalent, the asset price of labor increases by 0.74 1980 U.S. dollars for a 35-year-old. For a 50-year-old the comparable hourly increase is 1.10, which is about 7% of the $15.72 asset price.

The layoff cost has been converted into a unit hourly measure to conform to the other data. This tends to understate the effect of redundancy payments on flexibility in employment decisions. At the margin, with the worker already employed, it can be less expensive to retain than to lay off the worker. The wage, or user cost, could exceed the marginal product of labor in the short run, with the worker continuing to be employed.

The problem is more acute in Germany, but quantifiable evidence is less forthcoming. The effect of access to labor courts and threats of litigation cannot be easily measured. The qualitative implications are that there are disincentives to hiring and firing when transactions costs arise.

By comparison, Canada has relied upon general unemployment insurance to provide security. In 1975, unemployment insurance payments were 2.14% of gross domestic product in Canada, compared with 1.19% in Germany, 0.41% in the United Kingdom, 0.49% in the United States, and virtually zero in Japan.

Returning to the supply side, unemployment insurance programs are compared in benefit terms to workers for 1981. The average non-agricultural hourly wage is expressed in 1980 constant U.S. dollars for all countries except Japan. It is assumed that the worker is covered by the program. This wage is multiplied by the benefit ratio after tax and annualized duration of coverage. This produces the following present value of future jobless benefits per hour in 1980 U.S. dollars, as of a 1981 hiring date, discounted backward from termination date, with Japan set at zero:

Canada	3.33
Germany	2.49
United Kingdom	1.14
United States	2.06

The duration of benefit payment is set at the maximum period in all countries. This is the second term in equation (9-25), and represents the asset price per career hour of the future unemployment insurance benefits. In this category, Canada is ranked first.

Analogously, there is a difference between calculations at hiring date and firing date. A worker facing layoff in Canada is eligible for up to 51 weeks of benefits. The relative weight of unemployment insurance benefits to wages rises at the firing margin. Partly, this is because there is no discounting of the unemployment insurance benefits. The duration of benefits increases with service. A complete calculation would require estimation of the value of time while unemployed.

The full calculation of all the costs and benefits to employers and employees of accepting and terminating a job requires modeling of extensive institutional arrangements. The rank order on the benefits of unemployment insurance to workers is the same as the overall cost as a percentage of gross domestic product.

The qualitative conclusions on the behavior of labor market institutions in the five countries can be summarized:

- Canada: relatively high unemployment benefits to employees, not experienced rated;
- Japan: relatively low benefits or redundancy payments legislated, though part of agreements;
- Germany: relatively high unemployment benefits, but high costs of dismissal and termination;
- United Kingdom: relatively low unemployment benefits, high cost of dismissal and termination; and
- United States: unemployment benefits experience rated, low severance costs.

The results suggest that institutional arrangements can affect differences in international labor costs. Japan has the highest labor costs, but the lowest levels of general labor market job protection. It is possible that workers in Japan have demanded security from the employer directly, or that employers, knowing their workers to be risk-averse, and that there is no other source of security, have found it profitable to offer it themselves.

IV. Concluding Remarks

It has become popular doctrine that the removal of publicly provided income support in labor markets will increase efficiency, employment, and output. Our evidence suggests that this is not so obvious. Much depends on the underlying preferences of workers, which may be revealed by the existing institutional arrangements.

This applies both to programs that reduce turnover, such as severance payments and redundancy, and to programs that may increase it, such as unemployment insurance. Germany and the United Kingdom have extensive doses of the former, through direct legislation. Institutions tending to inhibit turnover are, however, even stronger in certain industry sectors in Japan, without the benefit of legislation. Were unemployment benefits to be removed in Canada and the United States, for example, the endogenous alternatives could have severe effects on the flexibility of labor markets. The costs of these programs have been extensively documented, but some of the benefits, such as more efficient markets, may not have been ascribed to the programs.

The data show that for employment, Canada and the United States have exhibited secular growth over the period examined, while Japan, Germany, and the United Kingdom have stagnated. This is particularly the case for young people. The relatively low participation rates for youth in the last three countries indicate that these people are delaying entry into the labor market, through increased schooling and nonlabor force activity.

Japan has the highest direct price of hiring and retaining workers, and its employment growth has been restrained. While Germany and the United Kingdom have lower user costs of labor than Canada and the United States, these costs have increased relatively more rapidly during the period. Further, Germany and the United Kingdom have legislated restrictions on dismissing workers that appear to be qualitatively important but which we are unable to quantify. Markets work more efficiently because of the presence of unemployment insurance. Where such insurance is less comprehensive, the response is higher labor costs to the employer, more rigidity, and less ability for the market to adjust. Smoothness in adjustment is not a plausible property in labor markets. Complete estimation of models of labor demand requires taking account of worker preferences as constraints in the production process.

Some of the structural problems in the labor markets can be disguised. If labor costs are high, firms hire better workers. Observed productivity is high, but the adjustment is borne by those not employed, either through unemployment or nonparticipation. Welfare and productivity comparisons between countries must be interpreted carefully to account for the cost of underutilized or unutilized human resources engendered by labor market institutions.

We have derived user costs of labor. These are the appropriate prices to apply as costs of labor services during the employment period. We have constructed the asset price of labor for adding one person to the work force. In so doing, we have taken account of wage levels per hour, tenure, discounting, payroll taxes, and redundancy and severance costs. Such data are required in estimation of labor demand functions. For actual estimation of these models, quantal choice models that mix discrete and continuous variables are required to deal with the jumps these user costs take over alternatives such as retaining a worker or hiring another.

Notes

1. Youth unemployment in Europe is a major topic in policy discussions. See the Organization for Economic Co-operation and Development [1984a, pp. 69–86]. This is not to minimize the problems of youth unemployment in the United States, as in Leighton and Mincer [1982] and in related chapters in the same book. Rather, we argue that labor market institutions have been more accommodative to youth employment in Canada and the United States than in Japan and Western Europe.

2. The possibility that nonzero unemployment insurance can be socially optimal has been noted in Burdett and Mortensen [1980].

3. For production functions, this has been recognized by Johansen [1961]. Firms can have fixed coefficient production functions, with the industry or economy, aggregating over these firms, having a neoclassical technology. It was suggested by Oi (1962) that labor should be treated as a quasi-fixed factor.

4. Optimality can exist without differentiability, but a further problem is that convexity properties for the technology may not be satisfied.

5. This has been observed for the United Kingdom by Feldstein [1967]. Our classification of labor markets does not necessarily imply that elements of rigidity and flexibility are not present in all markets.

6. Quality of working life surveys are in Barbash [1976]. An exit-voice explanation of why dissatisfied workers remain on the job, along the lines of Freeman [1980] for unions, may be an incomplete explanation. The presence of channels to voice complaints is not implied by a rigid market.

7. While q is either 0 or 1 for the firm, as an aggregate over firms at either corner, $0 < q < 1$ for the economy or industry.

8. Hall [1982] indicates that 28% of U.S. workers have jobs with an eventual tenure length of at least 20 years. This includes the self-employed and public sector employees. Also, 23.5% are employed in jobs with tenure length of two years or less. Similar results for the United States are obtained by Clark and Summers [1979]. Hasan and de Broucker [1984] indicate that 25.4% of Canadian workers have eventual job tenure of 20 years or more, with 19.7% in jobs of two years or less.

9. Schwartz [1982] makes a similar argument.

10. The conversion by exchange rates is applied to facilitate comparison. For actual decision making, workers are not mobile across borders, and firms do not have access to costless international relocation. Also, wages include those for workers in nontradable goods sectors.

11. Source: United Kingdom Department of Employment, *Ready Reckoner for Redundancy Payments*.

References

Barbash, J. 1976. "Job Satisfaction Attitudes Surveys." OECD Industrial Relations Programme, Special Studies. Paris: OECD.

Burdett, K., and D.T. Mortensen. 1980. "Search, Layoffs and Labor Market Equilibrium." *Journal of Political Economy* 88: 652–672.

Clark, K.B., and L.B. Summers. 1979. "Labor Market Dynamics and Unemployment: A Reconsideration." *Brookings Papers on Economic Activity* 1: 13–72.

Feldstein, M.S. 1967. "Specification of the Labour Input in the Aggregate Production Function." *Review of Economic Studies* 34: 375–394.

Freeman, R.B. 1980. "The Exit-Voice Tradeoff in the Labor Market: Unionism, Job Tenure, Quits and Separations." *Quarterly Journal of Economics* 76: 643–673.

Hall, R.E. 1982. "The Importance of Lifetime Jobs in the U.S. Economy." *American Economic Review* 72: 91–123.

Hasan, A., and P. de Broucker. 1984. *Unemployment, Employment and Non-Participation in Canadian Labour Markets*. Ottawa, Ontario: Economic Council of Canada.

International Labor Office. *Handbook of Labor Statistics*. Geneva: ILO, various issues.

Johansen, L. 1961. *Production Economics*. Amsterdam: North Holland.

Koike, K. 1987. "'Japanese Redundancy': The Impact of Key Labor Market Institutions of the Japanese Economy Compared to the United States Economy." This book.

Leighton, L., and J. Mincer. 1982. "Labor Turnover and Youth Unemployment." In R.B. Freeman and D. Wise (eds.), *The Youth Labor Market Problem: Its Nature, Causes and Consequences*. Chicago: University of Chicago Press.

Oi, Walter, 1962. "Labor as a Quasi-Fixed Factor." *Journal of Political Economy* 70: 538–555.

Organization for Economic Co-operation and Development. 1984a. *Employment Outlook*. Paris: OECD.

Organization for Economic Co-operation and Development. 1984b. *Main Economic Indicators*. Paris: OECD.

Organization for Economic Co-operation and Development. 1984c. *Tax Benefit Position of Production Workers, 1979–1983*. Paris: OECD.

Raisian, J., and M. Hashimoto. 1985. "Short-Run Wage Adjustments in Japan and the United States." This book.

Schwartz, A. 1982. "The Implicit Contract Model and Labor Markets: A Critique." Department of Economics, Northwestern University, Discussion Paper 513.

United Kingdom Department of Employment. 1967. *Ready Reckoner for Redundancy Payments*. London. Her Majesty's Stationery Office.

10 COMPENSATING DISPLACED WORKERS—WHY, HOW MUCH, HOW?

Daniel S. Hamermesh, Joseph J. Cordes,
and Robert S. Goldfarb

I. Introduction

Even accounting for cyclical changes there has been an apparent rise in the fraction of the labor force that has lost jobs because of plant closings. Among household heads in the Panel Study of Income Dynamics (PSID), only 1.6% reported themselves as having left their most recent job (been displaced) between 1974 and 1976, when the unemployment rate was 7.1%. Between 1979 and 1981, when the aggregate unemployment rate was 6.8%, 2.2% reported themselves as having been displaced because the plant closed. Roughly 2½ million workers reported in the January 1984 Current Population Survey (CPS) that some time during the previous five years they had lost a job they had held for at least three years because the plant closed.[1] Since the CPS tabulation excluded workers with less than three years of tenure, while the PSID included all workers, it is reasonable to conclude that around 1 million workers have lost jobs annually in recent years because

Helpful comments from Larry Iannaccone and from John Goddeeris have been incorporated.

their place of business closed.

Other industrialized nations have undertaken a variety of programs to deal with the labor market phenomenon of displacement. For example, Italy has a special program of unemployment pay for blue collar workers who have been displaced by technical changes, and Luxembourg provides special benefits for workers displaced from the steel industry.[2] In the United States the only special program (other than unemployment insurance) has been Trade Adjustment Assistance, which was paid only to workers who could demonstrate their jobs ended because of import competition, and for which workers were eligible only if they remained unemployed. No programs in the United States provide compensation for worker displacement per se other than income maintenance during the period of unemployment displaced workers may experience.

In this chapter we examine whether such compensation should be provided, by discussing the various rationales that might be adduced for it. Both efficiency and equity grounds should be considered in deciding what losses should be compensated and how the compensation should be structured. Having identified what we believe to be the loss that should be compensated under various rationales, we then construct a method for measuring the magnitude of that loss. That measurement in turn provides the basis for constructing a scheme consonant with certain minimum requirements of the rationales for compensation and with the size of the losses that are incurred when plants close.

II. Rationales for Compensating Job Losers

Should displaced workers be compensated for their job losses as a matter of public policy? Answering this question requires that two broad issues be addressed. First, under what circumstances, if any, should displaced workers be entitled to compensation for job losses? Second, if such entitlements are granted, should their cost be defrayed directly by the government, or should private parties be compelled to pay?

To answer these questions it is necessary to examine some suggested rationales for compensating workers. It is useful to distinguish between two different causes of job loss: government policy changes and changing private market conditions. Examples of the former include job losses resulting from airline deregulation and those caused by cuts in defense spending. Examples of the latter are shifts in market demand, technical change, changes in other input prices, and so forth.

The principal focus of this chapter is on the latter type of job loss, but we refer to an emerging literature that has examined various rationales for compensating those who suffer economic losses—including job losses—as a result of public actions. (See, for example, Hochman [1974], Tullock [1978], Cordes [1979], Goldfarb [1980], Cordes-Goldfarb [1983], Cordes-Goldfarb-Barth [1983], and Cordes-Weisbrod [1985].) What general criteria are offered by this literature concerning appropriate creation of entitlement to compensation, and which of these guidelines applies to job losses attributable to the "vagaries of the market"?

Compensation for Job Losses Caused by Government Action

Insofar as job losses are caused by public actions, two general principles of policy emerge from the literature. First, the case for compensation is strongest when there is evidence that the job loss could not have been anticipated by the affected worker. Second, even though there may be a strong case for limiting compensation to "unanticipated job losses," not every unanticipated job loser necessarily deserves compensation.

The role of anticipations is illustrated by the distinction between job losses caused by shifts in defense procurement and those caused by airline deregulation. It is plausible to assume that people know that defense industries experience large swings in employment. Accordingly, informed and rational workers choosing between employment in those industries and otherwise similar but more stable jobs elsewhere will require a wage premium in defense related industries. Hence, in a well-functioning market, jobs in defense industries would pay a higher wage to compensate for their relative instability. Since the wage premium already compensates workers for the greater risk of job loss, compensation for any subsequent job loss would be double payment and hence unjustified.

This case can be contrasted with that of job losses arising from airline deregulation. It is at least arguable that fundamental changes in the "rules" by which a market operates can be very difficult to anticipate. If so, it is likely that long tenure employees of airlines made large industry-specific human capital investments before deregulation could have been anticipated. In this case, compensation for such unanticipated losses might be appropriate.

However, determining that a job loss is unanticipated is only the first step in assessing whether compensation is appropriate. The second step requires the application of various efficiency and equity criteria, several of which have differing implications. For example, one efficiency consideration is whether compensation is needed to buy off politically powerful interests that would otherwise block passage of socially desirable changes in rules.[3] Under this criterion workers who suffered genuinely unanticipated losses, but who were not politically powerful, would not be granted compensation.

Insofar as losses are deemed compensible, the literature is unanimous (at least implicitly) that the cost of compensation be borne by the public sector. For example, when harm is imposed on specific individuals by a rules change designed to raise the general welfare, it is ethically appealing that the general population of gainers should pay. One obvious means is through the taxing power.

B. Compensation for Job Loss Caused by Market Forces

The issue of whether workers should be entitled to any form of compensation for job losses caused by market forces has not received as much attention. The distinction between anticipated and unanticipated losses holds for both privately and publicly caused job losses. However, if potential entitlement to compensation is based on whether the loss was unanticipated, it is difficult to tell which losses that result from market forces are unanticipated. Since a case-by-case determination is impractical, broad classes of job losses that have a high probability of being unanticipated have to be identified.

Consider, for example, the distinction between job losses caused by layoffs and those caused by plant closings. Between January 1979 and January 1984, 49% of the people who had held jobs for at least three years, but lost those jobs, were displaced by plant closings, with the remaining 51% laid off from plants that did not close.[4] Both categories are thus important in analyzing the problems of job losers. In many cases demand fluctuations are frequent enough so that past experience suggests that periodic layoffs are a predictable aspect of employment at the firm. By contrast, plant closings are less frequent, and hence less predictable. Thus job losses caused by plant closings are more likely to be unanticipated than are those caused by periodic layoffs.

Our earlier discussion of wage premiums implies that this conjecture can be tested empirically. If plant closings are unanticipated events, then the probability that a plant will close will not be reflected in the wage structure observed prior to plant closings. Specifically, if information about an impending plant closing were known in advance by both employers and employees, then one would observe a decline in specific training at that plant because the expected return would have decreased. In this case plausible assumptions about utility functions would leave unchanged the division of the cost of specific training between workers and firms produced by a Nash equilibrium solution to bargaining over sharing this cost. The combined impact of reduced specific training and unchanged cost-sharing would make the wage-tenure profile flatter, as differences in the amount of firm-specific capital by tenure diminish.

On the other hand, if employers anticipate before employees that the plant will close, the amount of specific training will decrease, but "uninformed" employees will overvalue the future returns to such training and pay a larger share of its cost. Indeed, if workers were completely ignorant, one might observe a steepening of the wage-tenure profile. This is unlikely, insofar as workers have some inkling that things are not going well.[5] However, to the extent that the profile does not flatten we may infer how well the plant closing is anticipated by employees. If the profile does not flatten out much as the date of job loss approaches, we may infer that workers are paying for specific training shortly before plants close, suggesting that they did not anticipate the closing very well.

C. Justifications for Compensating Unanticipated Job Losses

Even if job losses resulting from plant closings were unanticipated, it would not automatically follow that workers suffering such losses are entitled to compensation. This conclusion awaits the application of additional efficiency or equity criteria. To this end it is useful to examine those criteria discussed in the literature on compensation for publicly caused harm that apply most directly to the case of plant closings.[6]

1. Better Calculations. One argument advanced by Tullock [1978] for compensating those harmed by public policies is that such compensation compels decisionmakers to make "better calculations" of the presumed costs and benefits of public actions. This rationale has a natural analogue in the case of plant closings. Markets will generally fail to allocate resources to their best uses when price signals are incorrect. Two types of incorrect signals may be associated with plant closings. First, if information about the closing is asymmetric, potential and actual employees will make labor supply and human capital investment decisions that are incorrect. Second, to the extent that costs associated with plant closings are not embodied in management's calculations, the decision to close the plant, though profit-maximizing for the firm, may not be socially optimal.

In both cases, requiring that workers be compensated for job losses could lead to a better use of scarce resources. In the case of asymmetric information, requiring firms to compensate workers would reduce the incentive to withhold information about possible plant closings from workers. Moreover, if the management knew it must compensate for job loss, and such compensation were set at a level commensurate with the external costs of plant closings, the decision to close would reflect social costs and benefits more closely.

If payment of compensation is justified because it leads to better calculations, who should pay, and how should the compensation program be designed? Several points should be noted. First, just as this rationale requires public financing of compensation for publicly caused losses, it requires private financing of compensation for plant closings. The desired correction to price signals would not be achieved by government compensation payments. The problem under this rationale is that there are too many plant closings. Indeed, public financing would reduce the incentive for both firms and workers to account fully for the relevant benefits and cost of closings and result in still more closings. Of course, in attempting to create such incentives, it is necessary to distinguish between plants closed by bankrupt and by solvent firms, as private compensation would not be feasible nor necessarily desirable in the former case.

Second, calculating the correct level of compensation may not be an easy task, as it requires information on all omitted costs. Even if a technician could determine the proper amount of compensation in any given circumstance, it is unlikely that such calculations could be easily codified.

Third, if the only omitted costs in management's calculations are the human capital losses suffered by ill-informed employees, an alternative to cash compensation in the event of job loss would be a program that improves employees' information about the true probability of a plant closing. This suggests that instead of providing a legal entitlement to compensation one might offer firms sufficient incentives to disclose information about potential plant closings to their workers.

Fourth, unionized firms may face appropriate incentives as a result of private contracts. If workers are concerned about job losses resulting from plant closings, they can negotiate a "tax" to be paid each time a plant is closed, thereby raising the costs of the closing to management. The recent United Autoworkers-General Motors contract provides a pertinent example. The settlement contains a training program for displaced workers and a job security provision that requires the employer to contribute to a job security "bank." As one observer noted, "If GM chooses to restructure faster than the rate of attrition, it pays a $1 billion penalty."[7]

Finally, the efficiency argument requires only that management pay a corrective plant-closing tax. It does not require that the proceeds be paid to those who lose their jobs. Indeed, it can be argued that such payments will actually inhibit efficient adjustment (job search) by workers. Some aspects of this problem are considered in section IV.

2. Political Buyout. Another efficiency rationale is that compensation may be necessary to "buy out" the opposition of politically powerful groups to otherwise beneficial changes in policy. The analogous argument in the case of plant closings would hold that paying compensation may reduce local opposition to economically efficient plant mobility. Under this view the number of plant closings is below the optimum. Support for this rationale has several striking features. It implies paying compensation only for those plant closings involving relocation; plants that closed because of bankruptcies would not qualify. Also, since the motivation is to facilitate mobility, it implies that compensation be financed by government rather than the firm. The implication of this rationale is at odds with the "better-calculations" rationale, which requires that the firm be held liable for the compensation payments. In addition, compensation schemes based on a buyout rationale would require that the compensation actually be paid to job losers.

These sharp differences suggest that the two "efficiency" rationales for compensation for privately caused job losses are mutually exclusive. The "better-calculations" rationale is most consistent with the view that there are too many plant closings because managers ignore certain relevant costs; the buyout rationale is relevant if there are two few plant closings because of opposition by interest groups.

3. Issues of Fairness. An argument for compensation in the literature on government-caused job losses is based on the work of John Rawls [1971] and its application to government seizure of property, by Frank Michelman [1967].[8] The arguments ask whether the typical individual who is assumed to be unaware ex ante of where he would end up in the distribution of income would favor a particular policy given this assumed ignorance. Would individuals in this hypothetical original position choose a set of social arrangements that provide entitlements to compensation for losses caused by vagaries of the private market, such as plant closings? In making this determination, individuals in the original position would have to compare the expected social costs of providing entitlements to compensation to the costs of failing to do so. But the expected cost of granting entitlements to compensation depends on the actual design of the entitlement scheme. For example, if the scheme imposed extremely rigid compensation requirements on the firm the scheme might act to prevent plant movements that would in the long run contribute to greater aggregate output. Similarly, if the scheme reduced the incentives of displaced workers to seek new employment, it would be quite costly.

Such entitlements are also more likely to be adopted when the individual losses from plant closings are expected to be large—so that the potential cost of not compensating is high—and when the cost of identifying losers and delivering "fair" compensation is small. Losses from plant closings will be higher the lower the probability is of reemployment at the same wage, and the larger the ratio is of specific to general human capital embodied in the displaced workers. This implies that the fairness argument is most applicable to the subset of job losses caused by plant closings that involve large losses of specific human capital.

The Rawls-Michelman fairness criterion is consistent with a variety of financing schemes. The critical question is whether rational individuals in the original position who decide what compensation for plant closings is fair would want it to be privately or publicly financed. It is plausible that many of the considerations identified in the discussion of the "better-calculations" and "political-buyout" rationales are relevant here. Any entitlement to compensation would have to recognize the distinction between bankrupt and solvent firms. Moreover, the gain from restricting plant mobility by requiring firms to pay the compensation would have to be weighed against that of facilitating plant closings by paying public compensation.

4. Transitional Aid.   Another argument in the literature on publicly caused job loss is the "transitional-aid" rationale. The existence of un-employment insurance (UI) is taken to reflect a social judgment that it is appropriate to provide no-fault transitional aid for job losers. The very existence of UI might appear to contradict our earlier claim that it is appropriate to distinguish between anticipated and unanticipated losses; eligibility for unemployment compensation does not explicitly depend on whether the loss was expected. However, a closer examination of the UI program suggests this is not so. Some state regulations do limit payments where the losses can be anticipated, chiefly by using weeks-worked require-ments to restrict benefits for seasonal workers.

This argument suggests that the "transitional-aid" rationale may implicit-ly recognize the distinction between anticipated and unanticipated losses. However, there is a competing interpretation that is also of interest. In emphasizing this distinction, one is adopting what Pauly and Willett [1972] have termed an ex ante view of equity, that focuses on expected outcomes, as distinct from an ex post view, that focuses on actual outcomes. The classic example of this distinction is military conscription based on a draft lottery. This gives each eligible individual an equal ex ante chance of being drafted, though not all will actually be conscripted ex post. To the extent that UI does not emphasize this distinction, it may be viewed as reflecting a social judgment that compensation be decided on the basis of ex post rather than ex ante equity.

Lastly, the existence of UI may seem to suggest that there is already a system in place for compensating those who lose their jobs due to plant closings. However, this view ignores the fact that UI payments generally bear little relation to the size of the long-term loss. Rather, UI is based on lost income while the worker is unemployed, which, as we discuss, may differ substantially from the losses that should be compensated under the various rationales for compensation. The "transitional-aid" rationale may not suggest that full or nearly full compensation be paid; but surely the size of the lost human capital needs to be considered. If UI covers a much smaller percent of the true losses from plant closings than of other types of job losses, perhaps a second program explicitly compensating these losses should be established.

It seems obvious that compensation based on this rationale should be publicly financed, as it is "society" that has made the choice to ease the pains of adjustment. However, several features of the current UI program suggest that the issue is more complex. Suppose, for example, that all job losses were due to layoffs and none to plant closings. Then if UI were perfectly experience rated, the firm, its workers, and its customers would in fact be paying for the job losses. Of course, the current program is only partly experience rated (see Hamermesh [1977]). That many students of the program argue for more complete experience rating suggestes that the case for society paying the cost of transitional aid is not indisputable. An additional complexity is that even if experience rating is desirable, it could not be used to deal with payments triggered by plant closings associated with bankruptcy.

5. Other Considerations in Providing Compensation.   An additional consideration is based on a compensation-limiting argument. In some cases it may be inappropriate to compensate even for unanticipated losses if they are attributable to monopoly gains. One possible outcome of the elimination of government-sponsored monopoly positions is a reduction in the losers' earnings to the level they would have attained in the absence of monopoly. In this case, those affected would be no worse off in the future than they would have been had the monopoly position not been created. However, they would have enjoyed the benefits of their monopoly during its existence. Compensation is therefore unwarranted. An alternative outcome is a reduction in losers' earnings below the level attained in the absence of monopoly. Determining whether compensation is justified in this case is more complex. Those affected would be worse off in the future than in the absence of the monopoly, but such losses would have been at least partly offset by excess earnings during the monopoly's existence.

Applying this argument to the case of market-caused plant closings requires that the following questions be answered: (1) What proportion of the current earnings of job losers involves monopoly rents, and (2) even if there are no rents, what proportion of current earnings cannot be replaced because they represent returns on prior investment in specific human capital that is still not fully depreciated? We know that earnings of union workers contain substantial rents. Best estimates of the union relative wage gap are between 10% and 20% [Lewis, 1986]; and recent evidence suggests any positive effects unions may have on productivity do not offset this gap completely [Clark, 1984]. Based on this limitation argument, losses of such rents should not be compensated. On the second question, one needs to discover how much of current earnings reflects investments in specific training that have not yet yielded a reasonable rate of return. An implication of the "monopoly-gains" rationale is that workers with similar total losses of earnings might qualify for quite different percentages of compensation.

A final consideration is that we have concentrated on four rationales for compensating *workers* displaced by *plant closings*. It is quite conceivable that, to the extent shifts in product demand are unanticipated, owners of firms will lose their investments in firm-specific human and physical capital. While we recognize the validity of this argument, providing rationales for compensating the owners of firms that incur losses because of market-induced shifts is a different subject from ours. So, too, even if the plant stays open because its workers have accepted wage cuts, a loss has nonetheless occurred on prior investments in firm-specific human capital. While all the rationales for compensating the losses of displaced workers apply to the losses of workers whose plants do not close when market demand drops, the difficulty of identifying such losses makes it infeasible to construct empirically useful compensation schemes.

III. What Is the Magnitude of the Loss?

The discussion of what is lost by displaced workers suggests that compensation is most appropriate for unanticipated losses of firm-specific human capital.[9] This approach is fundamentally different from that taken in the substantial literature examining Trade Adjustment Assistance. The losses were generally categorized there as the value of the time the dislocated worker spent unemployed (e.g., Jacobson (1978) and Neumann (1978)), or the value of the wage loss between the job that disappeared and the job the worker eventually obtained (e.g., Bale [1976] and Jenkins-Montmarquette [1979]).

Both of these methods have problems that suggest they are not closely linked to what is actually lost. Thus, the value-of-time method mixes job-search considerations with the value of the lost rights to the previous job; workers whose reservation wage falls rapidly, or who are efficient searchers, will be deemed to have lost little. It also fails to answer the question of the appropriate wage at which to value the time spent unemployed. The wage-loss method also bases any estimate of the loss on the worker's search behavior, for those who search carefully (or luckily) will obtain a higher wage and be considered to have lost less. Moreover, anything that lowers the wage from its level in the lost job, including the loss of the rents that accrue to union status or to ascriptive characteristics such as race or sex, will be counted as a loss resulting from displacement. As we discussed in section II, such rents do not merit compensation except under the "political-buyout" rationale.

In the literature on wage determination it has become conventional to infer the importance of firm-specific investment from equations estimated over samples of workers and specified as:

$$\log W = F(TEN, X, Z), \qquad (10-1)$$

where W is the wage rate, TEN is years of tenure with the firm, X is total years of experience, and Z is a vector of control variables describing other characteristics of the worker and the job.[10] Since the effect of experience on wages is reflected in the coefficients on X (and its quadratic), any effect of TEN must indicate a difference between the effect of experience in the firm and experience elsewhere, which is exactly the impact of firm-specific investment that we seek to measure.

Each data point in the estimation of $(10-1)$ is of one worker observed in the last year before involuntary separation from a job. If workers had expected the impending separation, they would have stopped investing in firm-specific training and allowed the stock of capital built up by past investments to depreciate. If that were so, we would observe that $\delta W/\delta TEN$ has decreased. If the wage-tenure profile has not changed immediately before displacement, we may infer that the displacement was not perfectly foreseen by the worker. Indeed, the magnitude of the slope allows us to infer the size of the loss incurred.

Equation $(10-1)$ is estimated for a sample of workers who left their jobs between 1977 and 1981, either because the plant closed or because they were laid off permanently. The data include 362 heads of households from the

Table 10.1 Estimates of Equation (10−1)[a]

	(1)	(2)	(3)	(4)
X	.0119	.0107	.0134	.0096
(16.45)	(2.36)	(2.09)	(1.74)	(1.75)
X^2	−.00026	−.00024	−.00032	−.00024
	(2.48)	(2.24)	(2.24)	(2.08)
TEN	.00896	.01748	.01019	.00873
(5.11)	(2.40)	(1.99)	(2.07)	(1.81)
TEN^2		−.00037		
		(1.07)		
X·LAIDOFF			−.0045	
			(.43)	
X^2·LAIDOFF			.00015	
			(.68)	
TEN·LAIDOFF			−.00473	
			(.63)	
X·UN				.0040
				(.26)
X^2·UN				.00008
				(.08)
TEN·UN				−.00304
				(.40)

[a]Means of the variables are listed under their mnemonics. The mean wage rate was $5.56 per hour. The absolute value of t-statistics are presented in parentheses below the parameter estimates.

Panel Study of Income Dynamics. X is measured as years of full-time experience since age 18, while TEN is measured as years of service with the employer from whom the worker is later separated. Included in the vector Z are measures of years of schooling attained, union and marital status, race, sex, region, city size, and occupation and industry. The dependent variable is the worker's average hourly wage rate, measured in 1980 dollars using the private nonfarm average hourly wage as the deflator.

The discussion of rationales for compensating job losses suggests several distinctions should be tested. We noted that layoffs may be anticipated by workers, so that the market establishes a compensating differential for such risks.[11] This suggests examining wage-tenure profiles of layoffs and displaced workers separately as well as together. Also, insofar as unionized workers earn rents, and most rationales for compensation suggest lost rents should not be compensated, we also examine the wage-tenure profiles in the sample disaggregated by union status.

Table 10−1 presents the means of the variables of particular interest here. They suggest that job losers are somewhat younger than the average labor force participant (34 years, assuming an average school-leaving age of 18, versus 37 years for the average worker).[12] The typical worker has had five years of experience with the current employer, though 20% have at least ten years of tenure with the firm.[13]

Columns (1) and (2) of table 10−1 present estimates of the parameters describing the effects of TEN and X on wages from equation (10−1), first without a quadratic term in tenure, then with that term included.[14] As the estimate in column (1) makes very clear, there is a distinct positive slope to the wage-tenure profile even in the year before this group of workers was separated involuntarily. Moreover, the estimates in column (2) indicate that the profile has the usual inverted-J shape, with a peak at 23 years of tenure with the employer. This peak is remarkably close to the peak at 22 years found by Mincer-Jovanovic [1981] for a much larger sample of male workers (most of whom presumably were not later separated). Though the two wage-tenure profiles peaked at the same point, the profile estimated here is somewhat flatter than that found by Mincer-Jovanovic in the sample of all workers. However, estimates of these profiles among nearly identical samples of displaced and laid-off workers two, three, and four years before separation show slopes essentially the same as those implied by the results in columns (1) and (2) [Hamermesh, 1987]. This suggests that there was no change in the wage-tenure profile, and thus in patterns of investment in firm-specific training, as workers approached the date when they were separated involuntarily by their employer.

Column (3) of the table presents a version of the equation in column (1) expanded to include variables indicating whether the worker was laid off permanently, as opposed to having his or her plant closed.[15] The results indicate that the wage-tenure profile is much steeper among workers whose plants closed ($\delta\log W/\delta TEN = .0102$) than among those who were laid off permanently ($\delta/\log W/\delta TEN = .0055$). This suggests that, in addition to the compensating differential for the risk of layoff, workers who actually are laid off anticipate some of their specific risk and respond by reducing their investment in firm-specific human capital. The same does not appear to be true for workers who lose their jobs in plant closings. It indicates that a compensation scheme that ignores workers who lose jobs through layoffs rather than plant closings will not depart too far from our criteria for appropriate compensation.

In column (4) of the table we present estimates of the basic equation (10–1) expanded to include interactions of X, X^2, and TEN with a dummy variable indicating union status. The results show that the wage-tenure profile is flatter among union workers ($\delta\log W/\delta TEN = .0057$) than among nonunion workers ($\delta\log W/\delta TEN = .0087$).[16] In addition to the rents they receive, the estimates indicate that union workers anticipate involuntary separations more accurately than nonunion workers and reduce specific investment accordingly.[17] Even though the political concern about plant closings is stimulated in part by the trade union movement, our results suggest that, among otherwise identical job losers, nonunion workers' losses of firm-specific capital are greater. Through collective bargaining, unions appear to avoid part of the costs of plant closings, perhaps because they offer a mechanism that provides better information to workers than does individual wage determination (see Freeman [1980]).

Having demonstrated that there is a loss of firm-specific investment—that is, workers do not perfectly foresee an impending displacement and allow their investment to depreciate fully by the time it occurs—we need to measure the magnitude of that loss. The displaced worker is left with a stock of firm-specific human capital at the time of displacement. This stock would, in the absence of additional investment, have depreciated at some rate δ each year the worker remained with the firm. Also, there is some probability q that the worker would have quit the firm each year, and, of course, the stream of (probabilistic) returns that the stock would have generated must be discounted appropriately back to the date of displacement at some discount rate r.

These considerations require us to specify all three of the parameters. We assume the real discount rate ranges between 0 and .10, with a median value of .05; we assume that the depreciation rate on firm-specific investment ranges between .05 and .15 per year, with a median value of .10, following Johnson's [1970] evidence. To estimate the probability of quitting, we need to capture the decline in quit rates that occurs as the worker's tenure with the firm increases. Four studies—Freeman [1980], Mincer-Jovanovic [1981], Mitchell [1982], and Viscusi [1980]—estimate quit rates as functions of tenure for broad samples of individuals. Using each worker's economic and demographic characteristics and their implied effects on quits, as estimated in each of the four studies, we calculate the quit rate at each year t, $t = TEN + 1$, $TEN + 2, \ldots$, up through an assumed retirement age of 68. We use the implied quit rates from each of these studies to calculate alternative estimates of the present value of the lost stream of returns.

The hourly returns on the lost stock of specific training at the time of

Table 10−2. Average Present Value of Lost Specific Training (in thousands)

	(r, δ)		
	(0, .05)	(.05, .10)	(.10, 15)
Quit Function			
Freeman [1980] PSID 1968−74, logit, all workers	$11.5	$6.5	$4.7
Mincer-Jovanovic [1981] PSID 1975−76, OLS, men	10.6	6.2	4.6
Mitchell [1982] QES 1973, 1977, probit, men and women separately	15.7	7.8	5.3
Viscusi [1980] PSID 1975−76, logit, men and women separately	12.1	6.8	4.9

involuntary separation are the difference between the wage the worker received, gross of any investment in specific training being made at that time, and the wage of an otherwise identical worker with $TEN = 0$. These are all based on the estimates in column (2) of table 1. To derive the lost annual returns (at the time of separation) we assume the worker was employed for 2,000 hours. Coupling these calculations with the ranges of assumptions about δ, r, and q yields the present values shown in table 10−2.

The estimates in table 10−2 are all in 1980 dollars. They suggest that involuntary separation induces a fairly substantial loss of firm-specific human capital. Taking the median values of the parameters for each of the four quit functions, it appears that this part of the loss is the equivalent of over six months' wages (remembering from table 10−1 that the mean hourly wage in the sample is $5.56). Since the estimates in column (3) of table 10−1 show a steeper profile for displaced workers, and since displaced workers have above-average seniority in the sample, we may infer that their loss is far above the equivalent of six months' wages suggested by the calculations in table 10−2. This implies that the loss to be compensated is hardly trivial, but instead could represent a significant decline in lifetime income for some workers, particularly those workers displaced at the peak of their wage-tenure profiles.

IV. How Should the Losses Be Compensated?

If one of the equity or efficiency rationales favoring compensation is found convincing, how should the losses actually be compensated? As we saw in section III, the loss incurred by displaced workers is the lost present value of their firm-specific human capital. A stream of returns that the workers expected, and for which they had invested, disappears. In this section we use the analysis above to determine the appropriate structure of compensation for this loss. It must be remembered that any such compensation must be linked to the amount and nature of the loss, and must be designed to minimize any detrimental side effects on the efficiency of the labor market. Whether these are sufficient to overcome the arguments for compensation is not the issue here. We are merely suggesting practical schemes that meet the objectives of compensation and try to minimize the negative side effects.

No compensation structure can, in practice, be based exactly on the kind of calculations presented in section III. Rather, any such scheme must devise proxies that represent the amount of lost firm-specific capital. Newly hired educated workers in union jobs will have higher wage rates than will high seniority, nonunion workers with little formal education; yet we have seen that the latter may lose more firm-specific human capital when the job ends suddenly. Since lost rents probably ought not be compensated, one should thus not base compensation entirely on the worker's prior wage rate or earnings. Also, compensation based solely on years of tenure in the firm will not proxy the loss well, because the effects of an additional year of tenure vary with the wage rate and with the worker's tenure.

A compensation scheme that avoids the problems outlined above is:

$$C = kw[TEN^* - |TEN^* - TEN|], \qquad (10-2)$$

where C is the total compensation, k is some constant we shall discuss, TEN^* is some tenure level, and w is the worker's annual earnings.[18] This proposal bases compensation on both the wage and years of service, thus representing better the value of the lost specific human capital than would compensation based on any single proxy. The compensation is structured very much like that of many severance pay plans, which is appropriate since severance pay also represents compensation for the specific loss. However, by specifying that compensation declines after some peak seniority is reached, this scheme recognizes in part that the wage-tenure profile has an inverse-J shape. Very senior workers nearing retirement, whose firm-specific investment is nearly fully depreciated, receive little compensation under this scheme. The appropriate value for the parameter TEN^* should be linked to empirical wage-tenure profiles. The profiles discussed in section III and those based on

larger samples (e.g., Mincer-Jovanovic [1981] and Bartel-Borjas [1981])
tend to suggest that wages stop increasing with tenure in the firm after about
20 years. That being the case, TEN^* might appropriately be set at 20. The
value of k should be based on the magnitude of the loss we estimated in
section III, between $6,000 and $8,000 in 1980 dollars. Using the hourly
wage of workers in our sample and annual employment of 2,000 hours yields
annual earnings of $11,100. (Alternatively, since average hourly earnings in
1980 in private nonfarm industry were $6.66, assuming 2,000 hours per year
implies average annual earnings of $13,300.) Both considerations suggest
that the lump-sum compensation payment should average 50% of the
worker's full-time annual earnings. Because the average worker in our
sample had five years of tenure with the firm, k should be set at 10% to
compensate appropriately. The particular compensation scheme will thus
be:

$$C = .1w[20 - |20 - TEN|]. \qquad (10-2')$$

Though this scheme does pay lower compensation to very senior workers
than to some others, in fact very few workers are likely to receive no
compensation. In our sample of 362 displaced or laidoff household heads,
only 4% had seniority of more than 19 years; in the Current Population
Survey data, only 9% of workers with more than three years of tenure whose
plants closed or who were laid off had more than 19 years of seniority.[19]

It is interesting to note that the structure of this scheme is similar, but by
no means identical, to compensation schemes that exist in European
countries. For example, the current British system of redundancy payments
compensating for plant closings or the disappearance of jobs increases
payments with years of service up to 20 years of service. However, there is
no reduction in benefits for service beyond 20 years [Metcalf, 1984].

To avoid the endless debates about eligibility that surrounded Trade
Adjustment Assistance, the eligibility requirement for compensation for
displacement should be a demonstration that the employer closed the plant
permanently. While a broader program that includes layoffs is possible, it
would be much more difficult to administer. Moreover, we showed in
section III that the value of lost firm-specific human capital is much less for
workers on permanent layoff than for those whose plants closed, confirming
the arguments of section II that layoffs are more likely to be anticipated than
plant closings. As with most labor market compensation programs, this can
be certified by the state employment service. To avoid administrative
burdens, though, eligibility should be limited to workers with at least one
year of seniority in the plant. This allows the calculation of annual earnings
in the plant. More important, it avoids compensating workers for short

duration jobs on which they are not likely to have accumulated a significant amount of firm-specific human capital that could be lost when the job ends unexpectedly.

Trade Adjustment Assistance was paid on a weekly basis in a manner similar to the payment of UI benefits. Payments ceased when the worker became reemployed. Linking payment of UI benefits to employment status is justified, given the goals of the UI program, as a way of maintaining the consumption of households that might otherwise immediately spend a lump-sum payment and be left with no income or savings to finance current consumption (see Hamermesh [1982]). Periodic payment of TAA benefits made sense in light of the program's goals of compensating workers for a permanent job loss only on the "transitional aid" criterion and only then as a way of ensuring workers' liquidity. On the "political buyout" rationale a lump-sum payment would have been equally appropriate. The same arguments apply to compensation for displacement not caused by import competition, with an additional argument in favor of lump-sum payments: Only with such payments will the "better-calculations" rationale be well served. With periodic payments based on employment status the link between the size of the loss and the magnitude of the payment is weakened.

It is true that the lump-sum payment might be squandered by the recipient. However, this argument is irrelevant in terms of the justifications we have adduced for this type of compensation. Also, the lump-sum payment has the advantage that it does not reduce the marginal benefit to taking a new job, a problem that was apparently quite severe in the case of Trade Adjustment Assistance (TAA) (see Kiefer-Neumann [1979]). If the lump-sum payment is unattractive, the same rationales that justified it would justify paying the compensation over a period of time with the amount paid and its time path independent of the worker's employment status.

Implicit in the argument thus far is the assumption that the compensation would be a cash payment. The compensation could instead be paid in the form of a training or hiring voucher, a subsidy transportable by the worker either to an employer willing to hire and retain the worker for some specified period or to be used for training. This method of payment provides an additional screen on eligibility for the program: only those workers retaining a strong labor force attachment will accept and use the training voucher. Workers nearing retirement, who presumably had little firm-specific human capital but might nonetheless receive some compensation under the scheme in $(10-2')$, would be less likely to use the aid. Even more important, since what is lost is a stream of returns on firm-specific investment, a training or hiring voucher replaces the loss by giving firms an incentive to hire workers and allow them to reinvest in firm-specific capital. Unlike proposals to convert all or part of UI payments into training vouchers—proposals that jeopardize the consumption maintenance goal of that program—offering compensation in the form of training or hiring vouchers to displaced workers strengthens the link between the compensation and the loss.[20]

Regardless of whether one deems compensation in the form of cash or vouchers to be more appropriate, it is essential that compensation *not* be offered on a periodic (weekly or monthly) basis linked to employment status. The loss is of a stock of specific human capital. Periodic compensation that depends on the worker remaining unemployed merely lengthens the time until displaced workers can begin accumulating a new stock of firm-specific human capital to replace what was lost.

If a compensation scheme like the one suggested above is to be adopted, how should it be financed? The answer depends on which rationale for compensation is espoused. Under the "better-calculations" rationale the private firm relocating its plant should pay. Under the "transitional-aid" rationale the government as "society's agent" should pay. Under a "political-buyout" rationale it is at least arguable that both the firm and the government should pay, since society and the firm are gaining from the induced increase in efficiency resulting from increased mobility. Obviously, any rationale that requires the firm to pay must come to grips with the potential ability-to-pay problems of firms that are closing plants.

V. Conclusions

We have explored rationales for compensating individuals who suffer private sector job losses, estimated the size of these losses, and proposed a compensation scheme consistent with some of the minimum requirements of the rationales. Several conclusions may be drawn from our survey of the various rationales. First, a necessary condition for compensation is that the job loss be arguably unanticipated. This suggests that compensation associated with plant closings is more defensible than that for layoffs. Second, sufficient conditions for compensation vary with each of the specific rationales. For example, the "better-calculations" rationale may suggest that firms that close plants should face appropriate fines, but does not necessarily imply using the revenue collected for compensation. The rationale also implies that, if job losers are to be compensated, the firm—not the government—should pay. Third, some rationales strongly suggest that the loss to be compensated should not include rents.

For several reasons, identifying rationales consistent with compensation is only a first step in evaluating the desirability of compensation. First, the appeal of particular rationales involves fundamental value judgments. Second, one may espouse the underlying value judgments but still reject the implied compensation program because there are other sizable difficulties and costs associated with its implementation. One important example of such difficulties involves "induced property rights." Suppose a well-designed program for compensating losses of human capital were implemented. Its very existence would create political pressures to expand it to cover other job losses. The history of TAA is instructive here: a system of payments that was initially (1962) tied to lowering formal trade barriers was expanded in 1974 to cover all trade-related job losses. Another problem, more specific to the scheme we have suggested, is the potential effect on the accumulation of firm-specific human capital. By subsidizing the losses of such human capital, the scheme gives workers an incentive to overinvest in this asset, and it changes the incentives for optimal sharing of the investment.

We have also described a method for determining empirically whether job losses associated with plant closings are well anticipated. The results suggest that these job losses are not so well anticipated as those associated with layoffs. The method is also used to estimate the size of the firm-specific human capital losses associated with plant closings. The estimates indicate that such losses are quite large, especially for employees with long tenure who are still far away from retirement. Since the method ignores losses of industry- or occupation-specific human capital, even these large estimates may be understatements.

The payment scheme we propose has certain advantages over those proposed in other contexts. Unlike the payment of TAA, it eschews basing compensation payments on the displaced worker's employment and wage experience after the job loss. It thus recognizes that the time spent unemployed and the wage eventually obtained depend in part on search behavior, which is in turn influenced by the compensation scheme. If society wishes to compensate for time spent unemployed, it already does so through the UI system. That system and the rationale for it are logically separate from the rationales for compensating for the losses of specific human capital induced by plant closings. Accordingly, another payment scheme, such as the one we propose, is logically required to meet these different rationales.

Notes

1. Bureau of Labor Statistics, *News Release*, November 30, 1984.
2. See Grais [1983] for a discussion of these and similar policies.
3. For a version of this argument, see Tullock [1978].

4. Bureau of Labor Statistics, op. cit.

5. One might wonder why workers fail to infer from employers' behavior that the plant will be closing. This question is equivalent to viewing the bargaining process over investment in specific training as a supergame in which all information is eventually shared. Whether this view is correct is basically an empirical question that we examine in the next section (see Hamermesh [1987]).

6. Cordes and Goldfarb [1983] and Cordes, Goldfarb, and Barth [1983] list rationales or criteria for compensation in the case of job loss caused by government. Several of the rationales they list are clearly inapplicable to private-sector job losses and are therefore not discussed here.

7. Harley Shaiken, as quoted in *Washington Post*, September 22, 1984, p. A−8.

8. It should be noted that Michelman argues that there is a *prima facie* case for denying compensation to those suffering losses resulting from the vagaries of the private market. However, in our judgment his framework for thinking about the desirability of paying compensation is as applicable in the private as in the public sphere.

9. The discussion and estimation in this section is based on Hamermesh [1987].

10. See, for example, Mincer and Jovanovic [1981] or Bartel and Borjas [1981].

11. See Topel [1984] for good evidence that such a differential exists.

12. If the sample is broken down into workers whose jobs disappeared because of plant closings and those who were laid off, we find that this difference is due entirely to the laid-off workers. Those whose jobs ended due to plant closings had the same average experience as the average labor force participant.

13. Among displaced and laid-off workers with at least three years of tenure on the jobs from which they were separated, average tenure was over eight years (calculated from Bureau of Labor Statistics, op. cit., table 3).

14. The coefficients on the variables in Z are generally what is expected for a broad-based sample of micro data. The implied rate of return on education was 4 percent, perhaps a little low; the union relative wage effect was 30 percent; males received 35 percent more than women; wages in the South were 15 percent lower than elsewhere, while whites received 14 percent more than nonwhites.

15. In addition to the interaction terms reported in the table, the dummy variable itself was also included in the equation.

16. Inclusion of the interactions with both UN and LAIDOFF suggests our conclusions about the differences between union and nonunion workers, and between laid-off workers and those whose plants closed, hold in an expanded equation. However, probably due to the paucity of observations on unionized workers whose plants closed, the results are not significant.

17. Hamermesh [1987] shows that union tenure profiles are actually steeper until two years before the separation, at which time they become flatter.

18. To avoid problems produced by unstable earnings that may have faced the worker during the year before a shut-down, w could be an average of the worker's earnings in the plant in the three most recent years.

19. Bureau of Labor Statistics, op. cit.

20. In its proposed FY 1983 budget the Reagan Administration proposed allowing long-term unemployed workers to convert UI benefits into training vouchers for use with employers who could obtain tax credits if they hired the unemployed worker.

References

Bale, Malcolm. 1976. "Estimate of Trade-Displacement Costs for U.S. Workers." *Journal of International Economics* 6 (August): 245–250.

Bartel, Ann, and George Borjas. 1981. "Wage Growth and Job Turnover: An Empirical Analysis." In Sherwin Rosen (ed.), *Studies in Labor Markets*. Chicago: University of Chicago Press.

Clark, Kim. 1984. "Unionization and Firm Performance." *American Economic Review* 74 (December): 893–919.

Cordes, Joseph. 1979. "Compensation Through Relocation Assistance." *Land Economics* 55 (November): 486–499.

————— and Robert Goldfarb. "Alternate Rationales for Severance Pay Compensation under Airline Deregulation." *Public Choice* 41: 351–359.

—————, —————, and James Barth. 1983. "Compensating When the Government Harms." In Richard Zeckhauser and Derek Leebaert (eds.), *What Role for Government?* Durham, NC: Duke University Press.

————— and Burton Weisbrod. 1985. "When Government Programs Create Inequities: A Guide to Compensation Policies." *Journal of Policy Analysis and Management* 4 (Winter): 178–195.

Freeman, Richard. 1980. "The Exit-Voice Tradeoff in the Labor Market." *Quarterly Journal of Economics* 94 (June): 643–674.

Goldfarb, Robert. 1980. "Compensating Victims of Policy Change." *Regulation* 4 (September/October): 22–30.

Grais, Bernard. 1983. *Lay-offs and Short-time Working in Selected OECD Countries*. Paris: OECD.

Hamermesh, Daniel. 1987. "The Costs of Worker Displacement." *Quarterly Journal of Economics*, in press.

—————. 1977. *Jobless Pay and the Economy*. Baltimore: Johns Hopkins University Press.

—————. 1982. "Social Insurance and Consumption: An Empirical Inquiry." *American Economic Review* 72 (March): 101–113.

Hochman, Harold. 1974. "Rules Change and Transitional Equity." In Harold Hochman and George Peterson (eds.), *Redistribution Through Public Choice*. New York: Columbia University Press.

Jacobson, Louis. 1978. "Earnings Losses of Workers Displaced from Manufacturing Industries." In William Dewald (ed.), *The Impact of International Trade and Investment on Employment*. Washington, DC: U.S. Department of Labor.

Jenkins, Glenn, and Claude Montmarquette. 1979. "Estimating the Private and Social Opportunity Cost of Displaced Workers." *Review of Economics and Statistics* 61 (August): 342–353.

Johnson, Thomas, 1970. "Returns from Investment in Human Capital." *American Economic Review* 60 (September): 546–560.

Kiefer, Nicholas, and George Neumann. 1979. "An Empirical Job-Search Model, with a Test of the Constant Reservation-Wage Hypothesis." *Journal of Political*

Economy 87 (February): 89–108.

Lewis, H. Gregg. 1986. *Union Relative Wage Effects*. Chicago: University of Chicago Press.

Metcalf, David. 1984. "An Analysis of the Redundancy Payments Act." London School of Economics, Centre for Labour Economics, Working Paper No. 606.

Michelman, Frank. 1967. "Property, Utility and Fairness Comments on the Ethical Foundations of 'Just Compensation' Law." *Harvard Law Review* 80: 1165–1258.

Mincer, Jacob, and Boyan Jovanovic. 1981. "Labor Mobility and Wages." In Sherwin Rosen (ed.), *Studies in Labor Markets*. Chicago: University of Chicago Press.

Mitchell, Olivia. 1982. "Fringe Benefits and Labor Mobility." *Journal of Human Resources* 17 (Spring): 286–298.

Neumann, George. 1978. "The Direct Labor Market Effects of the Trade Adjustment Assistance Program." In William Dewald (ed.), *The Impact of International Trade and Investment on Employment*. Washington, DC: U.S. Department of Labor.

Pauly, Mark, and Thomas Willett. 1972. "Two Concepts of Equity and their Implications for Public Policy." *Social Science Quarterly* 53 (June): 8–19.

Rawls, John. 1971. *A Theory of Justice*. Cambridge, MA: Harvard University Press.

Topel, Robert. 1984. "Equilibrium Earnings, Turnover, and Unemployment." *Journal of Labor Economics* 2 (October): 500–522.

Tullock, Gordon. 1978. "Achieving Deregulation—A Public Choice Perspective." *Regulation* 2 (November/December): 50–54.

Viscusi, W. Kip. 1980. "Sex Differences in Worker Quitting." *Review of Economics and Statistics* 62 (August): 388–398.

Index